KV-050-530

D711·4 OSW

URBAN
CATALYST

The Power of
Temporary Use

Philipp Oswalt, Klaus Overmeyer, Philipp Misselwitz

CONTENTS

CULTIVATING TEMPORARY USE

Kees Christiaanse

This publication is the product of a long-term and intensive engagement with the phenomenon of temporary use. The initiators and editors of this book, collectively known as Urban Catalyst, have succeeded in generating an international public discourse on temporary use, and in developing their research findings into a new form of professional practice. The team formed in the late 1990s and the award of a major European Commission research grant created their first opportunity. Between 2001 and 2003 Urban Catalyst investigated the potential of temporary use as a motor for urban transformation using five European cities as case studies: Helsinki, Amsterdam, Berlin, Vienna and Naples. Based then at Berlin's Technical University, Urban Catalyst coordinated a network of twelve European partners. The strategic planning tools and action models which they developed during this research form an important background and basis of this book.

Formerly, a project like Urban Catalyst would have been seen by the investment establishment simply as a hobby for some left-wing, socially engaged planners of the leftist-scene. But today, business developers, municipalities and property owners alike have woken up to the fact that the sustainable and successful development of urban life cannot be achieved without a consideration of contextual aspects. This is true for physical structures, as well as for existing activities and programs. Traditionally seen as threatening the interests of owners and developers, informal uses are now increasingly embraced as valuable indicators for potential growth. Temporary use can provide impetus to new developments and influence the urban quality of those developments. This is nowhere more relevant than in urban wastelands and other residual spaces where traditional development methods have failed. High construction costs, the frequent popular resistance to homogeneous mass investment projects, the long planning processes and strict regulations, the uncertainties and risks connected to fixing use programs in times of economic and social change, the lack of municipal budgets to subsidize such developments and, most of all, low or even shrinking investment in many cities have left numerous spaces vacant.

Urban Catalyst demonstrates the limitations of established development tools, making a compelling argument for temporary use. This includes case studies of urban wastelands, developed into new forms of public space which provide a vibrant alternative to commercialized city centers—often perceived as homogeneous, boring and regimented. Rather than campaign for a dogmatic preservation of the status quo, Urban Catalyst advocates intelligent incorporation of temporary uses into a new form of urban planning based on the formalization of the informal and the informalization of the formal. When the members of Urban Catalyst started their research, most of these ideas were alien to planners and investors. Since then the stagnating economy experienced by many Western cities has catapulted Urban Catalyst strategies into the centre of this discourse. Instead of approaching temporary use as a problem, it is now increasingly considered a pivotal component of new development strategies. Urban Catalyst itself has initiated and participated in a range of projects that test these strategies in practice and demonstrate that this new approach has the potential to fundamentally alter the way we think about our role as architects, designers, city administrators or investors. For urban designers–or let's rather talk about urbanists– this generates tremendous new opportunities. Within this more holistic approach, urbanists become spiders in a web of stakeholder interests–filling a gap as coordinators, managers, and visionaries, even becoming developers themselves. A perhaps simplistic, but nevertheless illustrative precedent is the architects' role in communal participation projects in the 1970s and 1990s, or the stakeholder management that is already practiced by many architects. In the 1970s, however, squatters, residents and local councilors dominated such initiatives, taking a confrontational approach towards investors or central government, which often led nowhere. But in the 1990s there was an almost complete reversal: investors and central governments regained power and today's stakeholder management brings together a range of participants, capitalists and local activists alike, mediating conflicting interests within an integrated decision-making process.

Urban Catalyst has generated a thriving debate on the production of urban space involving numerous architects and planners, local authorities, property owners, and users from all over Europe. The debate has attracted public and professional attention through conferences, workshops and high profile public actions, such as the appropriation for temporary use of Berlin's most controversial building–the former East German parliament, known as Palast der Republik. Distant at first, public bodies like the German Ministry for Building or Berlin's Senate began to embrace the issue, commissioning further research on the subject and first implementation projects. Urban Catalyst has succeeded in opening up a new frontier of discourse on the city. This discourse has gained tremendous momentum and impacted on the way we engage with the urban environment.

Urban planning and urban reality are generally poles apart. In the past twenty years, for example, this has become particularly noticeable in Berlin. While in the euphoria following the fall of the Berlin Wall the city's Senate assumed vigorous population growth and commissioned a profusion of master plans for large-scale renewal areas, only a small number of these plans could actually be implemented. After a brief construction boom in the first half of the '90s, most projects were put on hold, planning goals had to be drastically reduced, and vacancy rates of the existing fabric rose considerably. Even the widely discussed, official "Planwerk Innenstadt" ("Inner-city Plan") was only partially put into effect. In many respects, it remained pure planning. At the same time, the city developed to an extent seldom seen before. However, it did so without planning. What constituted the "New Berlin" [1] at that time took place outside urban planning.

A vibrant temporary use scene developed on much of the derelict land and in many of the spaces between buildings that remained in Berlin after 1990. There were numerous nomadic bars or clubs. Close friends and casual acquaintances improvised parties in vacant buildings or former industrial areas, primarily in the eastern part of the city. New forms of leisure-time culture developed, as did a variety of migrant economies. Rents were often insignificant. Berlin became an attractive place for the younger generation, as the city allowed for an improvised, inexpensive lifestyle. Word got around.

It was precisely that which was officially considered a flaw—high vacancy rates, derelict land, slow economic development—that became the city's most valuable resources. None of these attractive sites appeared on the city administration's radar. Rather, the issue of temporary use was a taboo. Representatives from the local authorities as well as the real estate industry considered temporary use "uncontrolled growth," which at best had to be kept at bay. The opinion was that informal use would only interfere with urban development. Interim users neither fit in with what the "Planwerk Innenstadt" proclaimed to be "Stone Berlin," nor with the visions of shopping and office districts in investors' brochures. Planning seemed increasingly to operate beyond reality. After the Internet bubble and the New Economy burst, it was only a question of time before Berlin's planning bubble would burst as well. It was in this context that the idea for Urban Catalyst developed in the late 1990s. [2]

As architects, we, the authors of this book, are dealing with a progressively schizophrenic situation: the disparity between the surplus of non-implemented plans on the one hand, and on the other the large proportion of open, incomplete spaces that serve as breeding grounds for a multitude of temporary uses. What interested us was the contradiction between formal urban planning and informal urban use. After 1945, the bizarre political history had turned Berlin into a laboratory for urban derelict sites and temporary uses. Yet the current situation was revealing a trend that can be found in every other city to a lesser or greater extent. For us as architects and planners, this discovery led to posing the question of how the growing irrelevance of our own profession could be overcome. If temporary uses are an important factor for urban development, how can they be incorporated into planning and urban development? How can planning open itself up to the unplanned? And, conversely, can the unplanned be planned, the informal formalized?

In order to get to the bottom of this set of problems, Philipp Oswalt and Klaus Overmeyer developed a concept for the two-year research project "Urban Catalyst—Strategies for Temporary Uses," based at the Technical University of Berlin under the aegis of Kees Chistiaanse and funded by the European Union.[3] Philipp Misselwitz joined, as well as twelve partners from five research cities. After the research project was completed, Philipp Misselwitz, Philipp Oswalt, and Klaus Overmeyer founded the spin-off "Urban Catalyst" as a working group. The research approach was elaborated within the framework of new studies and interim use projects that had been implemented. The present book is an attempt to take stock of a nearly ten-year-long theoretical as well as practical examination of the issue of urban development through temporary use.

Our investigation of informal urban development takes up the traditional methods of works published in the 1960s and 1970s and which by means of an analysis and conceptualization of the real-life city served as a valuable impulse for a renewal of the urban planning debate. Whether *The Death and Life of Great American Cities* by Jane Jacobs (1961), *Learning from Las Vegas* by Robert Venturi and Denise Scott Brown (1972), *Collage City* by Colin Rowe and Fred Koetter (1978), or, published that same year, *Delirious New York* by Rem Koolhaas, all of these very different studies are based on the examination of unplanned and unconscious processes, of aspects of urban development that were repressed, went unnoticed, or marginalized whose potential for future planning practices was opened up. The structures of the unplanned were developed and harnessed. Thus, the investigation of the real-life city also served as a critique of the prevailing orthodoxies of urban planners and architects.

The issue of informal urban development virtually came into vogue in recent urban planning discourse. Yet it only made reference to the rapidly growing metropolises in the Southern Hemisphere. This perspective overlooks not the quantitative but the strategic relevance of the informal for the old industrial nations of the North. In view of advancing urbanization and the considerable number of existing buildings, unlike in the developing and threshold countries, advancing urbanization and the growing building stock in the North is not about the provision of new buildings for a quickly growing urban population but about creating new uses in the existing fabric. Urban planning has always moved in the field of tension between planned and unplanned development, with informal for the most part prevailing over formal processes.[4] It will consistently be necessary—precisely in the interest of planning—to call existing formalizations into question and subject them to an analysis of those processes that take place outside the established rules and structures. In view of this Sisyphean task, we will be bound time and again to dissolve existing formalizations and formalize informal practices and integrate them into established structures.

NOTHING NEW

Temporary uses are neither marginal nor novel manifestations. They have existed in the old industrial nations for a long time now. In their growth stage during the second half of the nineteenth century, shanty towns were widespread on the urban periphery. In the wake of the Great Depression, in the late 1920s and early 1930s squatter settlements and self-built structures flourished. After World War II, emergency housing and subsistence food cultivation were widespread in Europe's devastated cities. In the course of the 1970s and 1980s, politically motivated squatting occurred in numerous large European cities that engendered alternative lifestyles and housing models in protest against clean-sweep planning and speculative vacancy rates.

With the collapse of the socialist states and the end of the East–West confrontation in 1989, new streams of migration developed in Europe accompanied by informal trade. In lieu of planned economies, the small-scale capitalism of informal economies flourished in Eastern Europe. Yet what is decisive for the boom of temporary use in Europe over the past two decades is first and foremost the transition from Fordism to knowledge-based economies. It was not only the culture economy that gained in importance: the economy and urban structures were entirely transformed. What had previously been permanent unraveled. What had been life-long employment was replaced by a flexible, dynamic, and often precarious working world. Welfare-state security was relaxed and cut back. The relocation of industrial production to low-wage countries as well as the advancing rationalization of production led to the emergence of vast industrial wastelands in Europe, North America, and Japan. On the other hand, new working, consumer, and recreation programs were concentrated in new exurban centers and sub-centers such as shopping malls, leisure parks, or office districts. This resulted in enormous vacancy rates in inner-city strip malls and office buildings. In many places, out-migration and falling birth rates led to population loss; residential buildings fell empty.

These empty spaces are often condemned to a waiting loop with no prospect of being made use of in the medium term. Hence, the transformation process leads to a spatial polarization: on the one hand, zones with high development pressure and a shortage of space are created at both a regional as well as a local level; on the other hand, areas of stagnation and shrinkage develop where there is a surplus of space. Decay and growth frequently occur hand in hand.

TEMPORAL INSTABILITY

Post-Fordism is characterized by a flexibilization and dynamization of social processes. This is also reflected in the use of space. Temporary uses are only one example of a broader tendency of particular interest to us that includes the "eventization" of urban spaces as well as the spatiotemporal dynamization of services. Where employees are often in transit or work at home, they no longer have a fixed workplace in an office but various working options in a differentiated environment such as hot-desking a lean office space. Permanent ownership is increasingly being replaced by sporadic access, as shown, for example, by the growing number of car sharing schemes.[5] These developments are being reinforced by opportunities for mobile communication and site-related information, by locative media and social networks.[6] The potentials of this augmented urbanism stimulate—and indeed generate—completely new urban practices, of which flash mobs and virtual urban games were only the first, early examples. Architecture is for the most part too sluggish for the innovations of the post-Fordian knowledge society, which has led to the emancipation of numerous new urban practices from building production.

FROM ISLAND URBANISM TO THE URBANITY OF IN-BETWEEN SPACES

These developments are accompanied by a changing planning culture. In the initial decades following World War II, urban planning policies were shaped by the ideas of classical modernism influenced by social democracy, above all in Western Europe. Integral and comprehensive urban planning was to ensure quality living conditions for the entire population. Yet by the 1970s, this model fell into a state of crisis and was replaced by the concept of the "corporate" city. The primary goal of planning was now the stimulation of private investment. However, a policy of this kind only has its eye on the financially sound, solvent strata of the population. A typical example of this is public–private partnership, in which urban planning increasingly occurs on the part of the investor. In terms of land management, this concept manifests itself in a kind of island urbanism: sites that are relevant for investments are planned as projects, while the territory in between disappears from the public consciousness. Enclaves develop in which everything is planned down to the last detail—such as influencing buying patterns by means of color, music, and the design of floor surfaces. But the territory between the investors' islands is ignored. And along with that, the socially and financially weaker residents as well. What was once a continuum of urban space ultimately disintegrates into two areas with virtually opposing characters.

Yet it is precisely those areas neglected by the state, capital, and planning that often stand out due to their special urbanity. Because here, the city is designed and influenced by financially unsound players who are excluded from the projects supported by corporate urban policy. By exhausting non-monetary resources—such as derelict spaces, unofficial network and people power—these players succeed in inhabiting another form of city in zones that are temporarily unusable in traditional real-estate terms. Only here, beyond the controlled enclaves, can such temporary, informal, and innovative practices unfold.

THE NEW UNDERCLASSES AS THE AVANT-GARDE

The social background of many temporary users is prototypical for the changing social composition in what were once the industrial nations characterized by Fordism. Temporary users are the pioneers of different uses of space and increasingly unstable, deinstitutionalized ways of life. This development is reflected, for instance, in ever more rapidly changing employment relationships as well as in the abundance of the self-employed, of small-scale business enterprises, and of part-time employees. Alongside the obsolescence of the ideal of permanent employment, today's knowledge society demands additional qualifications. Networking culture and the development of a diversified knowledge environment are not only of growing importance for the individual, but for cities as well.

The departure from traditional working structures is reflected in the working biographies of today's temporary users. In many cases their activities alternate between project-related work, unpaid involvement, unemployment, or illicit, temporary, and part-time employment, while these different types of work are frequently combined. Depending on the perspective, these players are either members of the new underclasses or of the avant-garde. Knowledge society's innovations tend to develop outside the classic economic apparatus and are frequently based on the principle of traveling light: free not only from the architecture of large businesses and institutions, but also from their inflexibility and from the obligation of large-scale investments. The heroes of our epoch are the garage do-it-yourselfers. With solid know-how, with ideas and their power of imagination yet with few means they succeed in developing the innovations of our new age. The lack of institutionalization or financial means is not an obstacle, but more a precondition for success.

CULTURES OF MIGRATION

The current practices of urban use are at the same time strongly influenced by migration and shifting sociocultural processes. Self-confident new players thrust themselves into the public space of traditional European cities and have a profound influence on conventional, everyday practices and established points of view. European metropolises are increasingly colorful and culturally diversified, and while the children of earlier immigrant worker generations are aspiring toward emancipa-tion, many of the newcomers who joined the regional and international labor migra-tion movements have also contributed to cultural diversification, in particular in the last two decades. The gradual opening of Eastern Europe, increased migration within Europe through the liberalization of the job markets, as well as the growing global networking of European cities fueling increased migration from countries outside of Europe explain this new reality. Informal markets and new forms of trade, imported from threshold countries, are progressively defining the everyday image of our cities. Immigrants have in many cases occupied niches that play a subordinate role for established social classes. The acceptance of lower standards opens up new scope for immigrants, which they skillfully exploit for the development of their own networks and economic cycles. In metropolises such as London or Paris, parallel, largely informal economies developed long ago that ensure the livelihood of many newcomers as well as many refugees, asylum seekers, and illegal immigrants without financial resources.

FROM ENCLAVES TO MAGNETS

Middle-class bohemians and destitute newcomers frequently meld into temporary use environments. Unlike the sub-cultures and protest movements in the 1960s, '70s, and '80s, whose attempts to implement an alternative or counterculture also made them interim users and squatters, today's temporary users are generally skeptical about all too high political demands. Their actions are less oriented toward a utopia of liberated society and more toward personal visions, be it entrepreneurial self-fulfillment or a specific cultural project.

Temporary uses also distinguish themselves spatially from the sub-cultures mentioned above in the sense that these tended to form enclaves of a collective shaped by political leanings, whereas contemporary informal urban users operate almost diametrically. Instead of creating self-contained areas, they create public places as magnets that, if they are successful, function as urban hot spots. The basic principle is not exclusion, but creating attractors, even if these places target a very specific public. In terms of politics and culture, today's temporary uses are marked by a great deal of permissivity, if not promiscuity. The importance of the spaces and platforms that develop is for the most part attributable to their public character, which plays a considerable role with regard to life in the respective city and thus for its identity and image. These places act as breeding grounds for innovations, and even as trendsetters for the mainstream.

"CREATIVE CITY": A MISUNDERSTANDING

While temporary uses continued to be almost a non-issue in the public debate into the late 1990s subsequently the situation has radically changed. On the one hand, a large number of architects, planners, and urbanists entered the debate, which rapidly became more dynamic and led to new research, new publications, and new projects.[7] On the other hand, many municipalities have opened themselves up to the issue, to the extent that temporary uses have almost become an integral part of official urban planning jargon. However, many of the urbanist and urban policy debates are marked by fundamental misunderstandings and instrumentalizations that should be judged critically, as city administrations and landowners often attempt to strengthen their own interests by way of temporary uses.

While cities still liked to adorn their advertising brochures with classic investor projects until well into the 1990s, today one finds attractive illustrated descriptions of a "creative micro-milieu of temporary users," small businesses, and start-ups from the area of the so-called creative economy. In the meantime, even small and medium-sized cities chant the mantra of the "creative class," which has become the primary beacon of hope for investments and economic growth. But does the concept of the "creative city"[8] really lead to a new municipal policy that is not only more positive toward temporary uses and takes advantage of them for the purpose of site marketing but also actively supports them? In most cases, talk about the "creative city" is hardly more than an urban marketing slogan that has no impact whatsoever on established political practice.

Subsuming temporary uses under the term "creative economy" also means that—as far as something is really undertaken—only the entrepreneurial temporary users are acknowledged and assisted. But efficiency is not the goal of all interim users. They operate to a substantial extent in the gray zone of the non-profit sector, experiment irrespective of economic gain, cooperate with voluntary initiatives, and make a considerable contribution to the social equilibrium and the social stabilization of neighborhoods. Yet it is precisely in cases of a temporary use oriented toward the common welfare or culture that the florid words are often followed by little action that could lead to the improvement of the conditions for the development of that specific activity. While the urban marketing rhetoric is being updated, urban policy adheres virtually unchanged to its traditional methods, player networks, and policy concepts.

FROM PARTICIPATION TO DO-IT-YOURSELF

With the island urbanism of postmodernism, not only were extensive areas of the city marginalized, so also was that share of the residents that does not develop any market power, thus does not participate in shaping the city through its purchasing power or investment of its own. An effort has been made since the late 1970s to involve urban dwellers in urban planning by way of participation. However, this process often led to unsatisfactory results on both sides. While planners and investors for the most part view participatory planning as a bureaucratic complication of their work, the participating residents and their representatives experience a frustrating powerlessness, because while they have a say in things, they are not allowed to make their own decisions or map things out. Temporary uses solve the stakeholders' dilemma in a different way. A do-it-yourself takes the place of what is often only the formal participation of marginalized players. The most important condition for this is that space as a resource is available at a reasonable cost or even at no charge. Individual initiative, sociocultural capital, and the principle of minimum intervention take the place of financial means.

THE BUILDING AS THE STARTING POINT—SPHERES OF ACTIVITY OF A NEW URBAN VISION

Until now, urban development was primarily understood as an act of colonization—initially about the designation and development of land for building, and then erecting new buildings. However, since the old industrial nations have, as it were, become completely urbanized and their populations are stagnating or even shrinking, the idea of colonization has lost its justification. In the post-colonial age, so to speak, it is more about addressing what has already been built and how it accumulated over a long period of time. In this process, the view is reversed: the built environment is no longer the goal, but the starting point. A different perception of the existing city is associated with this change. And new perspectives on development open up from this perception.

The present book is devoted to the city's open spaces, all of those areas whose future is vague for a definite or indefinite period of time; which find themselves in a state of no longer or not yet. The book still attempts to pay tribute to the acute need for a better understanding of structures, activities, and demands in this diffuse zone. It formulates models of action for dealing with the open city.

NOTES

1 See the cover story, "New Berlin," of the news magazine *Der Spiegel,* no. 36 (1999).

2 The idea for the project Urban Catalyst developed out of the study *Berlin Stadt ohne Form: Strategien einer anderen Architektur* by Philipp Oswalt with the collaboration of Anthony Fontenot (Munich: Prestel, 2000). The book examines Berlin's automatic urbanism and treats the temporary as one of a total of nine themes.

3 The research project Urban Catalyst was stimulated and led by Philipp Oswalt and Klaus Overmeyer. It was funded by the European Commission, Key Action 4 "City of Tomorrow and Cultural Heritage" within the Energy, Environment and Sustainable Development Program as part of the European Union's 5th Framework Program (2001–2003). The project was coordinated by the Technical University of Berlin and participated in by eleven partners from Berlin, Helsinki, Amsterdam, Vienna, and Naples. Further information at www.urbancatalyst.net.

4 See Michelle Provoost, ed., *New Towns for the 21st Century: The Planned vs. the Unplanned City* (Amsterdam: Sun, 2010).

5 See Jeremy Rifkin, *The Age of Access: How the Shift from Ownership to Access Is Transforming Modern Life* (London: Tarcher, 2000).

6 See the Web site www.themobilecity.nl.

7 See, for example, the Web sites www.zwischennutzung.ch, www.zone-imaginaire.ch, and www.zwischennutzungsagentur.de.

8 Charles Landry's book *The Creative City: A Toolkit for Urban Innovators* (London: Earthscan, 2000) took up the discussion of the concept of "creative industries" introduced in the mid-1990s. This was the first publication to formulate the urban-policy model of the "creative city." More influential, however, was Richard Florida's book *The Rise of the Creative Class* (New York: Basic Books, 2002).

ZU VERKAUFEN

(030) 98 23 879
0173 2010 401

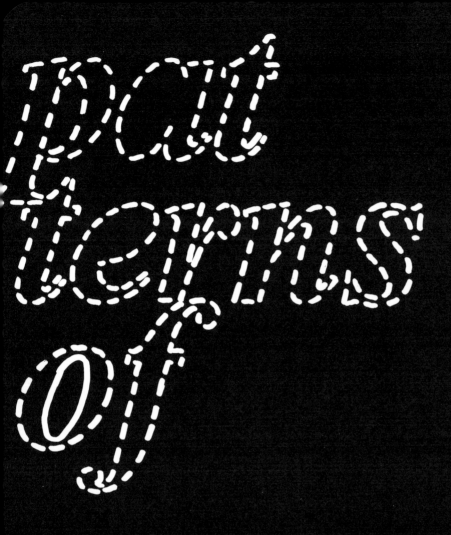

patterns of

Urban development through temporary use has long been a reality. But can it be planned? How can city planners learn from temporary users and integrate informal practices into their planning? In open-source city planning, the planner's task is less to establish facts than

the un plan ned

to create new possibilities. The users themselves become producers of the urban environment. On the basis of such experimental projects, six different strategies can be described. These approaches highlight a new field of possibilities in dealing with city planning and temporary use.

STAND-IN

The stand-in has no lasting effect on the place. It merely uses the gap between the last use and the next. Such a low-impact approach makes realization easier at the cost of transitoriness.

ÖFFENTLICHES GOLFZENTRUM BERLIN-MITTE
(BERLIN-MITTE PUBLIC GOLF CENTER)

Berlin / Germany
1995–2006
leisure / golf

Built in 1950, the Stadion der Weltjugend (Stadium for the Young People of the World) was demolished in 1994 to make way for the planned Olympiasporthalle (Olympic Sports Hall). But Berlin failed in its bid to host the 2000 Olympic Games and the plans fell by the wayside. A residential complex was planned as an alternative, and a town planning competition was held for it in 1995. But there was no demand for it either, so the private investors were lacking. Eventually, the unused and increasingly garbage-strewn area gradually came to be used—illegally at first—as a golf course in the wild, in which the terrain is left in its natural state rather than being turned into a conventional golf course. Then in 1996, as a result of private initiative, the Öffentliches Golfzentrum Mitte (Mitte Public Golf Center) opened at the site with a training area of approximately 100,000 square meters. Over the following years it was equipped with covered teeing grounds and a driving range. Open year-round, it received more than 40,000 visitors yearly. Additional athletic complexes sprang up on neighboring sites, and the area developed into a popular cult sport facility. Throughout this entire time, however, the lease remained a fixed-term temporary use agreement with no entitlements on the part of the operators. In 2003 the decision was made to move the Bundesnachrichtendienst (BND, or Federal Intelligence Service) from Munich to Berlin to the former grounds of the stadium. In fall 2006 the cornerstone was laid and the temporary use of the area as a golf and athletic facility was put to an end.

FREE FLOW

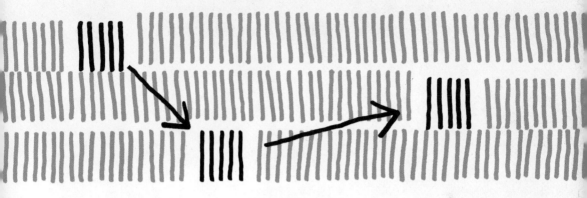

**The use continues indefinitely by moving to new locations as the opportunity arises.
This approach skillfully combines the pragmatism of the stand-in with long-term development,
as it also uses the change of location to update its own activity.**

CLUB WMF
Berlin / Germany
1991–2010
nightlife

The club was created in the context of a clandestine squat in the basement of the former building of
the precious metals manufacturer WMF, from which it took its name. Since then the WMF regularly
opened as an electro house club for a limited time in a series of new locations. The buildings and
locations served not only as physical spaces but also as thematic backdrops that were incorporated
into the furnishings or taken up as an element of the design. In 1994 the club's status changed from
illegal gathering to corporation. Thereafter the spaces that it occupied were rented on a short-term
basis and for modest amounts, and run as a "bar- or counter-served food establishment with regular
public dancing." The club continued to take over new spaces, but from this point on it was no longer
the location that determined its design but the club that came up with new ideas for the location.
For the conceptual redesigning of the spaces, artists and groups of designers recycled scrap material
and furnishings from the club's previous locations and "discarded" Berlin sites. Over the past nearly
20 years, the club has moved approximately 10 times within a 3.5 kilometer radius. Although it had no
fixed address, it succeeded in becoming a permanent fixture on the Berlin club scene, even spawning
its own electro record label. The operators saw constantly moving as an opportunity to reimagine the
club permanently without running the risk of losing its image. On the contrary, the aspect of temporariness became a kind of trademark that, in addition to the musical performances that it housed,
substantially contributed to the nightclub's notoriety and appeal. However, in spring 2010, the club
filed for bankruptcy due to internal conflicts of interest.

IMPULSE

In-between use can generate decisive impulses for the programmatic profiling of its location: it establishes a new activity profile that is carried on in a new form even after it ends.

KUNSTPARK OST (ART PARK EAST)
Munich / Germany
1996–2003
leisure / nightlife

In 1996 the abandoned site of the old Pfanni factory near Munich's Ostbahnhof (Eastern Railroad Station) was leased to the entrepreneur Wolfgang Nöth. An event and recreational center sprang up at the site with discotheques, clubs, bars, restaurants, amusement arcades, artists' studios, and small businesses. Concerts and art and antique flea markets were also held there. Some 250,000 visitors came to the Kunstpark every month. In January 2003 the lease on the site ran out and the old factory structures were slated to be torn down to make way for office buildings. In its structure Kunstpark Ost resembled a commercial enterprise that established a recreational area and event center at the site. In January 2003, when the lease expired, this impulse was directly taken up and continued. In April 2003 the Kultfabrik (Cult or Culture Factory) arose in the immediate vicinity–modeled on Kunstpark Ost, it is Europe's largest party zone with 60,000 square meters of floor space. In addition, in 2004 the exhibition venue whitebox opened with a surface area of 1,000 square meters. Meanwhile, the former management of Kunstpark Ost opened another smaller facility specifically for clubs and discotheques, which is also running successfully. Called Optimol-Werke (Optimol Works), it occupies the former premises of the company of the same name, not far from the Kultfabrik.

CONSOLIDATION

Former temporary use becomes established and turns into long-term use. Informal arrangements are replaced by long-term leases and regular permits.

CABLE FACTORY (KAAPELITEHDAS)
Helsinki/Finland
1989 onward
leisure/culture/cultural production

Nokia began to rent out the empty factory on a temporary basis as early as the 1980s, when it ceased cable production at the site, in order at least to finance the maintenance of the buildings. The tremendous rush on the relatively inexpensive studio spaces, which were renovated by the users themselves, led to the creation of the Pro Cable Society, in which the users developed an alternative plan for preserving the buildings and reviving the surrounding area and submitted it to Nokia and to the city, the latter as the future owner of the property. The declared objective and demand of this concept was to secure access to the spaces for the promotion of cultural production in the public interest. The city accepted the proposals and in 1991 formed the municipal Cable Factory Real Estate Company for the purpose, which offered Nokia another building in exchange. In 1992 the change of ownership took place. This company continues to be responsible for renovating the site and managing the Cable Factory today. Over the past ten years the site has been developed for the expanded cultural use. Today the Cable Factory is the leading cultural arena in the region, with 53,000 square meters of floor space. Its declared objective remains to make affordable spaces available to artistic and cultural producers and the creative sector. Its use now includes leasing studio and workshop spaces; TV and radio stations and theatrical, educational, and athletic facilities; and even large-scale entertainment events and restaurants. The Cable Factory Real Estate Company is entirely self-financed from event proceeds and from leasing studios.

CO-EXISTENCE

Even after the appearance of new commercial uses, the informal temporary use continues to exist on a smaller scale. A niche existence makes coexistence possible.

SCHWARZER KANAL (BLACK CANAL)
Berlin/Germany
1990–2010
residence/cultural use

In 1990 the Schwarzer Kanal (Black Canal) trailer park sprang up on a vacant construction site on the south bank of the Spree. One year later it received permission from the mayor of the Berlin borough to occupy the site until the beginning of construction of the planned headquarters of the service workers union ver.di. The trailer park evolved into a residential colony with legal status in the middle of the city and an alternative and noncommercial performance space in the borough. In 2002, when construction began, the residential settlement had to give way. After tough negotiations with the building sponsor HochTief, the project received medium-term usage rights for a site in the neighborhood—an area of the city that has been marketed since 2004 as the Media-Spree-Quartier (Spree Media District) for modern office space. In this context, in 2005 the neighboring Deutsches Architekturzentrum (German Architecture Center) and the real-estate company Office-Grundstücks-verwaltung (Office Real Estate Administration) successfully contested the trailer park's legal perma-nence before the Berlin Administrative Court, claiming that this presence diminished the value of their properties. While the residents filed an objection and an appeal, they continued to be tolerated sympathetically by HochTief and ideologically supported by ver.di. The trailer park was forced to move a second time when construction finally started in 2010 and now occupies a new site in the neighboring district of Berlin Neukölln.

PARASITE

The temporary use exploits the potential of an existing long-term use by operating next to it.

DISUSED ELECTRICAL EQUIPMENT COLLECTORS
Berlin / Germany
informal trade / informal economy

Something has been happening for years in front of the recycling centers in Berlin that no doubt goes on at recycling facilities everywhere–an informal trade in waste electrical and electronic equipment. Cardboard signs reading "VCR, TV, Refrigerator, Hi-Fi, CD" announce that the men behind the cars and VW buses are interested in the old appliances the users have come to dispose of. All day long the parking lanes are full of cars with signs and men sitting a short distance away on the sidewalk. At night one constantly finds old TVs and stereo components that didn't pass the second inspection. The deal is quite simple: the traders take everything and the owners of the electronic waste don't have to give money to the recycling center or take the trouble of actually driving into the center to dispose of the equipment in compliance with waste regulations. Instead of simply throwing them away, the old appliances are put to further use. The "collector" repairs the appliances that are still in relatively decent working order and then resells them, in Germany or in other countries where old electrical equipment finds buyers. In doing this the waste collectors aren't breaking any laws–the only illegal aspect is the littering that occurs with the unusable residual waste.

PIONEER

Hitherto unused territory is at first temporarily appropriated by the simplest means and used in a transient manner. With the success of the temporary use, the activities continue indefinitely and take on increasingly permanent forms.

ARIZONA MARKET
Belgrade / Serbia
1990s
informal trade / informal economy

As in the rest of Eastern Europe, the new residential areas in Belgrade were characterized by large and often unused open spaces as well as by a shortage of infrastructure and shopping opportunities. With the emergence of the market economy, a thriving street trade developed at nodal points of traffic systems such as intersections and public transit stops. At first it was often poor women offering just a few items for sale, some of which they produced themselves, such as fruit and vegetables, hand-knitted sweaters, and shoes. They held the goods in their hands, spread them out on the ground, or sold them out of the trunks of cars. Not long after, booths and kiosks sprang up as the first formalization and consolidation of the street trade. Over the years, these were expanded or even replaced by storefronts, sometimes even small shopping centers. In a reversal of the usual trajectory, the use emerged first and then its built manifestation. Similar processes of urban development take place through the seizure and occupation of land and the building of informal settlements in the cities of the Global South.

SUBVERSION

The temporary use strategically occupies the spaces of a long-term use in order to disturb and transform it. Although such occupations and sit-ins are usually short-lived, they often effect a marked transformation of the institutions concerned.

FREEDOM CAMP
Kiev
winter 2004 / 2005
political

In the fall of 2004 presidential elections were held in Ukraine. Already in the run-up to the elections, international observers and opposition groups had criticized the undemocratic conduct of the campaign and harassment of voters in the first round of elections. The runoff election of November 21 prompted massive demonstrations and calls for new elections and led to the so-called Orange Revolution—a peaceful, weeks-long protest against the government in power. The national movement was politically independent, decentralized, and self-organized. Centrally located Independence Square was blockaded for weeks and occupied with tents. For the national liberation movement, Pora—as this freedom camp in the city's central square was called—served as their base. The site's centrality facilitated improved organization and communication as well as the movement's symbolic visibility with respect to foreign media. This strengthened the movement and guaranteed freedom of information. The tent camp was to remain in place until democratic and lawful new elections could be held. The occupation lasted more than four weeks and achieved its political goals. Under international pressure and with a decision passed by the Supreme Court on December 26, 2004, the runoff election was repeated and the opposition candidate Viktor Yushchenko was duly elected president.

DISPLACEMENT

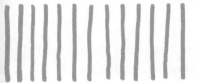

Permanent uses are temporarily displaced and continue in an improvised fashion until they are able to return to their permanent location. The temporary displacement can generate impulses for the reinvigoration of the program.

STEDELIJK MUSEUM
Amsterdam
2004–2008
art

Because of conversion and renovation work on the Stedelijk Museum, the former post office building in Amsterdam was adapted for the temporary incorporation of portions of the collection. Under the name Stedelijk Museum CS the temporary use of the building not only pointed to its address–the former post office building is located very near the main railroad station, Centraal Station–but also to the joint use of the building together with other offices and institutions to which the museum saw itself as being linked. The temporary space housed one of the largest design centers and the renowned Club 11, both of which were devoted to contemporary trends in design and art. From 2004 to 2008, while the conversion of the Stedelijk Museum continued, portions of its collection and special exhibitions were displayed on the third and fourth floors of the structure. During this time the museum cooperated with other institutions in the building. The program was initially oriented toward art from the period of student revolt in the 1960s and provided an interdisciplinary crossover. With the final phase of intermediate use, the focus shifted to contemporary media art, also because humidity and variations in temperature posed a risk to historical exhibits. In terms of content, the concept of the temporary solution represented an important stimulus to the reopened museum's program.

PATTERNS OF THE UNPLANNED

Temporary use is unplanned, but it is present in every large city. Often, it plays an important role in a city's public and cultural life as well as in its urban development, but it has thus far been almost completely ignored in official policymaking and city planning circles. But why does temporary use occur in the first place? And how does it develop? Can structures be discovered in the unplanned?

VACANCY AS A RESOURCE

Every temporary use has its starting point in empty buildings and disused sites that go unused for some period of time, whether shorter or longer. What is traditionally regarded as a failure on the part of city planners and real estate developers not infrequently represents an opportunity and a resource when seen from the perspective of other actors.

Since the end of the World War II, inner-city spaces in the developed, industrialized countries have repeatedly fallen into disuse. While the first to do so were areas that had been destroyed in the war, since the 1960s enormous industrial and infrastructural sites have been abandoned as a result of deindustrialization and modernization. Suburbanization, structural economic transformation, and the change of political system from the socialist to the postsocialist states; real estate speculation, failed planning projects, as well as the withdrawal of military units from numerous sites and the departure of portions of the population—all of these have contributed to the emergence of various forms of vacancy. Former industrial areas, waterfront areas, railroad stations and airports, unused commercial parks, empty residential neighborhoods and public institutions, as well as vacant lots of various sizes constitute seemingly functionless zones that linger for years and often decades in a state of transition between their old uses and new ones. Property owners, project developers, and city planners are in many cases unable to develop such properties within a reasonable period of time.

The causes of this are numerous and complex. In many cases, the sheer size of an area leads to long development timeframes. Often there is no demand for the new envisioned use, so that real estate developers wait for market conditions to improve. Soil contamination, the requirements imposed by departments of historic preservation, and the need for extensive development measures can make for high development costs. An ownership situation that is murky or complex can also impede the development of a property. Sometimes, sites are intentionally left undeveloped as part of a process of long-term infrastructure planning.

Today, there are vacant spaces and structures in every city, sometimes on a considerable scale. These spaces and structures can be used at low cost for limited periods, provided those who use them are willing to put up with their relatively poor condition. In large part thanks to the increasing supply of such spaces and structures, a special clientele has long since emerged for their use: the so-called temporary users.

Thus, the constant process of change and redevelopment in cities leads to a kind of urban three-field crop rotation system. Just as in medieval agriculture fields would lie fallow for a season after two periods of use so the soil could regenerate—that is, become fertile again—so urban spaces now "lie fallow" from time to time during the transition from one use to another, a process in which the periods of ostensible disuse in fact possess strategic significance.

WHO ARE THE TEMPORARY USERS?

Temporary users have little in the way of financial resources, but they have a large amount of social and cultural capital, a high degree of energy and commitment, and great willingness to improvise. Generally speaking, new spaces are not taken over by longtime residents of an area but by newcomers, people whose lives are in a state of flux. Three groups of actors can be distinguished on the basis of their relationship to established social structures.

The first group consists of young entrepreneurs and hatchers of schemes who use these urban niches as a springboard for the realization of an idea. With little starting capital, a concept can be tested and then—if it is successful—firmly established and further expanded. In other words, temporary use offers a low entry threshold and possible avenue for the potential establishment of an economic, cultural, or social concept. Typically, the actors in this category are young, well-educated people between school and career; they include students, migrants, and others.

The second group consists of actors who engage in temporary use as a kind of hobby. They have a regular income and look, for example, to sociocultural projects or the initiation of sports-related uses to provide them with enriching experiences beyond conventional categories. These actors belong to established social structures, but parallel to these they seek the freedom to pursue experimental life practices.

The third group includes trailer- and houseboat-owners as well as homeless people. This relatively small subset of temporary users is looking for opportunities to "drop out" of society and build alternative living arrangements.

Common to all temporary users is a tendency to set to work quickly and spontaneously in their chosen location and a willingness to work with existing conditions, a process in which experimental, often improvised solutions are frequently used to adapt the space to their needs. For the opportunity to use a site or building at low cost or even no cost, they are willing to

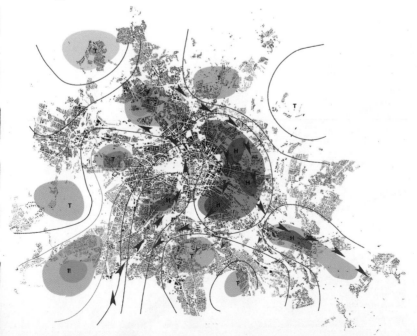

A "weather map" shows areas that facilitate (H) or complicate (T) the location of temporary uses. Due to its good traffic connections, available areas, and high density of young strata of the population, the eastern part of Berlin offers attractive temporary use environments.

53

accept an element of temporal insecurity, whether in the form of a short-term rental agreement, the absence of a rental agreement, or the illegal status of the use. The question of a larger time frame rarely enters the picture at the beginning of a use; it can begin to do so, however, if the use is successful. The notion of temporariness encompasses various concepts of time-limited use, from one-time events to projects that last a single season all the way to initiatives that were originally designed to be short-term but later turn out to be lasting as a result of their gradual growth and increasing professionalization.

WHAT LOCATIONS ARE CHOSEN?

It may seem surprising, but in terms of centrality of location and accessibility, the spatial preferences of temporary users are often no different from those of the conventional real estate market. With their cultural, recreational, gastronomic, and neighborhood offerings, temporary users seek to attract a lively walk-in clientele, which sooner or later not infrequently places them in competition with financially powerful commercial activities. Temporary users are quicker, however, since they need very little in the way of material requirements in order to get up and running in a given location. They are also a great deal more flexible, since they manage quite well with even marked qualitative limitations. They are also more creative. They discover urban architectural potentials, have a flair for unusual locations, and worry very little about the existing image of the site they have selected. Unlike those in the mainstream real estate market, temporary users do not expect a site to meet established standards of structure, state of renovation, and surroundings, but attach importance to the unknown and unexpected. They benefit from sites that are currently devalued both socially as well as in terms of the real estate market and hence are often undervalued as well.

The types of spaces chosen for temporary uses are as diverse as those selected for conventional uses. Specific types of use look for types of spaces that are suitable for them. Conversely, specific kinds of space attract temporary uses that match their particular

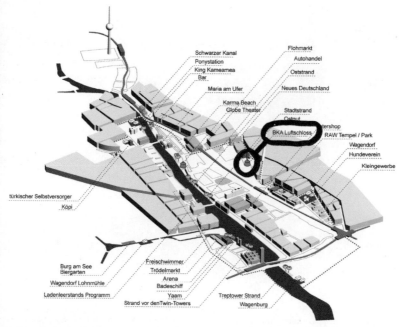

Eastern Spree region 2004. More than 60 projects had located to the abandoned industrial and railroad areas. The construction of a sports arena has meanwhile displaced numerous experimental uses.

character. For example, users engaged in informal commerce look for locations with high pedestrian traffic and thus prefer locations near railroad stations, department stores, and major intersections. Clubs wish to be easily accessible. They often use unusual facilities in order to make themselves distinctive, but they avoid residential neighborhoods because of the noise problem. By contrast, sociocultural institutions depend precisely on a close connection with a neighborhood. Start-up offices and galleries also value the connection with a neighborhood, in part because of the availability of walk-in customers, in part because of the presence of service providers in the immediate vicinity, e.g., restaurants and cafés.

Generally speaking, uses benefit from the presence of similar activities nearby, which has a favorable effect on the development of larger areas and neighboring spaces. Many temporary users choose a site less for its location than because of the temporary user milieu that already exists there. They want to participate in precisely that milieu. Because of their more or less public character, most temporary uses are located near city centers. In outlying districts, by contrast—to the extent that they arise in such areas at all—most temporary uses are located near homes.

By no means all disused urban sites are suitable for temporary use. Generally speaking, the more intact a site's infrastructure, the more accessible it is, and the denser the network of potential actors, the greater the likelihood that a temporary use will arise there. If the investments required to renovate it are too high, if it lies too far off the beaten track, or if suitable users are unavailable, it will remain unused. This latter point becomes especially clear in the case of many smaller, shrinking cities where the younger, more active population has moved away and there is virtually no influx of new residents. In such cases, the large supply of vacant spaces and structures does not provoke uses, because the initiators are lacking.

WHAT ROLE DO NETWORKS PLAY?

As a rule, temporary users do not arise in isolation but in clusters, whether in a large disused industrial area or scattered throughout a neighborhood with a high vacancy rate. These clusters generate specific identities. Whereas in the case of shopping centers the formation of such images is artificially generated by project managers through the selection of lessees and directed by a centralized leadership, with temporary use such identities emerge over time. They are the result of social networks and the values of all the individual participants. If the supply of space is adequate, the first pioneers are followed by friends and acquaintances. Particularly in the initial phase of projects, conditions are ideal for rapid "cell growth."

Since most temporary users have only a small amount of capital, their social and professional networks are among their most important resources. On the one hand, it is these that make it possible to initiate a temporary use in the first place; on the other, temporary activities in turn lead to new cooperation. It is possible to distinguish two kinds of network formation.

The melting pot: For many temporary users, the shared site becomes a melting pot. This experience is the result of mutual support, communal activity, and professional cooperation. Temporary users deal with their lack of financial resources and the inadequate condition of their spaces with mutual aid. Professional cooperation also gives rise to local economies, which in turn engender relations of nonmonetary exchange among the various temporary users. Moreover, as a result of their communal appropriation of the site, the latter acquires an aura that is initially internal but develops a public component as their activity increases, an aura by means of which the users also identify themselves as a group. This communally generated identity compensates for the instability of the situation, above all for the uncertainty regarding the duration of the use. The existential endangerment of a temporary use community tends to reinforce it rather than lead to its dissolution. The need to assert their own interests against owners and authorities—to negotiate regarding the duration of the use and the granting of additional permits while mobilizing public awareness at the local level: all of this strengthens cohesion among the users. Finally, it can also lead to the emergence of formalized structures such as associations or corporations.

Branching: Conversely, the temporary character of temporary uses leads to the formation of networks through branching. Once a joint project is over, the participants often go separate ways and initiate multiple new temporary uses in parallel in different locations. Thus, a temporary club may spawn a bar, a booking agency, or a record label. The offshoots of the initial project are independent entities, but they are closely linked through cooperation. On the one hand, temporary uses are dependent on networks; on the other, they themselves contribute intensively to the formation of new ones.

HOW DO TEMPORARY USERS APPROPRIATE SPACES?

The spaces of temporary uses were often built for entirely different purposes. They usually lack the necessary amenities; not infrequently, they are slated for demolition; sometimes they are building shells. Heating, the supply of electricity, light, and water, health and safety, and fire protection are inadequate for the purposes of virtually any conceivable use. The owners, however—because they receive little or no rental income—have no interest in investing in construction measures on behalf of the temporary use. For their part, the temporary users not only lack the capital for larger investments but also the long-term security that would make such expenditures worthwhile.

Temporary users confront this dilemma with the principle of maximum adaptation. At least in the beginning, they usually use the spaces and structures as is, improvise a lot, and recycle whatever they can. They accept limitations on use, avoid or ignore official requirements as far as possible, and in the process sometimes accept illegal conditions.

Temporary users make a virtue of necessity. Thanks to the fact that the site is largely left in its original state, it becomes possible to preserve its aura and historical character. This allows for unusual aesthetic experiences, particularly as it has often been a long time since the spaces have been seen by the public. Historical artifacts—for example, from industrial culture or postwar modernism—are appropriated and carried forward into the present and the future. Characteristic and also visible to the visitor is an easily readable multilayeredness: the site is overlaid with a series of interventions that decidedly belong, aesthetically, to the present, and culturally to contexts different from that of the site. These interventions provide important stimuli to the design-related fields—the visual arts, graphic design, and architecture—stimuli that reach far beyond the actual temporary use.

WHAT ACTORS ARE INVOLVED?

In addition to the temporary users themselves, a whole range of other actors is also involved in temporary uses. The first of these are the agents, who usually instigate larger temporary use projects and help them get off the ground without ever being users themselves. They create framework conditions that make it possible for others to launch a temporary use, including lease contracts with owners, official permits, political and administrative support, and organizational structures. A crucial factor in the effectiveness of such agents is their ability to function as a bridge. They not only enjoy the sympathy of the temporary users; they also have a good understanding of their informal mechanisms, because they themselves come in part from the same milieu. At the same time, they can also speak the language of the authorities and the owners, which puts them in a good position to mediate between these opposing milieus. Once they have initiated a project, the agents usually withdraw and leave its subsequent development to the temporary users themselves.

Originally, the agents have purely idealistic motivations and act without a contract or financial incentive. They are initially found in the temporary user milieus and municipal agencies, especially those that are responsible for the administration of real estate. Thus far, the agents in government offices have primarily operated "under the radar." They act from their own sense of personal engagement, with no contract from the administrators or municipal policy-makers and politicians. Instead, they use the freedom of maneuver that goes along with their position to engage in a kind of micropolitics that supports the social and cultural intentions of weaker actors in the city by offering them the opportunity to launch a temporary use and in this way also promotes a better development trajectory for the city as a whole.

In recent years, the phenomenon of temporary use has been discovered by municipal policy-makers and politicians, and the result has been that there are now official agents in addition to informal ones. Their work has emerged as an important factor in the development of temporary uses, and this in turn has resulted in that work becoming formalized and professionalized. Cities now create special administrative offices to coordinate temporary uses or contract with private entities to do so, as in the context of neighborhood management. Because of the high demand, private agencies have been created in many locations; such agencies work on behalf of owners and municipalities to bring spaces together with temporary users. With an office on site and in keeping with a concept developed in coordination with their client, they attempt to attract and, as it were, "curate" specific temporary user milieus. With the skill of experienced pilots, they support the temporary users in building organizational structures, planning, marketing, obtaining funds, and securing permits. They coordinate local programs and actions. At the same time, they attempt to recruit owners to make spaces and structures available on a temporary basis, advise them in selecting temporary users, and help resolve legal problems.

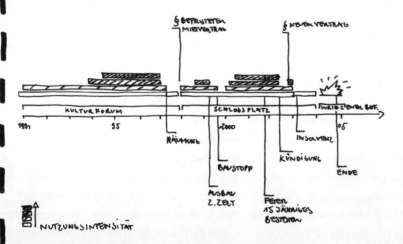

Development path of the tent theater BKA Luftschloss, Berlin

Next to the users, the owners of properties are the most important party. It is a prerequisite of every temporary use that it be tolerated—either explicitly or implicitly—or contractually permitted by the owner. In view of the fact that, in either case, the owner is also responsible for the safety and security of his property, making it available for use involves an element of risk, depending on the condition of the buildings. Moreover, the expense of managing and caring for the property is disproportionate to any possible rental income the owner might receive.

On the other hand, there can also be many non-monetary advantages for the owner. Such advantages may include a new and positive image for the location, the creation of a specific identity, public awareness of the site, and the prevention of squatting vandalism and decay. Temporary users may attract permanent users or become long-term tenants themselves. And with all this, the investment costs to be shouldered by the owner are low if not nonexistent. For these reasons, more and more owners are accepting and even initiating temporary uses.

However, even in situations where their properties have stood empty for many years, many owners are unwilling to take this step. Temporary use does not meet their expectations of a high return on their investment. They are also afraid that the use will become permanent or that they will have to contend with conflicts when seeking to end it. This attitude is especially common among investors who have purchased abandoned areas with the intention of developing them immediately. Whereas large real estate portfolio companies that have owned properties for decades can afford to let them stand empty—or be the scene of temporary uses—for long periods of time, investors have loans that they need to repay within a limited time frame. They depend on developing the property as quickly as possible and therefore view temporary users as an obstacle. In a number of countries, however, there are laws limiting the power of disposal of owners who no longer use their properties. Such owners are required to tolerate temporary uses.

Policymakers and administrators are involved in processes of temporary use in multiple ways. First, every use of a built structure is subject to legal regulations and official licensing requirements, compliance with which is controlled by the government authorities. Depending on how the authorities interpret regulations regarding fire protection, health and safety, and a great deal more, temporary uses can be enabled or prevented. It is no accident that temporary uses sprang up throughout the countries of Central and Eastern Europe after the collapse of the socialist system, since governmental authority only continued to operate to a limited extent. Once the administrative structures had become consolidated again in the new political conditions, the boom was over.

Although temporary uses largely go against the classical control and organizational practices of government entities, for a number of reasons they have now become an attractive urban development option for policymakers and administrators. Facing increasingly tight budgets, city administrations hope that by cooperating with pioneers from civil society they will be able to stabilize socially weak neighborhoods, reactivate vacant sites, and create new public spaces, all without any significant financial expense. Temporary use milieus create new images for entire neighborhoods, images that are usually viewed quite positively by the majority of residents as well as being attractive to investors. From a city planning perspective, this creates new options for developing sites that have long ago defied all classical city planning attempts to work with them. In addition, city and location development become possible even for sites that have no hope of attracting investments even in the medium term.

All this has led to a situation in which many cities have not only become more tolerant in their licensing practices but also stimulate and enable temporary uses in other ways. For example, in cases where a private owner makes his property available to temporary users, cities are sometimes willing to offer a payment guarantee or release him/her from liability and property taxes. Moreover, many cities own a large amount of property themselves, which they are able to make available for temporary use when it is not being used. Beyond this, some cities promote temporary uses by creating temporary use agencies, making such use a subject of planning processes, and including it in city planning contracts.

In the mediation and negotiation process, indeed in the entire process of communication among temporary users, property owners, and municipal authorities, the media sometimes play an important role. As financially weak as temporary users may be, their activities often remedy the social and cultural deficits of particular neighborhoods and open up possibilities that are positively viewed by a majority of the residents. For this reason, media reports tend to serve the interests of temporary users and hence strengthen their position vis-à-vis owners and authorities. Press coverage also helps to win over politicians, persuading them to champion particular projects. Hence it is not surprising that—especially in conflicts—temporary users engage in targeted public relations campaigns. However, a good press is by no means a guarantee of success in negotiations. Not infrequently, the owner, the administration, and even politicians disregard public opinion.

At the same time, municipal policymakers and property owners can also benefit from reaction in the media. If temporary users have settled in a particular location and a creative milieu has grown up among them, this changes the external perception of the location and leads to a change in its image. In the increasing competition for locations, informal activities are that extra something special in the arsenal of "creative cities," a title to which many cities seek to lay claim today. In this connection, subcultural hotspots are discovered and exploited more rapidly today than ever before, not only by the mass media but also by city marketing. Prominent examples of cities that have changed their image thanks to temporary uses are "Cool Manchester" in the 1980s and "das Neue Berlin" ("the New Berlin") in the 1990s. Media attention can help to consolidate temporary uses, but it can also hasten their end. If a location becomes attractive to investors because its image has been enhanced by

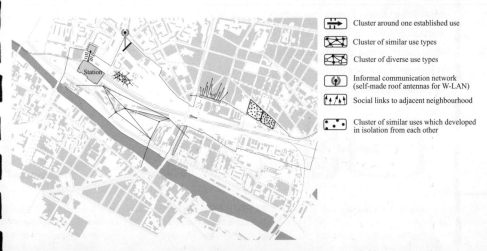

Cluster around one established use

Cluster of similar use types

Cluster of diverse use types

Informal communication network (self-made roof antennas for W-LAN)

Social links to adjacent neighbourhood

Cluster of similar uses which developed in isolation from each other

Network formation of temporary uses in the eastern Spree region, 2003

temporary use, that usually spells the end for temporary users.

Even before the media enter the picture, direct public awareness has a role to play as the "customer" of temporary uses. For temporary users are rarely sufficient unto themselves, but seek to appeal to a public—whether it is broad and inclusive or a small niche audience—to whom they offer culture, excitement, or particular services. Consumers initially learn of the activities of temporary users by word of mouth, through flyers, or through emails from friends and acquaintances; the novelty of the use and the fact that it is so little known tend to make for a certain exclusivity, which naturally contributes to the appeal of the temporary use. Often, the activities cannot be detected from the street without specific instructions, which is also advantageous in view of possible legal violations. In contrast to classical economic and cultural life, the boundaries between suppliers and demanders are often not clearly drawn; a single person can switch sides quickly or even play both roles at once. It is also possible for an area to be used informally without temporary use being involved. This occurs when consumers appropriate it directly, playing games and engaging in athletic activities there, going for walks, having picnics and camping, or having parties in the absence of any special facilities for the purpose.

HOW DO TEMPORARY USES DEVELOP?

The simplest case is that of the "stopgap," whose plans for a site involve only a limited time period, whether it be a day, a month, or a year. However, many temporary actors do not see themselves as temporary users at all, but display a clear interest in consolidating their use or even making it permanent. For this group, temporary use offers an opportunity to circumvent the usual start-up difficulties and clear away obstacles to the realization of their ideas.

When perpetuating temporary uses, the initiators confront the task of formalizing informal structures. Informality has its price. For the continued existence of a temporary use, it is simply cheaper—and sometimes even necessary—over the long term to consolidate the hardware and the software. This affects the internal organization of the temporary users, their relationship to the owners and authorities, and the design of the site. For example, in Germany, in the course of consolidation, what was initially a loosely structured group of like-minded people acting more or less as a collective, without any hierarchy, must be converted into the formal and contractually capable structure of a registered association (*eingetragener Verein*, or *e.V.*), a limited liability corporation (*Gesellschaft mit beschränkter Haftung*, or *GmbH*), or some other kind of association provided for in the German Civil Code. In the process, some portion of the—initially often enormous—spontaneity of the participants is often lost. Beyond this, rivalries and even power struggles often develop among the initiators, which may end with one or another of the founding participants feeling completely marginalized. However, without such conflicts and the hierarchization and marginalization that accompany them, it is

Types of Temporary Use

Niche / Temporary use as a shelter and refuge from the established social system

Playing Field / Changing worlds: temporary use as a parallel universe and experimental space alongside everyday working life

Incubator / Temporary use as a springboard for one's professional career and social integration

virtually impossible to apply for financial assistance, obtain loans, or enter into contracts.

In terms of the temporary users' relationship to the owners, formalization means that instead of merely being tolerated, they strive to obtain a rental contract, if possible with the option of a long-term or even hereditary lease or purchase of the property. Many temporary uses come to an end when the owner refuses to accept any further temporary use of his property. This often leads to conflicts, which temporary users then deliberately publicize. Often, municipal city planning and cultural agencies intervene in the public interest and attempt to mediate between the opposing fronts. Not infrequently, temporary users are able to avoid the threatened end of their use by moving to a new location, a change that usually also involves the updating of their concept and further formal consolidation.

However, problems may also be caused by the requirements of the authorities, for the legal regulations regarding temporary uses are ultimately no different from those for permanent ones. If, on the one hand, with the perpetuation of a temporary use, the authorities demand the fulfillment of a wide range of requirements, and if on the other the building fabric and technical infrastructure of the site are too poor and necessary investment costs too high, the result may be a predicament that can quickly lead to the end of the temporary use.

WHAT DO TEMPORARY USES ACHIEVE?

First of all, they stimulate the development of the location in question. Programs and profiles become established. Their influence continues to be felt even after the end of the temporary use. For, in many respects, they can continue to determine the use of the site long after its temporary use is over. Sometimes, it is the temporary uses themselves that turn into permanent ones. In addition, temporary uses change the image of their location and attract other uses to settle there. Often, temporary uses cause buildings that were previously slated for demolition to be preserved, renovated, and modernized.

Even independently of their original location, temporary uses can establish new use concepts. Hitherto unknown types of uses are developed on the basis of temporary uses, and when they are successful they continue to unfold and develop in other locations. In the process, temporary uses may become the nuclei for new companies and new cultural and social institutions. Finally, temporary uses also have an impact on the biography of their initiators. The calling becomes a profession; new occupational profiles come into being; the actors acquire much of the knowledge of their new professions as autodidacts. Even if in most cases temporary uses only exist for a limited time, they may have lasting and long-term effects on the development of locations, economic sectors, and cultural fields. In this case, they serve as an urgently needed rejuvenating treatment for established structures that are no longer capable of renewing themselves by their own efforts.

CLAIMING A NO MAN'S LAND: ARIZONA IN BOSNIA

Azra Akšamija

Protagonists: SFOR troops as initiators; traders and vendors at a later stage

Use: Black market, trading and selling of goods

Status: Legal with illegal spill over areas at the periphery of the market

Site: Arizona Highway in the Brcko district, Bosnia-Herzegovina

Transformation: 1996-2000 informal growth of the market; 2000-2002 conflict over closure versus legalization; 2002-2007 transformation through construction of a 100,000 square meter shopping mall (ItalProject)

Cost: € 120 million for the construction of the shopping mall

Financing: Joint venture between the Brcko district and the Italian investor ItalProject

Arizona Market was the largest black market in the Balkans. It developed at an unbelievable rate alongside Arizona Road—the military term given to Bosnia-Herzegovina's main north–south highway.

Emerging in 1996 in an unstable border-zone, Arizona Market flourished as the only regional shopping and service center. At its peak state of development in 2001, the market consisted of 2,200 businesses, sixty-five cafes, and seven nightclubs. It was situated about 15 kilometers southwest of the border-town of Brcko. Some 30,000 people made a living from it and its daily turnover was estimated at € 0.5 million, which doubled on weekends. Smuggled articles, copies of designer brands, women–everything could be bought and paid for in any currency. Many aspects of the market reflected the new political, social, economic and urban conditions that have arisen as a consequence of the war in Bosnia. Illustrating the new Bosnian economy of survival, the market knew only one rule: it had to be cheap!

A chain reaction of paradoxical circumstances and governmental interventions led to the development of informal and unplanned "urban" configurations along Arizona Road. As the market was not regulated by any institution, everyone was able to build and sell whatever he or she desired. While this lack of control strengthened organized crime, the market's autonomy also attracted people from all ethnicities.

Already during the war, Arizona Market had become the first space of communication between the

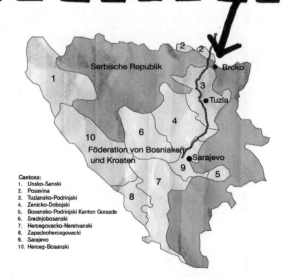

Cantons:
1. Unsko-Sanski
2. Posavina
3. Tuzlansko-Podrinjski
4. Zenicko-Dobojski
5. Bosansko-Podrinjski Kanton Gorazde
6. Srednjobosanski
7. Hercegovacko-Neretvanski
8. Zapadnohercegovacki
9. Sarajevo
10. Herceg-Bosanski

"Arizona Road" is the military designation for the main north–south transit route in Bosnia and Herzegovina. The road runs through the district of Brcko, a zone that has been demilitarized since 1999 and enjoys political privileges.

country's warring entities. It thus provided a unique opportunity to observe the birth of a self-organized city as a spatial mediator of peace in Bosnia and Herzegovina.

THE FORMATION OF ARIZONA MARKET

The strategic importance of this region where three countries come together conically–Bosnia and Herzegovina, Croatia, and the remaining part of former Yugoslavia–had made this area one of the most violent war fronts. In the wake of the Dayton Peace Agreement in 1995, the state of Bosnia-Herzegovina was divided into two entities: the Serb Republic and the Federation of Bosnians and Croats. The area around the border town of Brcko remained an unresolved political issue. Then, the "Arizona Corridor" that was not a part of any of the entities, was established along Arizona Road. The International Community supported this territorial compromise, as it was supposed to bring peace to the region. Given the catastrophic political and economic situation after the war, there was hardly any communication between people or sufficient supply of food and other necessities in the Arizona Corridor. For all these reasons, the establishment of a market in this no-man's-land seemed to be a good idea.

Traveling displays: "Traveling displays" developed due to the extreme concentration of businesses along the road. The displays of the surrounding businesses were experienced from the car.

Arizona Market was intended to become the first point of communication between the warring sides. Providing the minimal infrastructure and space for growth, the International Community did not necessarily plan the market, it rather initiated its self-organized development. In 1996, the American SFOR soldiers leveled an area of 40 hectares close to their checkpoint, thus establishing the basis for the emergence of trade along Arizona Road. Such an institutional initiation of an informal market represented a unique act of political creativity in Bosnia and Herzegovina. Subsequently, in 1997, the market was also officially founded by the Ravne Brcko administration.

Facilitated by the lack of official governance, the market quickly became the most flourishing commercial center in the country. Many different stalls and traders began to set up business along about 20 kilometers on both sides of Arizona Road. Merchandise was sold directly to people passing through, either from cars or from portable crates. On a field bordering on a minefield, the trade grew into a "bazaar" whose area doubled every six months. The biggest profits were made by selling products directly from trucks. There was no domestic production and therefore all goods were imported. However, a lack of government control in post-war Bosnia also allowed a network of organized crime to evolve very quickly. Corruption

Differentiation: The density of the businesses in the bazaar mall meant that they differed in terms of their accessibility and business outlooks.

was already widespread within the first few years following the war and remains very powerful to this day. Consequently, Arizona Market soon became the main source of crime in the country, trading in illegal articles such as weapons, drugs and women. Another problematic aspect of the market were epidemics and fire risks, as there was hardly any investment going into fundamental infrastructure such as electricity, water, or sewage.

While protection rackets and the slave trade market in women earned Arizona Market the soubriquet "hell on earth," its business success melted the rival nations together. Arizona Market represented an important model of peaceful coexistence. It was one of the rare places in Bosnia and Herzegovina where people spoke all three languages characterizing it as "the greatest peace in the world." It is no coincidence that Arizona Market also became known as "the United Colors of Bosnia."

SELF-ORGANIZATION AND PLANNING: PROCESS NAVIGATION

In 2000, the market had reached a critical size that made the growth of the self-organized city unsustainable. Organized crime, exploitation, trafficking and unbearable living and working conditions made it necessary to quickly solve the question of its future. If its development had gone on as it had, the market could have collapsed. The authorities made unsuccessful attempts to enforce a new regime of control on the market, and it eventually became necessary for the Office of the High Representative to order its regulation. The regulation plan worked out by the Brcko district included drawing up a master plan, establishing fiscal measures, regulating ownership, fighting crime, carrying out inspections, and regulating different types of market activities. All contracts and work permits were to be checked and reissued and the opening times

PATTERNS OF URBAN BEHAVIOR

Area occupation

Dock

Traveling display

Bazaar mall

Exclusion

Route

Public space

Tap

of the market were immediately set from 6 a.m. to 6 p.m. The masterplan provided for the resettlement of the market on a neighboring area, the demolition of the existing market, and the transformation of the resulting "tabula rasa" into a shopping center. To this end, an "open" international competition was organized. The winning entry was a regional shopping and recreation center entitled ItalProject submitted by an Italian investor.

However, the regulation plan faced immediate resistance from the market. The inplementation of these regulatory measures could have led to the break-up of the market or to its reemergence in the neighboring Republika Srpska, with the loss of the largest regional income generator as a consequence. And while the government's top-down strategy threatened the livelihood of many people, it did not provide any realizable solution to their financial problems. If the regulation plan was to be followed, the resettlement of the traders would have resulted in higher rents and therefore higher taxes. The market people were already barely surviving, having to pay protection money to the mafia in addition to the Brcko district's taxes. When tax inspectors came, stall owners ran into the surrounding minefield with their merchandise. In order to protect their livelihood, they were risking their lives.

When the government attempted to implement the ItalProject, marketeers periodically organized demonstrations that blocked traffic on Arizona Road completely.

In absence of any realistic problem resolution, the ItalProject remained just a plan for a few years, and the difficulties in its implementation exposed the parallel existence of the Arizona structure and the state system. They were too far removed from one another and worked only against each other. The government was not in a position to solve the market's many problems so it had to find a way to reconcile itself with the market and to cooperate with it. For this, alternative planning methods needed to be found that could really communicate

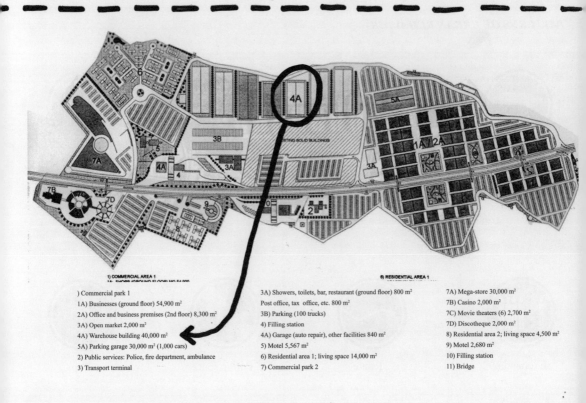

) Commercial park 1
1A) Businesses (ground floor) 54,900 m²
2A) Office and business premises (2nd floor) 8,300 m²
3A) Open market 2,000 m²
4A) Warehouse building 40,000 m²
5A) Parking garage 30,000 m² (1,000 cars)
2) Public services: Police, fire department, ambulance
3) Transport terminal

3A) Showers, toilets, bar, restaurant (ground floor) 800 m²
Post office, tax office, etc. 800 m²
3B) Parking (100 trucks)
4) Filling station
4A) Garage (auto repair), other facilities 840 m²
5) Motel 5,567 m²
6) Residential area 1; living space 14,000 m²
7) Commercial park 2

7A) Mega-store 30,000 m²
7B) Casino 2,000 m²
7C) Movie theaters (6) 2,700 m²
7D) Discotheque 2,000 m²
8) Residential area 2; living space 4,500 m²
9) Motel 2,680 m²
10) Filling station
11) Bridge

with the market. The "wild" aspects of Arizona did not necessarily have to be preserved, but it was a matter of maintaining and developing those qualities that could be lost with the market's "domestication."

While there was an agreement to bring Arizona Road under control, it was difficult to convince stakeholders of its qualities and its potential for development. In the short term, even a simple positive evaluation of the existing market would not have promoted new development in Arizona, since it was fraught with extremely negative associations. And whereas the market's behavioral patterns showed that the rules of conventional planning are often circumvented and cannot always be successfully applied, small, temporary planning interventions could have created a platform for the market to continue to function while gradually becoming integrated into the state system. In this way, self-organization could have been deliberately used and guided in order to encourage new urban development processes. In the course of time new needs would have emerged, for which new instruments of planning would have been required. A fundamental reorganization of a situation in the case of a conflict provides the possibility to intuitively come to terms with the economic and political changes that ensue. By using existing conditions to create new ones that future users would come to terms with, the market would have been gradually reshaped without destroying its original character. Yet, the final product of such a planning strategy remains uncertain. The market might have disappeared, but it was more likely that we would have had the rare opportunity to witness the birth of a new city: the city of Arizona in Bosnia.

After several years of heavy struggle that even involved a military intervention, Arizona Market was destroyed and the ItalProject finally implemented in the form of a shopping mall with an overregulated traffic system and parking with surveillance. Paradoxically, the ready-made aluminum structure of the shopping mall still carries the name "Arizona black market."

- - - - - - - - - - - - - - - - -

Protagonists: the city as property owner and a network of users

Use: start-up offices and studios for the cultural sector

Status: short-term lease

Site: historically protected administration building with 15,000 square meters of floor space near Berlin-Alexanderplatz

Cost: rent of € 4.25 per square meter

Financing: sponsors/marketing

- - - - - - - - - - - - - - - - -

The temporary leasing of the Haus des Lehrers (HdL, Teacher's House) near Alexanderplatz in Berlin from August 1999 to June 2001 is a prime example of a temporary use initiated by the government.

On the one hand, the city of Berlin as landlord was in a position to revive and enhance an almost forgotten and abandoned piece of real estate in the consciousness of its citizens by leasing it temporarily.

On the other, a heterogeneous and spontaneously formed group of renters was able to develop into a professional network with a strong identity.

- - - - - - - - - - - - - - - - -

BACKGROUND

The government's willingness to initiate a temporary use had its roots in earlier town planning and social developments that had been taking place in Berlin since the early 1990s. Especially in the borough of Mitte, the exodus of much of the preexisting population after the fall of the Berlin Wall and the partial dissolution of the administrative infrastructure of the German Democratic Republic had resulted in a high vacancy rate in the area. At the same time there was an influx of young population groups from throughout the Federal Republic on an unprecedented scale. This influx made up to some degree for the exodus, but it also created a lifestyle based on the use of larger-than-average residential and commercial spaces for little money. Squatting and self-initiated reuse and redevelopment became an everyday occurrence. For a long time the supply of new space seemed inexhaustible. The bar for appropriating space was especially low in the late 1990s, since successful precedents had now been set throughout the entire city. The government had gradually gone over from an attitude of strict protectionism to a more open approach, especially because that allowed it to avoid security and maintenance costs in view of vandalism and decay, and even to take in a small amount of income.

The HdL represents an architectural emblem of GDR modernity. As the "appendage" of a conference hall with a shallow dome, the twelve-story high-rise office building was constructed east of Alexanderplatz from 1962 to 1964 according to plans by the architect Hermann Henselmann. It has a total usable floor space of almost 15,000 square meters. After German reunification, in 1991, it became the property of the city of Berlin, which initially moved portions of the administration of the Senatsschule (Senate School) to the building. Since there was no long-term plan for how it should be used, from 1994 on it was rented to a succession of different tenants, until it finally stood totally empty as of August 1999.

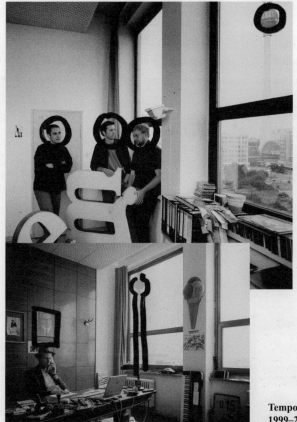

Temporary use at the former Haus des Lehrers, 1999–2001

THE RISE OF A NETWORK

With the building now standing empty, the Mitte Borough Council decided to rent it out as office and work space on a temporary basis. The initiative was primarily based on the motivation of two of the borough's employees, while the borough as an institution had reservations concerning the plan. The two initiators prepared a cost estimate and also pointed out the advantages of previous instances of temporary use, which had made at least enough money to cover the cost of building maintenance and security.

Thanks to contacts between the Borough Council and potential users that had filed earlier inquiries, news of the offer spread throughout the scene extremely quickly, and within two months the building was entirely rented out to interim tenants. Interested parties were required to submit a statement describing the use they wished to make of the space. They were then invited to discuss these plans with the two initiators in the city administration, on the basis of which the latter then selected the tenants so as to ensure a diverse and high-quality mix of uses by cultural producers. A heterogeneous group of people working mainly in the creative fields—artists, designers, graphic designers, musicians, students, and theater people—moved into the building. The group of approximately sixty new tenants primarily consisted of people under thirty with an academic background. They received lavish amounts of space for a moderate rent of €4.25 per square meter and an attractive setting in a central location where they could take the first steps in their independent careers and try out their skills. The building offered a playful way to make the transition from school to career.

The architectural peculiarities of the structure—for example, its wide hallways and light-flooded stairways—helped to build and promote internal communication. Short visits and mutual interchange from one end of the building to the other were the order of the day. As if in a vertical neighborhood, focal points of communal use soon emerged. The tenants created a cafeteria, a party room, and a joint exhibition space. Regular meetings and gatherings were held at which the new areas were planned and administered. Internal cohesion grew and evolved from a social phenomenon into a professional network—contracts were obtained and projects were jointly initiated. The end result was a dynamic commercial body of little start-ups in which the individual was able to benefit to a high degree from synergetic effects.

Former foyers and common rooms in the building facilitated mutual exchange and professional cooperation.

EXTERNAL CONSOLIDATION

During the period of its temporary use, the HdL evolved into a cultural milieu with a magnet effect. With exhibitions, parties, and happenings as joint activities held at the site, the tenants were increasingly able to present themselves to the outside world as a unit. The HdL came more and more to be perceived as a cultural site with a dynamic of its own, and its events were increasingly well attended. This evolution reached its high point with the use of the facade for the video art project *Blinkenlights* by the Chaos Computer Club in 2001 and the use of the HdL as the backdrop for the music video *"Nur die Liebe zählt"* ("Only Love Counts") by the band Die Toten Hosen in 2002.

Within the network, however–motivated by the growing notoriety of the building and its users–the temporary nature of the project was becoming a source of mounting dissatisfaction. Intent on consolidating their success, the tenants now set their sights on a long-term use. By contrast, the Mitte Borough Council remained determined to find a buyer for the property—a plan, however, that was difficult to realize. While the new activities at the HdL had drawn much attention to the property (which had been virtually forgotten until then), that attention was almost entirely restricted to a relatively self-contained milieu. As far as the perception of potential investors was concerned, the HdL was effectively invisible. Thus in the following period the temporary lease was extended four more times—for one year and then for six-, four-, and two-month periods. In spring 2001 a consortium of investors finally agreed to finance the purchase of the building. Their plan was to renovate the HdL and then sell it on the real estate market for a profit. At this point the HdL's tenants jointly launched a large-scale press and publicity campaign that targeted both the city of Berlin as owner of the building and the investors. This increased the notoriety of the property and users even further, and the headlines reached large parts of the population. In terms of the tenant–landlord relationship, however, nothing changed. In addition to mounting their public protest, the tenants also reorganized and embarked on a joint search for alternative spaces. In this phase they acquired the structural hallmarks of a corporate identity—a brand name, a logo, and a spokesperson—including building elements such as a standardized uniform that completed their public visibility.

After giving notice and moving out in 2001, the user community divided itself up into two groups: one moved to the Haus des Reisens, the other into the former Neues Deutschland building.

71

TERMINATION AND REORIENTATION

Despite the massive protests and the support of large portions of the Berlin press, the lease was not renewed, and the final move-out date was set for June 30, 2001. The users' goal shifted towards keeping the HdL network alive and to relocating as a collective, putting faith in their newly won popularity. The search quickly met with success. A smaller part of the group moved into the neighboring Haus des Reisens (HdR, House of Travel), while the larger part moved into the Neues Deutschland (ND, New Germany) building in the nearby district of Friedrichshain, which was comparable to the HdL in terms of size and historical significance. There was a slight fluctuation in the course of the move. Some users left the group, and some new users joined the community.

The ND group in particular succeeded in transferring the HdL network to the new rental relationship with its characteristic features intact, without giving up the cluster structures developed by the group. Also, the new private landlord was responsive to the group's needs, providing the community with an entire floor of the building and refraining from placing a fixed term on the leases. Thus the users were able to continue interacting as they had previously done in the spaces of the HdL. At the ND too, semipublic zones and large common areas facilitated and promoted mutual interchange and synergies. Moreover, the group was able to maintain contact with the other members of the former HdL network across building boundaries by means of a standing data link to the HdR. The primary difference with regard to the HdL is the peripheral location of the ND building and the resulting decrease in the degree of public attention.

A further temporary use after giving notice and moving out: the individually programmable light installation *Blinkenlights* by the Chaos Computer Club, 2001–02

CONCLUSIONS

In retrospect, it is clear that the temporary use of the HdL generated important benefits to the user network. Despite the limited time frame and the fact that they were ultimately forced to move, the tenants were able to build lasting structures as a social and professional cluster, and a group of start-ups and informal businesses was able to use the growing popularity of the building to position itself in the marketplace. The network was solid enough that it even survived the loss of its original space and the ensuing split and move to new locations without losing any of its vitality. This was only possible thanks to the inherent qualities of the community, which continually seized the initiative to organize and develop a public profile, and largely acted autonomously.

By contrast, the new owner of the HdL—a consortium made up of a private investor and the city-owned Wohnungsbaugesellschaft Mitte (WBM, Mitte Corporation for Housing Construction)—failed to derive any benefit from the temporary use for the value of the property and hence for itself. A consolidation model that would have allowed the users to transition to a normal rental relationship by raising the rent in stages and renewing the leases might have been more profitable over the long term and would have removed the need for large initial investments. Instead, the city of Berlin as part purchaser stifled the temporary use structure that it had encouraged in its previous role as owner. The total loss of the existing group of tenants and the resulting need to find new ones made for extra costs that—combined with the slow progress of planning and construction—increased the pressure to turn a profit soon after the building was ready to be occupied. However, the capital expenditure of more than € 33,000,000 that the WBM was called upon to shoulder (the purchase price of the property in 2001 amounted to € 8,180,000, while the renovation from 2002 to 2004 cost roughly € 25,000,000)–added difficulties to an organization that in summer 2006 was also marked by other failed speculations, including the controversial renovation of the neighboring Rathauspassagen (Rathaus, or City Hall, Shopping Arcades). At the same time, the HdL is still only partially rented, so that the target revenues are not being met.

What is more, the renovation destroyed the distinctive structural features of the building and replaced them with standard low-cost components that call the original architectural value of the building into question. In particular the HdL's two distinctive access cores, with their stairwells along the building's outer skin, and wide connecting corridors fell victim to optimization measures. Considering the fact that precisely these architectural features and the large proportion of common spaces inside the building decisively fostered the formation of a network among the users and in consequence ultimately enhanced the site, the benefits of this conversion are doubtful. The relatively brief period of the temporary use of the HdL remains to date an important and still remembered experiment in spatial appropriation of large institutional buildings in central locations of the city.

— — — — — — — — — — — — —

Further Information

www.blinkenlights.de

www.hausdeslehrers.de

Bettina Allamoda, ed., *model map. Kartographie einer Architektur am Beispiel vom Haus des Lehrers Berlin* (Frankfurt am Main: Revolver, 2003).

Gabriele Seidel, "Das Ensemble 'Haus des Lehrers und Kongresshalle' am Alexanderplatz. Transformation eines Baudenkmals der DDR-Moderne", degree dissertation, Berlin 2003.

URBAN CENTRE RELOADED: SUBCULTURE IN MANCHESTER'S CITY CENTRE

Kevin Ward

Protagonists: Independent music producers

Use: Create industries and music scene

Status: Rental

Site: Manchester city center

Transformation: 1980-1997, beginning with the appropriation of selected sites and gradually taking over the entire city quarter; 1997 Haçienda closes

Financing: self-financing clubs and music production businesses

Broken windows, empty buildings, run-down facades. This was the centre of Manchester at the end of the 1970s. A place through which to pass and not to linger as the mills, the factories, and the warehouses, disused and decrepit, proved a hostile environment. Firms either went out of business or relocated to elsewhere in Manchester, or further afield. Residents did likewise. Only those too poor to move out of the center stayed put. By the early 1980s the number of people living in the center of Manchester was a few hundred in housing developments like the one tucked away on Tibb Street, opposite Smithfield Market, in the area to the north of the city center now known as "the Northern Quarter." The houses small and poorly laid out, the estate altogether unwelcoming and rather edgy, where the only bars in the neighborhood were those outside the windows, reflecting the concerns of residents inside: this was city center living out of necessity, not out of choice—before the center of Manchester had cafés and delicatessens on every corner. Walking around the city center it was impossible not to be struck by the amount of redundant space, inside, between, behind, and in front of buildings. As Mike Pickering, one of the people involved from the beginning in Factory Records put it, "When we found the site for the Haçienda, that part of town, Whitworth Street up to Deansgate ... was a ghost town, derelict. None of the railway arches were in use for anything apart from some garages."[1]

But by the late 1980s the economic and cultural fortunes of this area of Manchester had radically turned. Old buildings were being renovated and new ones were being erected. Capital was returning to the city. More than just marking an important moment in the physical regeneration of the city of Manchester, the opening of the Haçienda in May 1982 came to represent a cultural transformation—some in the city saw its futures, visions that over time went on to be shared by those in political power.

THE HAÇIENDA: THE BEGINNINGS

Factory Records—home to Joy Division, New Order, and Happy Mondays, amongst others—was formed in 1978. Emerging out of the Hulme Crescents that were built in the 1960s as an answer to the squalor of the back-to-back houses of the industrial revolution but which by the 1970s were already showing signs of decay and degeneration that would lead to them being torn-down by the mid 1990s, Factory was initially the name of a Friday-night-club. The term "Factory" was appropriated by the founders, Tony Wilson and Alan Erasmus, because it embodied creativity, a place where things were produced. It was a rather ironic choice in a city in which fewer and fewer things were being produced as the manufacturing base was eroded. Wilson and Erasmus wanted to create music, initially using other people's music to run clubs. Then, with the formation of a record company, Factory Records, they turned to producing their own music. By the early 1980s Manchester was awash with music venues. The local music scene was vibrant. Low-key and informally organized, making use of the derelict buildings and the low demand for space, pockets of activity were dotted around the city center. It was not that there was no cultural life in the city—there was—but Rob Gretton, the manager of Joy Division, together with others such as Mike Pickering, Tony Wilson and Alan Erasmus wanted something different. So did New Order–the band formed out of Joy Division after singer Iain Curtis committed suicide in May 1980. Its members wanted a gig and dance venue of their own, and so began the search for a site in which to realize their vision, a search that would ultimately lead them to opposite Deansgate station, in a rather shabby part of town.

Its opening was confirmed when Tony Wilson announced "The Haçienda must be built"–quoting directly from a 1953 Situationist slogan by Ivan Chtcheglov. It drew inspiration from New York, on the basis of what Tony Wilson and others saw on New Order's and A Certain Ratio's first US tour. Various structural changes were made to the building. The pillars on the dance floor, for example, were seen as embodying what the whole movement was about. As Ben Kelly, Head of Design for the Haçienda put it, "the... iconography is to do with stripes on columns... they were structural, industrial, they were fantastic, and let's make something of them, and in the same way you would have any such hazards in a factory producing goods—well, let's put the hazard marks on the columns."[2]

For the first year the Haçienda functioned as a discotheque and was members-only, and it struggled. It had few members. When somebody took out his membership in the first year and in return received a stylishly embossed card, he was in a quiet minority. But by the time to renew the membership a year later, the numbers had begun to increase. More bands were being booked and the club was no long just a disco–it

Upper right: The later Haçienda Club building, 1972
Bottom: Vacancies and demolition in the center of Manchester in the 1970s

was also a venue for live acts. Artists like ABC, ACR, Heaven 17, and The Thompson Twins played over the first few years. And then club nights started to take off, and the music that was played–which was already pretty eclectic–diversified even further, to include Rap and Soul on a Fridays and "Nude Night." The Haçienda was part of a loud and getting louder majority. The venue's future was still not certain. And then the Haçienda and its owners struck lucky. New Order's *Blue Monday* stormed up the music charts, sold millions worldwide, and provided means for the band to underwrite some of the venue's initial losses. Of course there was much more to Manchester's music scene than just the Haçienda. Clubs such as Berlins, Home, Sankey's Soap and the Boardwalk were important pieces in the city's emerging clubbing jigsaw, and around them developed a "cottage industry." Some preceded the Haçienda while others were established on the back of its successes. Musicians, artists, designers, DJs, promoters, managers, bouncers: all played a role in a local division of cultural labor. Musicians needed somewhere to practice and to perform. Music that was made had to be promoted. Bands had to be managed. Flyers had to be designed. DJs had to have somewhere to buy their records. Clubbers needed somewhere to buy their clothes. And all of these activities required space, something that was not in short supply in inner city Manchester at the time. So across the city this fledgling industry began to make small changes in the built environment. At the same time Manchester's well-established but subterranean gay community continued to thrive, despite the city government's best efforts to ignore its presence. This was before it had realized the value of the "pink pound" and how some areas in the centre of the city, traditionally understood to be "gay spaces," could be used as part of a wider attempt to transform the downtown into one large entertainment complex. And of course Manchester's population was changing: industries had emerged around the migrants who had entered the city during the 1950s and 1960s, and new economies were emerging to meet the needs of these new populations.

Michael Winterbottom, scene from the film *24 Hour Party People*, 2002
Poster announcing the opening of the Haçienda making reference to a quote by the Situationist Ivan Chtcheglov

Across the city other railway arches, mills and warehouses were being transformed. Slowly but surely large swathes of the physical reminders of Manchester's industrial past were transformed into signs of Manchester's future. This redevelopment of the built environment continued unabated throughout the 1990s and into the twenty-first century. In 1983, when The Smiths posed at the Greater Manchester Central Station for one of their first photo shoots, it was hard to believe that just over a decade earlier the station had been a thriving enterprise. Even harder to believe, given the state of building at the time, was that just over a decade later the station would be re-born as the GMEX—a venue at which some of the best known names in dance and rock would play to packed audiences, a space in which the biggest names of the so-called "dance revolution" would perform.

FROM SUSPICION TO INSTRUMENTALISM

This "creative, local, young groundbreaking popular culture activity," as Dave Haslem has put it, raised the profile of Manchester so others became interested in the physical redevelopment of the city.[3] Not straight away, of course. Local developers with money to invest and who understood the returns to be made once the early pioneering work had been done began to sink money into the city's built environment towards the end of the 1980s. Very slowly and very unevenly capital began to return to the city center. However, this new investment was the exception: much of the city remained untouched. Yet slowly but surely a good "business climate" was manufactured, in order to provide the conditions for sizable investments in Manchester's building fabric. Together with Manchester City Council, whose position on the "ground breaking" activities changed from opposition and suspicion to one of encouragement and support, a series of high-profile developments began to occur. Renewal took place in buildings that lay along the rivers that cut across the city and which lay off the major roads in and out of Manchester. Factories and warehouses were gutted. Facades were often kept but internal restructuring turned large open spaces–ideal for formal and informal clubs–into smaller apartments. The Phoenix Initiative was formed in the mid 1980s but its attempts at redeveloping Castlefield did not get very far. More successful was the Central Manchester Development Corporation (CMDC), which operated from 1988 to 1996. It was given planning control over an area of 187 hectares in the center of the city, and working with the likes of AMEC, Bellway Homes, Bruntwood and Crosby Homes oversaw the creation of over 2,500 housing units. In other areas of the city, behind Piccadilly, and to the north around Oldham Street, Manchester City Council's new Special Projects Unit, led by Howard Bernstein, worked directly with private developers to renew the area's buildings, many of which dated from the industrial revolution.[4] With the 1990s there came a noticeable shift in the types of developer investing in the city. Local developers were gradually replaced by the large corporations. The pioneering work had been done. After their experience of working in partnerships like the CMDC these transnational multi-million corporations had been convinced that their investment would be both safe and very rewarding. High-end condominiums and penthouses began to spring up. Manchester got its first £1 million loft. With the new investment so the city's skyline began to be subject to change. No one building better embodies the coming together of these changes than the city's new Manchester Hilton Deansgate hotel.

The city government's role in the production and maintenance of a good "business climate" is reflected in their increasingly sophisticated strategies to market Manchester. With the stepping up of the redevelopment of the city center at the end of the 1990s the city council decided that there was a need to focus marketing efforts. It created a new organization–Marketing Manchester–and launched two marketing campaigns. Local reactions were mixed. Most noticeably those local cultural entrepreneurs who had invested in the centre during the 1980s and retained a stake in some of Manchester's most iconic bars were unimpressed.

They were unhappy at not being consulted in the launch and unhappy about how the campaigns portrayed the city. After a series of bust-ups the campaigns were dropped. Only some three or four years later, at the beginning of the 2000s, was there another attempt to run a series of marketing campaigns proclaiming Manchester's various cultural assets. More recently Peter Saville—whose early art work adorned many of the early Factory Record covers—has been appointed the city's Cultural Director.

When the closure of the Haçienda was announced in 1997, the headline of the *Manchester Evening News*, the local newspaper, read "How did the Haçienda go wrong?" The city's drug culture and the gangs that organize around their sale had proved impossible to keep away from the club. It was not the only one asking this question. Clubbers, local business bosses and others in the trans-national clubbing network were also perplexed. The Haçienda's shadow fell high and wide over the global clubbing community. Faç51, the spin-off from Factory Records, and its owners went into liquidation. Those involved protested and plans were made to re-launch Manchester's most famous nightclub. But it was not to be. The club never opened again. It was knocked down in 2002 by developers Crosby Homes, with the permission of Manchester City Council. In its place were built high-end apartments and luxury penthouses, the company explicitly using the name "Haçienda." As they put it on their web-site, "The Haçienda, once the coolest club on the planet, is now one of Manchester's premiere residential addresses." A long way from how the term was used by the early Situationist International. From leading-edge, and challenging to mainstream and conformist, the Haçienda's fate reflected what some felt was those in charge of Manchester's short-sightedness.

With escalating residential prices other forms of land use became less profitable. Residential development literally transformed the city's physical landscape, challenging those with political power to think smartly about the city's future. Not all agreed with the decision to allow the residential development of Haçienda. At the marketing launch some of the audience–perhaps ex-clubbers–booed!

CONCLUSION

Outside of the city, the Haçienda and other clubs are understood as examples of a deeper change in the city's psyche, of re-energizing a city and its population. The December 2005 issue of the dance magazine *Mixmag* listed the top 30 events in clubbing history. New York's Studio 5, Chicago's Loft party and Ibiza's Amnesia were all there. Number one was though Manchester's Haçienda and its 1994 nights of disco, funk, hip-hop and house. The building may have gone but the memories continue to linger. The "emotional revolution," as Paul Morley put it, continues to cast a shadow over contemporary Manchester.[5] The physical reclamation of the city center by the urban pioneers may only have been temporary but the consequences of their activities are more pervasive. Emotions, feelings and memories of that time in the city's recent history remain strong in the city and outside. And this was a profoundly political uprising. It was of the streets and for the streets. It was about reclaiming buildings and about envisioning a positive future when most people, state agencies and developers had given up. Finally, it was about use and not exchange values, as Marx would say. Unfortunately, as Marx would also have told us, capitalism's restlessness and desire to seek out new revenue generating activities meant it was only a matter of time, once the risks had been taken, before it flowed back into the city, transforming social relations as it went.

Acknowledgements

Thanks to Bob and Helen Pleasance for their insights into pre-1990s Manchester.

Notes

1. Dave Haslem, *Manchester, England: the story of the pop cult city* (London: Fourth Estate, 2000), 149.

2. Ben Kelly in John Savage, *The Haçienda Must Be Built* (Essex: International Music Publications, 1992), 21.

3. Haslem, *Manchester, England*, 253.

4. Jamie Peck and Kevin Ward, *City of revolution: restructuring Manchester* (Manchester: Manchester University Press, 2002).

5. Paul Morley, 'A northern soul, in: Observer Music Monthly', no. 33 (May 2006), 29.

Further Readings

Harvey, David. *The Urbanization of Capital* (Oxford: Blackwell, 1985).

King, Ray. *Detonation: Rebirth of a City* (Warrington: Clear Publications Limited, 2006).

Merrifield, Andy. *Dialectal Urbanism: Social Struggles in the Capitalist City* (London: Routledge, 2002).

Label transfer: After the club closed, the Haçienda building was demolished and replaced by a luxury apartment high-rise of the same name.

WHAT CITY PLANNERS CAN LEARN FROM TEMPORARY USERS
Peter Arlt

A temporary user is someone who uses buildings free of charge or on very favorable terms in order to bridge gaps in their utilization. Temporary users are in many respects the opposite of investors. They think of and define themselves in terms of content rather than financial return, and they attempt to (re)use existing circumstances and structures for their own purposes. The investor, by contrast, has a clear plan. He creates new circumstances and structures. His problem is rather the staging and use of the newly created structure. At the risk of over-statement, the temporary user might be described as a software specialist who has to go to the "marketplace" to procure the appropriate hardware. Or more precisely: in the junkyard of the marketplace—among the things that the market has ceased to value or values very little—the temporary user looks for objects that inspire him. To find out how temporary users operate, in 2001 I conducted lengthy individual interviews with more than a dozen cultural temporary users from Berlin and Vienna.[1] For all their individual differences, my conversations with them make it possible to elaborate a set of general principles and structures. The cases examined certainly do not cover the entire spectrum of temporary uses. They do, however, cover those that have led to a (new) boom of the phenomenon both in practice and in the realm of public discussion.

HOW TEMPORARY USERS FIND THEIR PROGRAMS

Temporary users define themselves in terms of their "own thing," in terms of what they want to do and what they can realize by means of temporary use, which they would otherwise not be able to do because of their lack of capital. Typically, they not only lack economic power; their "thing" also tends to lie far afield from credit-worthy ideas for new businesses. What they want to do does not have its origin in the desire to make money but in a content-based ambition or programmatic idea, which initially brooks very little compromise. Money and profit are of secondary importance. The harmony of person and project gives rise to a certain authenticity. The fact that temporary users lack necessary training and experience is in no way detrimental to their cause. On the contrary, the fact that they believe in their project despite these unfavor-able conditions reinforces its supposedly authentic character. The fact that, on the other hand, many fall by the wayside for these and financial reasons is simply the fate of the temporary user. Experience comes by doing, and it grows with each new project, so that if the majority of temporary users approach their first use with little expertise, they acquire considerable profes-sionalism over time.

Even if their belief in their own project eclipses everything else, that doesn't mean that their idea is clear from the very beginning. On the contrary, it starts out as something vague, and it is only as a result of their own activity, the site, their partners, the circumstances, etc., that special emphases begin to crystallize out, emphases with which they then continue to work. The impor-tant thing is to keep moving, react to the environment, and continue to evolve. The content that emerges is linked to the space or the site as well as to one's comrades-in-arms. Every time temporary users change their location, they start over from the beginning. The only things they take with them are the know-how they have acquired, a constantly expanding and increasingly specific network, and their "name" as a kind of trademark.

HOW THE SITE IS FOUND AND ADAPTED

Sometimes it is impossible to say which came first, the idea or the site. Temporary users may discover a site without immediately knowing how they would like to use it. But the opposite may also occur—a clear idea for which only certain highly specific sites can be considered. However, since temporary users are almost never in a position simply to take possession of a given site, they are always dependent on the circumstances, that is, on sites that lie outside of current economic interests—as well as on accommodating property owners.

These circumstances exert a determining influence upon the temporary user's choice of site. Thus, temporary users know what sites and neighborhoods have fallen, not out of fashion, but out of the economy, and from within that pool they now seek out those spaces and sites that nevertheless—or for that very reason—possess an appeal, a special spirit, for themselves and their projects. Temporary users see themselves very much as trendsetters. At an "uncool" site, even the very best of programs will be useless. What is important in the temporary user's decision to choose a given site is the possibilities it contains. The determining factor is not its present state but the degree of inspiration it is capable of arousing. In this process, the original idea is influenced decisively by the site that is found. In this case, the site is the entire complex of the surroundings, the physical facilities, the atmosphere, the objects that belong to the place and to the temporary user himself, the owner and abutters, as well the site's history and possible future. It includes everything that can possibly be associated with the site. Not everything is then actually included; rather, certain things are specifically selected; the program is gradually elaborated and concretized together with the site itself. The idea is adapted to the site and vice versa, until finally idea and site become one and something new comes into being.

COMMUNICATION: OWNERS, AUTHORITIES, MEDIA, VISITORS

Temporary users are dependent on others, but they are not at their mercy. They look for partners who will help them realize their own aims, and they will only settle for a site where the deal with the owner leaves them breathing room, financially as well as with respect to their activities. Otherwise even the best location makes no sense. The relationship with the authorities is more complex. Here their motto is: never communicate more than is absolutely necessary; this is often nothing at all, so that temporary use often takes place in a legal gray area. However, this gray area is not just the result of this mutual agreement to look the other way; it is also the result of a legal vacuum. Temporary use—from building regulations all the way to trade regulations—is actually not something that is envisioned by the law, and the legal assessment of it is therefore fluctuating and unstable. Put another way: communication with the authorities is marked by a high degree of creativity, ideally on the part of the authorities as well.[2]

Precisely because temporary use exists in a legal gray area, temporary users often have an ambivalent relationship with the mainstream media. They seek them out only as allies when they have difficulties with the authorities. Normally they have tended to refrain from generating widespread public awareness, also in part because word of mouth is regarded as a quicker and more contemporary medium and—like unlabeled entrances—almost as a mark of quality. Temporary users know exactly which visitors they want to attract, even if that can change on a daily basis. Those visitors are an integral part of the whole; it is they who round out the project and make it complete. For this reason, widespread publicity is counterproductive, because then the "wrong" people will also come, those who want to watch. Spectators are the death knell for every temporary use; they destroy the setting and drive away the active visitors, who ideally constitute a tight-knit and exclusive community, an in-group. Success consists precisely in the harmony of the idea, the site, the installation, the music, and the visitors, so that the finely coordinated interplay of all individual elements is extremely important.

HOW THE SITE IS RUN

One characteristic of temporary uses is that the activities are complete in themselves, whereas the physical premises never reach a finished state. They are constantly being updated, transformed, and adapted to new needs. As soon as one element of the "total artwork" is modified, there are repercussions for all the others. The associated effort and expense lead to a basic configuration that is inexpensive and flexible and therefore highly versatile. The fixed furnishings are restricted to the bare necessities.

A use may end for many different reasons. The time allotted for it may be over, or the tight-knit, exclusive community—the in-group—may go elsewhere, where there is something better on offer. Sometimes the authorities close down the activities; sometimes the operators are exhausted and need distance and rest or simply want do something else. It also sometimes happens that the site or the program "wears out." The temporary users cease to be able to wring new facets from it; it ossifies, and what was an adventure becomes routine.

Strictly speaking, however, there are no such things as endings in the world of temporary uses, at least not in the sense of a loss, for it was never the intention of the temporary users to remain at a single site "forever." The goal was to try something out for a while, and when temporary users fail to achieve that objective, it is sometimes because they failed to stop in time. A site cannot be lost; the only thing that can be lost is that special harmony that must be rediscovered again and again. Thus, for professional temporary users, withdrawing from the public sphere is part of standard operating procedure—pausing to collect oneself, to stake out new positions, and to look for new sites and new partners in order to tackle the next "thing."

TEMPORARY USERS ARE TACTICIANS

For urbanists, the way temporary users approach and work with the city is worth analyzing. Their scope of action is marked less by the great battle plan than by a constant stream of small-scale reactive maneuvers. The action of the temporary user may thus be described as tactical rather than strategic.

Both of these concepts are military in origin. According to Clausewitz, "tactics teaches the use of armed forces in the engagement," whereas strategy teaches "the use of engagements for the object of the war."[3] The foundation of every strategy is one's own place (army, enterprise, city), which is divided off from the surrounding environment and constitutes the organizing basis for one's relations with the outside world. This place of one's own is the site of one's own power and one's own will. Here, nobody can tell me what to do. From this autonomous place, the strategist can "transform [the] foreign forces" that are situated outside of his place "into objects that can be observed and measured, and thus control and 'include' them within his scope of vision. To be able to see (far into the distance) is also to be able to predict, to run ahead of time by reading a space."[4] Having a place of one's own also makes possible "a certain independence with respect to the variability of circumstances. It is a mastery of time through the foundation of an autonomous place."[5]

Tactics, by contrast, has no place of its own and hence no boundary that could divide the other off as a visible totality. "The space of a tactic is the space of the other."[6] Tactics is marked by lack of power; it is the art of the weak. The weak individual must constantly seek to derive benefit from forces that are foreign to him. Tactics must work with what is there. "It does not have the means to keep to itself, at a distance, in a position of withdrawal, foresight, and self-collection."[7]

Because tactics has no place, it is dependent on time. It is constantly in motion, always looking to seize its advantage on the fly, to exploit favorable opportunities, to play with events, to manipulate the strategies and convert them to new functions. It is the "art of putting one over on the adversary on his own turf."[8]

Strategy banks on the establishment of a place, and its strength lies in (fore)seeing. By contrast, tactics banks on the use of time, and its strength lies in acting here and now, without "a view of the whole, limited by the blindness (which may lead to perspicacity) resulting from combat at close quarters. . . ."[9]

It may be safely assumed that "ordinary" temporary users have neither power nor money and are therefore dependent on foreign forces. What they want can only be achieved through clever cooperation. Whether they like it or not, temporary users have no choice but to ally themselves with the circumstances. Their relationship with the other lies somewhere between peaceful coexistence and necessary cooperation. This is also the reason why temporary users are not strategists: they have no overarching objective to which the individual engagements are subordinate. Their sole objective is the current project (engagement).

The classic example of the tactician is the guerrilla warrior. It is no accident that we speak of guerrilla tactics and not guerrilla strategy. For all the differences between temporary users and guerrillas—differences that are primarily rooted in the absence of an enemy to be destroyed—a comparison between them will clarify the structural similarities in their (tactical) approaches.

According to Che Guevara, the foundation of guerrilla warfare is the ideal of social justice, for the sake of which the battle is waged.[10] It is the political character of the struggle rather than private enrichment that dictates the guerrilla's action and thought. The struggle for the "just cause" also leads, according to Guevara, to moral superiority as well as to stronger motivation and morale.

While temporary users fight in their own cause, the principal element of their struggle always remains their belief in and enthusiasm for that cause, even where it goes against economic rationality. Their "own cause" is not regarded as having triumphed until they have succeeded in mobilizing allies—operators as well as visitors—who are familiar with the codes and secrets of the "scene" in question.

The concrete realization of the ideal requires "a perfect knowledge of the ground."[11] The guerrillero must be "constantly informed about everything that happens in the relevant area."[12] However, he does not fight on the open battlefield. Rather, "he forces his enemy into another space. In other words, he displaces the space of regular, conventional theaters of war to a different, darker dimension—a dimension of the abyss."[13]

In the same way, temporary users must be intimately acquainted with the relevant city, especially when it comes to seeking out a suitable location. Where is an area that is cheap and yet easily accessible? Which locations are cool and have, as it were, a surplus value or dimension of depth that casts a fresh light on what has thus far been overlooked? The part of the city that is significant for him can also be found in virtually all other big cities. Globalization may (perhaps) alienate him from most of his native city, but it does not alienate him from the hip neighborhoods that suit his objectives. Thus, "a motorized"—or globalized—"partisan" does not "lose his telluric character," as the political philosopher Carl Schmitt suggests, but finds his biotopes scattered throughout the entire world.[14]

A further hallmark of the partisan or guerrillero is his mobility and speed. He must be daring; surprise is his weapon of choice. "Hit and run!"[15] In addition, he is able "to adapt himself to all circumstances," "to identify himself with the environment in which he lives, to become a part of it, and to take advantage of it as his ally to the maximum possible extent."[16] Since the enemy is superior in number and in arms, the guerrillero can only strike where the enemy is weak: the worse conditions are for the enemy, the better they are for the guerrillero. Night and confusing situations are his accomplices. Finally, the guerrillero must possess a set of physical attributes that also provides a good description of the temporary user: an iron constitution, resilience, toughness, and staying power; but he must also "be able to produce another effort at the moment when weariness seems intolerable."[17] According to Che Guevara, forty is the "maximum age" for a guerrillero. At the same time, however, the guerrillero is not a man of grand rhetorical gestures: "Combat is the most important drama in the guerrilla life."[18]

STRATEGIC AND TACTICAL CITY PLANNING

The question of what city planning can learn from temporary use may be approached in various ways. One may look to temporary use to generate lasting urban structures, which sometimes amounts to the instrumentalization of temporary use and contradicts the self-conception of some temporary users. Another approach casts the municipality itself as a temporary user or an initiator of temporary uses. In this scenario, the search for actual actors on the ground becomes problematic, since the latter tend to see their activity as a job rather than a calling.

Softer variants merely envision a liaison office between owners of vacant properties and potential temporary users. Aside from the high cost and effort of updating the list of such properties, however—and the impossibility of capturing all relevant objects—one of the temporary user's specific abilities lies precisely in the discovery of the site. An empty building is only a prerequisite for temporary use; it is not the deciding factor.

In my view, the consequences for city planning lie deeper than this. They concern the fundamental self-conception, culture, and mentality of a type of city planning that might be described as *strategic city planning*.

In the period of rich municipalities, the planners sat in their offices and devised master plans. Sometimes entire neighborhoods were razed because they did not accord with the social and aesthetic ideals of the planners, or else they had to go to make room for a highway. The common good of the city—the objective of all city planning—was often nothing but the city planners' own (usually bourgeois) notion of what constitutes a "city." First they would identify problems with the actual, existing condition of the city, problems that were then in need of a solution. The prerogative of defining both the problems and their solutions lay in the hands of the politically powerful. Urban planning sought to rule out what it considered to be repugnant and then attempted to capture, organize, and control everything. The goal was the "clean city," the city with no "contaminants" or contradictions.

Those days are gone, not because people recognized that it was impossible to carry out plans like these, but simply because the money is not available to do so. Those who are planning and building here and there in the city today—private investors (with architects in tow)—also know what they want. They have a clear vision, pay architects to do the planning (and sometimes the realization as well), and define uses, inside and out. Problems only arise because of the reality on the ground.

That is why their favorite construction site is one where nothing exists yet, or where everything that does exist can be demolished. This way, their plan can be implemented on a one-to-one basis, and a deliberately and uniformly designed building or neighborhood can be created. This has very little to do with city planning that sets its sights on the city as a whole. With this choice-parcel-oriented type of planning, (more or less) separate, self-contained realities are created, realities that are indifferent to the rest of the city.

To summarize: strategic city planning (1) has a goal for the city, (2) knows when, where, and how the intervention is to take place, and (3) asserts and executes the plan with no possibility of compromise. The really existing city and unpredictable events are initially ignored or suppressed by the strength and power of their will (that is, of the plan).

But the actual city is distinguished by precisely these heterogeneous, scattered practices, which can never be definitively controlled.[19] Strategic city planning thus finds itself engaged in an endless attempt to bring order into the chaos of the city. Thus, there is a powerful incentive to adopt the current strategy of initiating such projects only partially and in financially lucrative areas while leaving the remainder of the city to its own devices (or its residents) and describing this inaction as "empowerment."

Tactical city planning, by contrast, continues to set its sights on the city as a whole and is also aware of the lack of money and power. However, there are three things that city planners must (re)learn:

First, a fundamental attitude that recognizes that the city is constantly changing and that a final or fixed condition is never attainable or even desirable. The city is a place with a tremendous variety of people who make widely varying demands upon it.

Second, in order to implement their program, they must find partners (allies) at the micro level, since that program cannot be implemented alone. In the case of large-scale projects and investors, this has already been done for a number of years. But this public–private partnership—and this is something planners have to learn—should also be applied to small-scale activities. In doing so, however, one cannot expect that these activists will always seek out city hall on their own initiative. Hence as a city planner one must leave city hall, keep one's eyes and ears peeled, and look for activities and ideas that can be connected with one's own program.

Third—and contrary to a common preconception—the tactician does not swing around in whatever direction the wind (the money) may happen to blow. The tactical city planner has a vision of the city that integrates strong and weak actors. He watches for a favorable wind and makes use of it when it comes.

Not everything will fit together on a one-to-one basis, but the program need not suffer as a result. Rather, it is honed and brought to life by the actual needs and notions of the many small-scale "urban activists."

Thus, what is called for is a capacity for reacting ad hoc: always underway, open in all directions, and ready for anything.

To summarize: tactical city planning (1) has a goal for the city, (2) watches for people who are already active, and (3) supports and supplements their activities wherever it finds them. The art of city planning consists of the attempt to bring one's own objective into harmony with unpredictable events while at the same time strengthening those events. The existing reality is a treasure trove and an ally, especially in areas that have ceased to be of interest to power and capital. This is what city planners can learn from temporary users.

Notes

1. Those interviewed include Benjamin Foerster-Baldenius (Lychener 60 and Bad Ly, Berlin), Martin Kaltwasser (Bad Ly, Berlin), Elke Knöss (Yaam, Berlin), Penko Stoitschev (Sensor, Ambient Lounge, Berlin), Ben de Biel (Tacheles, Eimer, Maria, Berlin), Gereon Schmitz (Visomat, Berlin), Gerriet Schultz (WMF, Berlin), Annette Mechtel (Rampe, Berlin), Helle and Max (HTC, Neues Problem, Berlin), Andreas Spiegl, Christian Teckert (studiocity, Vienna), Ula Schneider (Soho in Ottakring, Vienna), and Kurt Sedlak (Kabel-werk, Vienna).

   Additional interviews were conducted with Jutta Weitz, Michael Stiefel and Dolly Leupold.

2. Thus, the operators of an illegal public outdoor swimming pool were encouraged by the authorities to describe their operation as a temporary art installation.

3. Carl von Clausewitz, *On War,* trans. and ed. Michael Howard and Peter Paret (Princeton, NJ: Princeton University Press, 1976), 128. Clausewitz also writes (on pp. 347–48): "In strategy, the pace is much slower. There is ample room for apprehensions, one's own and those of others; for objections and remonstrations. . . In a tactical situation one is able to see at least half the problem with the naked eye, whereas in strategy everything has to be guessed at and presumed. Conviction is therefore weaker."

4. Michel de Certeau, *The Practice of Everyday Life,* trans. Steven Rendall (Berkeley: University of California Press, 1984), 36.

5. Ibid.

6. Ibid., 37.

7. Ibid. "Strategy is the science of military movements outside of the enemy's field of vision; tactics, within it" (von Bülow).

8. Ibid., 40.

9. Ibid., 38.

10. Che Guevara, *Guerrilla Warfare*, (Wilmington, DE: Scholarly Resources Inc., 1997).

11. Ibid., 56.

12. Ibid.

13. Carl Schmitt, *Theory of the Partisan: Intermediate Commentary on the Theory of the Polit-ical,* trans. G. L. Ulmen (New York: Telos Press, 2007), 69. As additional examples, Schmitt lists airspace as a new dimension since World War I, and also the submarine, which "opened up an unexpected deep dimension beneath the surface" of the sea (70).

14. Ibid., 22. Telluric: "the tie to the soil, to the autochthonous population, and to the geographical particularity of the land" (21).

15. Guevara, *Guerrilla Warfare* (note 10), 54.

16. Ibid., 59 and 75.

17. Ibid., 76.

18. Ibid., 91. Just as it "goes without saying" that the guerrillero is a man, so men are also in the clear majority among temporary users. The conquest of space is something that seems to carry decidedly masculine connotations.

19. Certeau, *Practice of Everyday Life* (note 4).

THE ECONOMY OF TEMPORARY USE
Rudolf Kohoutek, Christa Kamleithner

Language would have us believe that use is the most natural thing in the world. Even Marx trusted in "phenomenological good sense"[1] when he spoke of a thing's "pure and simple use value", before it becomes an exchange value and then a fetishized commodity. But the concept of use has two sides: it expresses a utility, and at the same time it speaks of the right of granting, as is expressed in the old term "usufruct." A single word contains within it the transition from a practice of use, or "function" (and therewith the suppression of construct-edness) to a legal relationship of disposition and profit, as regulated by civil law on the basis of private property.

Because the entire material world in Western societies is constituted as property, this civil right is the true constitution of the city and of architecture. On top of use as a quality of things, structures, and spaces, social relationship is superimposed in the triangle of owner-ship, control, and right of use. In this sense, use is a more or less precarious relationship between usage and commercial exploitation. But the elasticity of this relationship has grown in the last two hundred years. The enormous increase in the mobility of things and people began with industrialization and the growth of cities in the early nineteenth century. The ties that bind uses to particular places and architectures have loosened as a result. Land is traded as a commodity rather than being handed down from generation to generation. Land is set moving and turns into interest-bearing capital, especially when it is not owned by small property holders but by large-scale real estate and building capital that operates without any personal ties to a place.

DEREGULATION, VACANCY, AND USE CYCLES
The mobilization and flexibilization that characterized the modern city of the nineteenth and early twentieth centuries apply to an even greater extent to contemporary postindustrial urban landscapes, and in principle to all urban real estate. It is no longer just apartments and businesses that change ownership at a more or less rapid rate and are converted or torn down. Large industrial and infrastructural facilities too—like all goods, which now tend toward privatization—are subject to an accelerating dynamic. The duration of uses and the turnover of capital have gone into fast motion. On the one hand, lifestyles and forms of production and distribution are changing more and more rapidly, which leads to ever new notions of space, forms of organization, and aesthetics. On the other hand, the useful life of buildings is also becoming shorter as a consequence of ever shorter depreciation cycles with high required returns, poor construction oversight, space concepts and building methods with little flex-ibility, and a total lack of connection between the exploitation of land and capital and the "end users" of the spaces.

Thus, the notion of stable uses that is embodied in the instruments of city planning has less and less actual basis. Today, even "normal" uses are temporary, provided they haven't found a last refuge in the small-scale ownership of apartments and single-family houses. This raises the question of what we actually mean by "temporary" use and what the actual distinction is between "normal" and "temporary" use. This distinction seems to have less to do with length of time than with the issues of social recognition and adequate architectonic accommoda-tion—and ultimately with gaps in the cycles of capital exploitation. Temporary use in the sense intended by Urban Catalyst is especially exemplified by those paradigmatically "urban" uses that can't find affordable spaces in the established real estate markets and are forced to lodge in the periphery of that economic system.

This periphery is defined by the temporal windows of vacancy, or more precisely transformation, that occur between two economically and socially recognized uses that have the backing of the city's political establishment. They vary in length, depending on the degree of effort and expense involved in adapting the site for the new use: resettlement, vacancy lasting for years, demolition or clearing of the site, possible decontamination in the case of industrial facilities, renovation of the buildings, elaboration and agreement of a new zoning and development plan, new construction. And it can take time to find new investors, lessees, or tenants. Unresolved questions of ownership and liability, a lack of funds for planned conversions, and conflicts between the divergent interests of property owners and policymakers can drag out this interval even further.

Vacancies and urban wasteland are blind spots in a productive economy. They may be brought about intentionally for speculative reasons, be the product of a crisis situation, or simply be due to the regular turnover of use. A functioning market in apartments, office space, or real estate in general requires a small percentage of vacancies so that ownership and use relationships are able to change and so that there is some degree of mobility in the markets.

Thus, a certain level of vacancy is "normal." The owners, of course, would ideally like to skip the period of vacancy altogether: the old lessee should move out on the last day of the month, and the new one move in on the first day of the following month. Nevertheless, owners are accepting longer and longer periods of vacancy, especially big corporate developers that can politically push through redesignations and rezonings and thus make higher profits. Also, under certain conditions, owners tolerate periods of vacancy, deciding to forgo a quick but suboptimal exploitation so as not to jeopardize the higher level of return on the site and its surroundings that they deem attainable.

In an apparently contrary tendency, the flexibility of urban uses and spaces has always been kept in bounds by developers and investors with the support of city planners. While the development of the modern city brought an accelerating dynamic in the distribution of people and uses over the territory, that dynamic was supposed to unfold within the orderly paths of social and functional segregation, which assigned the various uses to a "tidy" frame. From an economic perspective, the goal was to stabilize submarkets, to create appropriate urban environments that protected the value of individual property, and thus to maintain or create "locations," a task to which architecture, with its reverence for images, is also called upon to make its contribution.

Within this order of things, empty houses and vacant lots must be barricaded and protected against any threat of informal appropriation. In some European countries—including Great Britain, France, and Germany—this has led to an actual professionalization of the safeguarding of unused properties: special products are supposed to hold unwanted temporary uses and vandalism at bay. Such an approach makes the divergent interests of owners and users visible in a paradoxical way, in that, within the "logic of ownership..., the assertion of the legal claim to space finds its clearest expression in the space *not* being used."[2]

However, there are many activities and uses for which only very low rents can be paid and for which the private real estate market has nothing to offer. Very often, the groups that generate this type of demand are unstable and cannot accumulate sufficient capital to compete in "normal" conditions in the real estate market. This affects the field of social services or communal activities that do not operate on a permanent basis but still have a recurrent need of spaces, such as activities for children and young people; or the cultural field, which can have difficulties adapting to the classic performance venues and needs flexible spaces of the most various kinds and sizes. A further variant are start-ups for the creative industries, which need special spaces and conditions of production that are seldom available in the normal real estate market, or offered at unaffordable prices. All these are uses that obviously fall through the cracks of the regular social and economic system.

In order to obtain space for such activities, users often accept laborious and legally precarious situations that, on the basis of the contractual conditions alone, imply a purely temporary use. It is still not the norm, but users are increasingly availing themselves of the possibility of free temporary use that can be terminated at any time. How to derive a positive notion of temporary use from this practice and introduce it into the discourse of planning, as Urban Catalyst seeks to do, is anything but obvious, especially since, in view of the usually poor state of renovation of these spaces and the uncertain legal situation, it tends to be a euphemism. It takes a certain amount of argument to show what value temporary use can possibly have for the development of cities and hence for planning, since this approach turns the existing logic of planning upside-down, a logic that has served to protect not only owners but also users. Nonetheless, it is a new situation when temporary uses earn partial acceptance from owners and investors as well as from the city's official political establishment.

THE ECONOMY OF ATTENTION—NEW PLANNING PARADIGMS

Temporary use—especially in the fields of art and culture—is becoming an increasingly mature and self-confident practice. It is no longer appropriate to regard it as a "naïve" improvisation, in which those in search of space resort to unconventional solutions due to lack of funds. On the contrary, temporary use often represents a deliberate intervention that is well aware of the possibilities and effects of short-term interventions. It forms part of the broader repertoire of a communication- and process-oriented planning that seeks to use it to set communication in motion, just as it is utilized by project developers for the targeted enhancement of sites. The two agendas may coincide, and it isn't always possible to clearly differentiate the various objectives that temporary uses pursue. On the whole, what is emerging is a new (professional) approach to dealing with attention-building as a resource.

An essential aspect of temporary uses and interventions is the fact that they generate a more or less substantial amount of social attention, locally as well as in the media. Their unconventionality breaks through the "normal situation" of regular use paradigms. Thanks to their singularity—both in the sense of being short-term and of being unusual—they arouse interest and help to make a place better known. They get people talking about it and spark conversations between urban actors who would otherwise be isolated. They have the capacity to make an important contribution to the social, cultural, and economic revitalization of an area, and they also have the ability to make local and citywide power relations, the commercial and the "other" interests, visible. In this way, conversational situations, indeed even local public spheres, can be generated—just as they can also be used to accumulate attention that operates selectively and intervenes in the constellation of the real estate markets. The "economy of attention"[3] interacts with the "normal" economy; the media of money and attention can enter into reciprocal interaction. An increase of one may lead to an increase of the other: the 89 increased publicity of a place leads to greater demand and hence to higher real estate prices. It is also one of the laws of temporary uses that such effects of enhancement then turn around and deprive those very uses of their foundation.

City planners as well as investors and project developers have now become familiar with these mechanisms. The discovery of social attention as a resource that can be harnessed for specific purposes correlates with the changed economic and social situation that has emerged in recent decades. Since the 1970s, a new liberal conception of planning has increasingly gained acceptance, in parallel with a general weakening of the public sector and the dominance of city planning by big investors. Unlike planning in the Fordist welfare state, this conception of planning is no longer based on comprehensive and area-wide predictability, nor does it attempt to produce homogeneous living conditions or set uniform planning goals. On the contrary, it seeks to bring about a differentiation of space that is supposed to take place processually through projects.

This new conception of planning can be partly traced back to the social changes of the 1960s and '70s, and particularly to the rebellion against paternalism and standardization. Plans issued like decrees with no communication and no regard for local peculiarities become discredited. The tabula rasa thinking of modernity is confronted with participatory planning approaches and the old patchwork city becomes the new guiding model. In aesthetic terms, this change manifests itself in concepts like "bricolage,"[4] which views planning as improvisation and rests on the utilization of "found objects." The new designer type of the "bricoleur" operates quite differently from the modern engineer. He doesn't create ideal designs but uses what is there: "The universe of his means is finite, and the rule of his game is always to make do with what is available."[5]

This change in the techniques and aesthetic concepts of city planning, which may be interpreted as a democratization of planning (though certainly more in the symbolic than in the political sense), also reflects a changed situation in the marketplace. The taking into account of differences plays a role here as well, because the markets have now reached a saturation point. The focus is now on the differences among the wishes of different consumers and the selective absorption of their purchasing power rather than on generalizable mass products, as in the immediate postwar period. The Fordist industrial system is replaced by the postindustrial, post-Fordist system, in which art and culture, aesthetics, space, and planning play a new role.[6]

What planning and design take up now is the interaction of space, architecture, and communication. The space of modernity, which is theoretically uniform, homogeneous, and "just" with respect to social demands, is dissolved. Social attention is not uniformly distributed in space. It concentrates in places of particular interest, and this process can be guided in both directions. Media presence in magazines, radio, and television can put places and spaces in the spotlight. Conversely, spatial interventions can generate attention and focus it on particular subjects. By way of the media, vivid and symbolic, memory-laden or new and attention-getting architectures associate places and projects with faces, images, and products. But it doesn't have to be architecture; events and festivals can assume this role as well. The festivalization of urban spaces also goes back to the 1970s and '80s, a development that also includes temporary uses and interventions, which often come from the field of art and culture.

Once modern planning had been discredited, a new approach to planning emerged that saw itself as a "politics of small steps" or "incrementalism," which no longer has a comprehensive strategy or overarching goals.[7] Instead, it uses individual decisions and realizations to generate impulses and set processes in motion that can then be reacted to. What looks at first like a crisis of planning and a retreat into pragmatism today turns out to be a process in which planning becomes more complex. Taking differences, changes, and the autonomous dynamic of communicative planning into account no longer allows for static, universal plans and makes planning punctual. That doesn't mean that planning is abolished; instead, it is tied to particular situations and regarded as a specific intervention, no longer as a directive.

This step-by-step approach brings about a concentration of organizational and financial forces in projects that are limited in space and time. For this reason, one speaks since the 1990s of "project-oriented planning"[8] in parallel with the paradigm of process-oriented planning. Within a "project," an enormous variety of different spheres—economic, cultural, constructional, ecological, etc.—are connected. Various actors are mobilized and networked, including important economic stakeholders and the civil society of a place or region as well as administrative officials from various departments. External consultants, city planners, economic experts, and cultural producers act as mediators, initiating communication and touching off processes of self-organization.

Temporary uses could become an integral part of such a processual approach. They would enable city planning to avoid preconceived spatial models and functional assignments, helping it instead to put the goals and projects themselves up for discussion and to determine them experimentally. Urban development planning has always tried to rely on definite knowledge. In fact, however, it has to deal with uncertainties: the future; the behavior of people, the markets, and policymakers; and future technologies that will influence city life. Planning means making decisions on these questions at a moment when not enough variables are known. Temporary uses can be helpful in decision-making processes like these. They set processes in motion that can be observed and from which new insights can be gained that then flow back into planning. Comparable approaches may be found in recent management theory: "Management is the ability to deal with uncertainty in a manner that makes it workable, without mistaking the outcome for certainty."[9]

Where can such processes lead? Today, city planning increasingly functions as city management and marketing and therefore functions competitively. The processes triggered by attention-generating projects—such as new museums, large-scale exhibitions and cultural and sports events—do not unfold entirely without direction but pursue a strategy of optimization. They seek to attract investments and a residential population that promises economic success. Klaus Ronneberger speaks in this respect of a "politics of privileged places"[10]: individual urban areas are enhanced, with the goal of tying promising sectors of the population to particular places. In a process like this, there are naturally also losers. Not all places can receive an equal amount of attention and profit from the associated cultural and economic upswings. Temporary uses and interventions are part of this development, but they include other potentials as well. When prestigious uses are at issue, such interventions may be employed for strategic culturalization and enhancement and may therefore lead to social and functional homogenization. The basic characteristics of a temporary situation—the unaccustomed juxtaposition of disparate uses and the atmosphere of the provisional and the variable—are thereby lost and give way to the social and functional segmentation that is typical of capitalist production of the city. However, temporary use may also have a compensatory effect within the economy of social attention and prompt new perspectives on hitherto neglected areas and clienteles.

They encourage the unconventional reuse of buildings and areas and confuse familiar and economically optimized functional models when they bring living and working, culture and industry together (again). It isn't always possible to predict what direction the processes touched off by temporary interventions will take; for that they are still too rare.

The introduction of temporariness and processuality is intended to force a rethinking of city planning by shifting it into the role of a mediator between disparate interests. Planning of this kind acknowledges the conflictual and even warlike character of the distribution of space and attempts to settle spatial conflicts in a civil manner—unlike the temporary uses of the 1970s, which assumed that such a reconciliation of interests was impossible within the capitalist order and therefore took the form of squats. The new forms of planning organization assume that the goals of every planning effort are themselves contested and must be permanently questioned—"organization" is now understood "as an independently goal-setting social system."[11] This open conception of planning is confronted with the tendency of city policy-makers and planners to regard city planning as city management in the service of investment projects, a tendency that is only now really coming into its own. As Dirk Baecker argues, it's worth remembering here that while city management may be combined with a communica-tive and dynamic type of planning, management itself is still the "application of an economic calculation to an object that is foreign to that calculation, i.e., organization"[12]—and that very quickly leads to closing down the openness of the situation.

Temporary uses of different types and scales have the increasingly urgent task of mediating between big investment projects and the substantially subtler processes of the city, strength-ening local and creative potentials, and endowing even the globally standardized large-scale projects with a less artificial life.

Notes

1. Jacques Derrida, *Specters of Marx: The State of the Debt, the Work of Mourning, and the New International*, trans. Peggy Kamuf (London and New York: Routledge & Kegan Paul, 1994), 150.
2. *An Architektur* No. 2: *"Anti-Vandal. Mietbare Eigentumssicherung,"* Berlin 2002.
3. Georg Franck, "The economy of attention" (English translation of: "Ökonomie der Aufmerksamkeit," in: *Merkur* No. 534/535 (1993)), in: Telepolis, http://www.heise.de/tp/english/special/auf/5567/1,html.
4. See Colin Rowe and Fred Coetter, *Collage City* (Cambridge, MA: MIT Press, 1978).
5. Claude Lévi-Strauss, *The Savage Mind* (Chicago: University of Chicago Press, 1966), 30.
6. A phenomenon that was described very early on, e.g., by David Harvey.
7. David Baybrooke and Charles E. Lindblom, "Zur Strategie der unkoordinierten kleinen Schritte (Disjointed Incrementalisms)," in: Gerhard Fehl, Mark Fester, and Nikolaus Kuhnert, eds., *Planung und Information. Materialien zur Planungsforschung* (Gütersloh: Bertelsmann, 1972), 139–166.
8. Walter Siebel, Oliver Ibert, and Hans-Norbert Mayer, "Projektorientierte Planung – ein neues Paradigma?", *Informationen zur Raumentwicklung* No. 3/4 (1999): 163–172.
9. Dirk Baecker, *Postheroisches Management. Ein Vademecum* (Berlin: Merve, 1994), 9.
10. Klaus Ronneberger, "From Regulation to Moderation," in: Florian Haydn and Robert Temel, *Temporary Urban Spaces: Concepts for the Use of City Spaces* (Basel, Boston, and Berlin: Birkhäuser, 2006), 49–57.
11. Baecker, *Postheroisches Management* (note 9), 157.
12. Dirk Baecker, *Organisation und Management* (Frankfurt: Suhrkamp, 2003).

potentials of

The establishment of rules and minimum standards was a major social achievement of modernity. Yet with the increasing formalization of all areas of life, the emancipatory potential of that accomplishment is threatening to turn into its opposite. As a counterreaction, cultures of the informal have emerged in the realms of architecture, cultural life, city

the informal

planning, economy, the legal system, new media, and advertising.
These cultures reveal the possibilities and dangers, costs and benefits
associated with informality. Rules must constantly be questioned and, if
necessary, abolished. On the other hand, productive informal practices
must be recognized and incorporated into the structures of society.

THE INFORMAL ECONOMY:

BETWEEN NEW DEVELOPMENTS AND

OLD REGULATIONS

Saskia Sassen

Note by the editors: In her 1994 text, Saskia Sassen discusses the strong growth of informal economies in large cities of the developed industrial countries since the 1980s. She explains why informality plays an important part in the newly emerged economic system. Sassen argues that it should be acknowledged as an important phenomenon. Instead of denigrating informality, regulatory systems should be modified to embrace it. Sassen's claims and suggestions are still highly relevant to contemporary cities today.

The growth of an informal economy in the large cities of highly developed countries prompts new questions about the relationship between economy and regulation today. As I shall employ the term, the "informal economy" refers to those income-generating activities occurring outside the state's regulatory framework that have analogs within that framework.

Until recently, theorization about the informal economy has focused on the shortcomings of less developed economies: their inability to attain full modernization, to stop excess migration to the cities, and to implement universal education and literacy programs.[1] The growth of an informal economy in highly developed countries has been explained as the result of immigration from the Third World and the replication here of survival strategies typical of the home countries of migrant workers. Rather than simply reassert the truth of such an argument, we must critically examine the role that Third World immigration might or might not play in the "informalization" process. Although immigrants, insofar as they tend to form communities, may be in a favorable position to seize the opportunities presented by informalization, immigrants do not necessarily create such opportunities. Instead, the opportunities may well be a structured outcome of the composition of advanced economies. The argument presented here is that informalization must be seen in the context of

1 *See* e.g. W. Arthur Lewis: *The Theory of Economic Growth* (London: George Allen & Unwin, 1955).

the economic restructuring that has contributed to the decline of the manufacturing-dominated industrial complex of the postwar era and the rise of a new, service-dominated economic complex.[2] The specific mediating processes that promote informalization of work are: on one hand, increased earnings inequality, and the concomitant restructuring of consumption in high -income and, very-low-income strata; and on the other hand, the inability of providers of many of the goods and services that are part of the new consumption to compete for necessary resources in urban contexts, where leading sectors have sharply bid up the prices of commercial space, labor, auxiliary services, and other factors of production. The growing inequality in earnings among consumers, and the growing inequality in profit-making capabilities among firms in different sectors in the urban economy, have promoted the informalization of a growing array of economic activities.

Increasingly, economic processes diverge from the model for which extant regulations were designed. As these divergences take on a recognizable shape of their own, it becomes meaningless to speak of regulatory violations; informal economic activity as here described is not a scattering of isolated deviations, but a recurrent pattern.

Rather than treat its components as isolated deviations from the norm, policymakers should recognize that a new norm has developed; rather than attempt to make this new norm fit the regulations developed decades ago, they should develop new regulations to fit this norm.

What makes informalization a distinct process today is not these small cracks in the institutional framework, but rather the informalization of activities generally taking place in the formal economy. While there are certain activities that lend themselves more to informalization than others, it is not the intrinsic characteristics of those activities, but rather the boundaries of state regulation, that determine their informalization. The informal economy is not a clearly defined sector or set of sectors. Neither is the informal economy a fixed set of activities undertaken solely for survival. Instead, the shape of the informal economy changes according to the opportunities created and constraints imposed by the formal economy. The key to an analysis of the informal economy is a description of the basic dynamics that make possible or even induce informalization, despite regulatory policies and pressure from institutions such as labor unions and enforcement agencies.

2 Bennett Harrisson and Barry Bluestone, *The Great U-Turn: Corporate Restructuring and the Polarization of America* (New York: Basic Books, 1988), chapter 1.

CONDITIONS FOR INFORMALIZATION IN ADVANCED ECONOMIES

The forms economic growth has assumed in the post-World War II era—notably capital intensity, standardization of production, and suburbanization-led growth—have contributed to the vast expansion of a middle class and deterred and reduced informalization. The cultural forms accompanying these processes shaped the structures of everyday life insofar as a large middle class engages in mass consumption and thus contributes to standardization in production. Large-scale production and mass consumption were conducive to higher levels of labor unionization and worker empowerment than had existed before World War II. It was in that postwar period, extending into the late 1960s and early 1970s, that the incorporation of workers into formal labor market relations reached its highest level.

The decline of mass production as the main engine of national growth and the shift to services as the leading economic sector contributed to the demise of a broader set of social arrangements, particularly a weakening of the larger institutional framework that shaped the employment relationship.

The groups of service industries that were the driving economic force in the 1980s were characterized by greater earnings and occupational dispersion, weak labor unions, and mostly unprotected jobs in the lower-paying echelons. Along with the decline in manufacturing, these trends altered the institutional framework that shaped the employment relationship in the 1980s. Changes in the employment relationship reshaped social reproduction and consumption trends which have had a feedback effect on economic organization and earnings. While in the earlier period a similar feedback effect helped reproduce the middle class and formalization of the employment relationship, currently it reproduces growing earnings dispersion and the casualization of the employment relationship.

The overall result of the transformation of the economic structure is a tendency toward increased economic polarization. The ascendance of finance and specialized services, particularly concentrated in large cities, creates a critical mass of firms with extremely high profit-making capabilities. These firms bid up the prices of commercial space, industrial services, and other factors of production, such as energy and business services. The high profit-making firms thereby make survival for firms with moderate profit-making capabilities increasingly precarious. My research indicates that even when moderate profit-making firms have a stable, or even increasing, demand for their goods and services from households and other firms, operating informally is often one of the few ways in which they can survive. In short, the sectors in which these firms operate may be thriving, demand may be sufficiently high to attract new entrants into the sector, but despite the high demand, the only way to succeed may be to operate informally. Alternatively, firms with limited profit-making capabilities may subcontract part of their work to informal operations. This alternative allows the contracting firm to operate formally and reduce its costs of operation.[3]

The polarization I have described does not simply constitute a quantitative transformation; it possesses the elements of a new economic regime. The centrality of mass production and mass consumption in economic growth and profit realization has been displaced by new sources of growth that feed the top and the bottom of the income structure. The expansion of a low-income population fuels the demand for very cheap goods and services; the informal economy can help satisfy that demand and, indeed, it can compete against low-priced imports in these markets. The expansion of a high-income stratum in cities promotes demand for customized goods and services; this market includes the rise of a designer culture in all forms of consumption, from food and clothing to furniture and home renovation. The production and/or distribution of customized goods and services frequently draws on the informal economy at some point in the work process.

The rapid growth of industries with strong concentrations of high- and low-income jobs has assumed distinct forms in the consumption structure, which in turn has had a feedback effect on the organization of work and the types of jobs being created. The expansion of the high-income work force, in conjunction with the emergence of new cultural forms, has led to a process of high-income gentrification that ultimately depends on the availability of a vast supply of low-wage workers.[4] High-income gentrification is labor-intensive, whereas middle-income suburbanization is capital-intensive. The latter phenomenon is characterized by tract housing, road and highway construction, dependence on private automobile or commuter trains, marked reliance on appliances and household equipment of all sorts, and large shopping malls with self-service operations.[5] High-income gentrification replaces many of these capital-intensive projects with operations that rely heavily on workers, directly and indirectly. Similarly, high-income residents in cities depend to a much greater extent on hired maintenance personnel than do middle-class suburban households, with their concentrated input of family labor and machinery. Producers that serve the middle-income market rely

3 *See* Christian Zlolniski, "The Informal Economy in an Advanced Industrial Society: Mexican Immigrant Labor in Silicon Valley," in: *Yale Law Journal* 103, June 8 1994, 2305.

4 *See* Saskia Sassen, *The Mobility of Labor and Capital: A Study in International Investment and Labor Flow* (Cambridge: Cambridge University Press, 1988), chapter 5.

5 *See* Paul Blumberg, *Inequality in an Age of Decline* (Oxford and New York: Oxford University Press, 1980).

heavily on specific customer input in designing their product line, and their small scales of production raise the relative costs of transportation and national distribution. Furthermore, unlike mass production and distribution, customized production and distribution do not facilitate labor unionizing.

The expansion of the low-income consumer population in large cities has also contributed to the proliferation of small operations and the move away from large-scale standardized factories and large chain stores for low-priced goods. The consumption needs of the low-income population are met in large part by small manufacturing and retail establishments that rely on family labor and often fall below minimum safety and health standards. Cheap, locally produced sweatshop garments, for example, compete with low-cost Asian imports. A growing range of products and services, from low-cost furniture made in basements to "gypsy cabs" and family day care, is available to meet the demand of the growing low-income population. [6]

Income polarization is also expressed spatially. Services in the formal economy for high-income customers have proliferated, as have services in the informal economy for low-income customers. Taxi services and banking services illustrate this pattern. The creation of a special, fully registered limousine line that exclusively services New York City's financial district stands in stark contrast to the increase in gypsy cabs servicing low-income neighborhoods, where registered cab drivers typically refuse to go.[7]

PATTERNS OF INFORMALIZATION AND THEIR IMPLICATIONS: A SUMMARY

My field research in New York City[8] has revealed several recurring patterns in the process of informalization. The first pattern concerns the source of demand for informally produced or distributed goods and services.[9] Most of the demand for informally produced goods in the garment, furniture, construction, packaging, and electronics industries comes from firms that operate in the formal economy. Other informally produced goods and services cater to the communities in which such activities are performed. Immigrant communities are a leading example, and probably account for much of this second type of demand.

The second set of patterns I have identified concerns factors influencing the supply of, and demand for, informally produced and distributed goods and services. One of these factors is pressure in certain industries, notably apparel, to reduce labor costs, given massive competition from low-wage Third World countries. Informal work in this instance combines very low wages with substandard conditions.

6 *See* Saskia Sassen-Koob: "The Informal Economy in Low-Income Communities in New York City", in: Alejandro Portes et. al eds., Informal Economy: *Studies in Advanced and Less Developed Countries* (Baltimore: Johns Hopkins University Press, 1989).

7 *See* Elliot Sclar et al., "The Nonmedallion Taxi Industry," in: *City Almanac,* New York, fall 1988.

8 *See* e.g. Sassen, *The Global City* (Princeton: Princeton University Press, 1991) at chapter. 9; Saskia Sassen and Wendy Grover, *Unregistered Work in the New York Metropolitan Area*, 1986 (research report on file with Urban Planning Department, Columbia University); Saskia Sassen and Robb Smith, "Postindustrial Growth and Economic Reorganization: Their Impact on Immigrant Employment" in: Jorge A. Bustamante. et al. ,eds., *U.S.—Mexico Relaet al.* (Eds.): *U.S.-Mexico Relations: Labor Market Interdependence* (Stanford: Stanford University Press, 1992), 372–393. *See also* footnote 7.

9 U.S. Department of Labor: *The Underground Economy in the United States*, Occasional Paper Series on the Informal Sector, No.2, 11 (1992).

Another important factor affecting supply and demand is the failure of enterprises operating in the formal economy to meet the demands of certain low-income consumers. Either their prices are too high for these consumers, their locations are inaccessible, or the seller provides no service at all to low-income consumers. Informal operations step in to meet the demand that regulated suppliers have failed to meet.

The existence of a cluster of informal businesses in a neighborhood may eventually generate agglomeration economies that induce additional entrepreneurs to move in or set up businesses. One observes the formation of auto-repair districts, vendors districts, or clusters of both regulated and informal small-scale manufacturers in areas not zoned for manufacturing. These districts can become magnets; they signal to other would-be entrepreneurs that the costs of entry in certain neighborhoods are lower than in the formal economy, and that there is a market in those locations for their goods and services. If the informal businesses choose their locations according to proximity to a relatively cheap labor supply, they signal to other businesses the existence of an informal "hiring hall."

A third set of patterns evident in the informal economy concerns the influence of locational constraints. Many shops engaging in customized production or operating on subcontracts are bound to New York City for some or all of the following reasons: (1) demand is local and typically client-specific; (2) the nature of the business requires proximity to design and specialized services and a quick turnover between completion of design and production; (3) the firms rely on the purchasing patterns associated with a highly dynamic overall economic environment; and (4) the firms cater to the specific tastes of local immigrant communities. Firms constrained by these factors must stay in New York City in order to have a clientele, whether of households or other firms. However, staying in New York City effectively means that these firms must operate informally. The high cost of doing business in the City, particularly the cost of land, can force small-scale customized manufacturers to set up shop in spaces not zoned for manufacturing.

A fourth pattern in the process of informalization concerns variety of jobs. Many of the jobs in the informal economy are unskilled, offer no training opportunities and involve repetitive tasks. Other jobs demand high skills or acquisition of a skill. The growth of informalization in the construction and furniture industries has required a re-skilling of workers in those sectors. There is no wage level typical of the informal economy. Generally, however, employers or contractors seem to save compared with what they would have to pay in the formal market.

How should government deal with the growing informal economy? The easiest course of action is to criminalize all economic activities that evade regulation, imposing fines and closing the renegade operations. New York City has enacted such a policy.[10] City authorities closed newsstands and small restaurants in low-income communities. The result was disappearance of the few available economic activities and loss of the few public space anchors in these communities. From an economic perspective, criminalization makes no sense. Instead of criminalization, cities like New York must find policy formulas that help reduce the tension between these new economic conditions and a regulatory framework rooted in an earlier economic era. Such policy formulas would encompass a range of interactions between government and economy. As one illustration, zoning legislation might be used to address the polarization in profit-making capacities that has become systemic in advanced economies. Zoning laws could allow firms in low-profit sectors to compete for space and other inputs in a place like Manhattan. Thus, the so-called West Side Industrial Zone in Manhattan keeps rents low and makes it possible for a wide range of industrial services to locate in the borough, close to their clients. Rezoning to allocate greater space to corporate offices—a major goal of New York City government in the 1980s—would likely force many of these industrial service firms to close or go partially or fully informal.

Policies such as zoning certain areas specifically for low-profit-sector use could be designed so as to induce an "upgrading" of informal activities by bringing these activities within the regulatory framework while minimizing costs to entrepreneurs. Upgrading is likely to demand greater flexibility in the implementation of existing codes and acknowledgment by city officials that compliance may require several phases. Lower thresholds of regulatory compliance would be applied to new, small-scale businesses in low-income communities than to well-established businesses that have had an opportunity to recover start-up costs. To encourage compliance with modified regulations and enforcement practices, city officials might offer informal operations technical and financial assistance as part of the long-term upgrading process. Beyond mildly accommodating policies, one might even envision a more drastic redrawing of regulatory frameworks, on the principle that current developments have rendered the old frameworks obsolete.[11]

The second question prompted by my study of New York City is: Why should we bother to upgrade the informal economy in low-

10 *See, New York State's Underground Economy: Underground Economy. Untaxed and Growing,* Report, Commission on Oversight, Analysis, and Investigation, N.Y. State Legislature (1982); New York City Department of Finance, *Unearthing the Underground Economy,* Report (1986); Deborah Sontag, "Unlicensed Peddlers, Unfettered Dreams," in: *The New York Times,* June 14, 1993.

11 *See* Edgar S. Cahn, "Reinventing Poverty Law", in: *Yale Law Journal 103,* June 8, 1994, p. 2133.

income communities? The informal economy is one of the few forms of economic growth evident in these communities. With the decline of manufacturing and the ascendance of finance and specialized services, economic growth has become disproportionately concentrated in central business districts and suburban office complexes. Economic growth, one might conclude, has abandoned low-income communities. We need to find anchors to regenerate these communities, to reconstitute neighborhood sub-economies. This task becomes particularly important in the absence of any sign that mainstream patterns of economic growth will find ways of locating growth in these communities. Informal economies bridge the divide between new high-income middle-class neighborhoods and low-income neighborhoods, a divide widened by the flight of the middle class from the cities.

This text has been shortened with kind permission of the author. The full version of this text was published in the *Yale Law Journal* June 1994.

INFORMAL ECONOMIES AND CULTURES
IN GLOBAL CITIES

A conversation between Saskia Sassen and Philipp Oswalt

Philipp Oswalt: In 1994 you published an article on informal economies in the *Yale Law Journal*; in retrospect, it proved to be an accurate forecast of many things to come. You mainly wrote about the American experience of migrant economies, but also pointed out that informal economies are not just about migrant economies—they are a central component of post-Fordist economies, especially in manufacturing and in the services sector, though for the most part quite hidden.

Since publication of that article, cultural economies around the world have become more and more informal; in Europe, for example, we see his process in Berlin, Vienna, Warsaw, Amsterdam, Barcelona, and London, where young start-ups, squatters, clubs and the arts scene, informal traders, and new forms of urban sports emerged in the 1990s.

Saskia Sassen: The same politico-economic restructuring that led to the new urban economy emerging in the late 1980s and onwards also contributed to the formation of new informal economies. It's important to distinguish these new informal economies from the old informal economies that are such a prominent part of megacities in the Southern Hemisphere, and to distinguish them from the pre-regulation era in all advanced economies. The decline of the manufacturing-dominated industrial complex that characterized most of the twentieth century and the rise of a new, service-dominated economic complex provide the general context within which we need to place "informalization" if we are to go beyond a mere description of instances of informal work.

Much of today's informalization is actually linked to key features of advanced capitalism. In this regard, they are new types of informal economies. This in turn also explains the particularly strong presence of informal economies in global cities. And it helps explain a mostly overlooked development:

the proliferation of an informal economy of creative professional work in these cities—artists, architects, designers, software developers. Yes, the cities you mention are key locations for this. And now we are seeing similar trends in the emergence of new types of informal economy in major cities in Latin America, Africa, and much of Asia. These new forms should not be confused with the older informal economies in the cities of these countries, which tend to be driven more by needs of survival than by the economic restructuring that began in the 1980s as part of the neoliberal era.

The new types of informalization of work are the low-cost equivalent of formal deregulation in finance, telecommunications, and most other economic sectors in the name of flexibility and innovation. The difference is that whereas formal deregulation was costly, and tax revenue as well as private capital went into paying for it, informalization is low-cost and comes largely on the backs of workers and firms.

In the case of the new informal economy among creative professionals, these negative features are mostly not there, and informalization greatly expands opportunities and networking potentials. Nonetheless, there are strong reasons why these artists and professionals operate at least in part informally. It allows them to function in the interstices of urban and organizational spaces often dominated by large corporate actors and to escape the corporatization of creative work. In this process they contribute to very specific features of the new urban economy: its innovativeness and a certain type of frontier spirit. In many ways this process represents a reinvention of Jane Jacobs's urban economic creativity.

CENTRALITIES

PO: Is there a spatial pattern to the kind of urban spaces that are occupied by the informal sector?

SS: What you see since the late 1990s in many big cities—and becoming progressively stronger—is a new vibrancy and a fascination once more in live performance and small spaces. The notion now is, "I prefer it imperfect; it doesn't need to be the most famous, but I want to be part of the experience. Better imperfect and live than perfect and recorded." That desire decentralizes activities. Spaces of centrality can also be constituted in what are considered peripheral areas. You have avant-garde groups in any big city whose geography is very different from that of the suburban middle-class person who goes to the opera. There are many spaces of centrality in the city; some of them occupy terrains which, from the perspective of the average citizen, might look way out. I like the example of live performance because it's very heuristic: once live performance is revalued, as it is today, it becomes a serious process that actively re-marks space. What may seem like marginal space to the operagoer, is central space to the world of live performance in a city. And that's great because it's about the active making of central space. Then the question of centrality plays on the recognition that there are many spaces of centrality that can inhabit a given terrain. A space that may seem slightly devastated, rundown—like old manufacturing and warehouse space—can also be a space that is central to artists in the city. For example, you have very tight finances for a certain kind of new media setup or for software development—at least, I know, tight in the case of London or New York. And then there is the new metropolitan scale for big corporate headquarters, which is another kind of space of centrality—it's multinodal. It still needs the gravitational force of a major city, but it stretches into what for most is experienced as suburban space, not central space. For performance art, that extension into the older geography of suburban space might not work, at least for now, because its context is embedded in a more urbanized area.

PO: Why do these different actors have different centralities?

SS: Why do they need financial centers at all? One way of thinking about it is the way in which different bits and pieces get assembled into a meaningful space for diverse actors or objectives: territory, network, geographic terrain, captive audience, marketplace … whatever it might be. One reason that the immigrant community was well positioned to seize on the opportunities for informal work produced by advanced capitalism—with a lot of exploitation, let's not romanticize it—was that it had captive markets, captive labor forces which were not necessarily running through formal channels, such as family labor or your neighbor's son.

The informal economy functions in what are commonly seen as peripheral spaces, but also in central spaces. When I was living in SoHo, in New York, an old warehouse district which had become very chic, I saw that a lot of informal work was happening inside these enormously elegant fancy lofts of designers. Whether it was making some kind of incredibly shaped piece of furniture or very beautiful clothing, they didn't want the materials in the houses of the immigrants, so instead the workers came to SoHo. The decorating work, the woodwork, and a lot of the construction work is not happening in peripheral spaces; it is happening right there in the gentrifying center.

One of the more confusing aspects of this question of centrality, and one I have worked on a lot, is why powerful global financial firms that can buy the most advanced technology and are all about electronic networks need financial centers. Why do they need a space of centrality at all? And they do. My answer to this question is that, insofar as they want to keep control over their globally dispersed set of operations, their central functions become enormously complex—even more so given the high speed at which they move vast amounts of capital. The problem of incomplete knowledge is acute for the global electronic sector. So these firms need a certain type of space of centrality, one that is different, let's say, from that of luxury shopping districts. The space of centrality they need is one that can produce what I call "urban knowledge capital"—a knowledge capital that is more than the sum of the knowledge of the professionals and of the specialized firms. It is more because of the multiple interactions and networks that a dense urban space contains, and the knowledge gets produced in this interactive space.

So this is a space of centrality that is different from that of performers, or of the new creative informal economy.

SPACE

PO: In your article you describe how informal economies and the informal labor market have grown since the end of Fordism. If you look to urban space, you can also say that with the end of Fordism, the urban territory has become fragmented, more unstable, with an increase in informal spaces, vacant lots, and disused buildings. There is a correspondence between the informalization and flexibilization of activity, on the one hand, and of space, on the other. Do these spatial informalities gain new meaning in the context of the informalization of the labor market?

SS: Absolutely. That's why I like your book *Berlin, Stadt ohne Form* [Berlin, City without Form]. Cities are full of *terrains vagues*. A place that doesn't have them is not a city; it's something else—perhaps an agglomeration, or a suburb, but it's not a city. The notion of *terrain vague* picks up on the layered spatial history of cities. It is both an opportunity for the informal, such as building a garden to grow vegetables, and the possibility of making public space. Modest spaces invite the *making* of public space, as opposed to *accessing* the beautiful and grand public spaces of crown and state, like those in Europe. These *terrains vagues* are potentially very productive spaces not just in terms of informal economies but also in terms of *making* temporary public space. Take Berlin, for example: ironically, the lack of development kept the city going as a cultural center after the Wall came down.

Even as massive projects proliferate, such cities contain many under-used spaces, often characterized more by memory than by their current meaning. These spaces are part of the interiority of a city, yet lie outside its organizing, utility-driven logics and spatial frames. These *terrains vagues* allow many residents to connect to the rapidly transforming cities in which they live, and subjectively to bypass the massive infrastructures that have come to dominate more and more of the spaces in their cities. From this perspective, pouncing on these *terrains vagues* in order to maximize real estate development would be a mistake. Keeping some of this openness might, further, make sense in terms of factoring in future options at a time when utility logics change so quickly and often violently—an excess of high-rise office buildings being one of the great examples.

This issue opens up a salient question about the current urban condition in ways that take it beyond the more transparent notions of high-tech architecture, virtual spaces, simulacra, and theme parks. All of the latter matter, but they are fragments of an incomplete puzzle. There is a type of urban condition that dwells between the reality of massive structures and the reality of semi-abandoned places. I think this condition is central to the experience of the urban, and it makes legible the transitions and unsettlements of specific spatiotemporal configurations.

TIME AND CHANGE

PO: The process of informalization is also a means of avoiding costs, as you point out in your article. But at the same time these informal economies often need to be in the center. So they have to use undervalued opportunities in time and space in a very flexible way.

SS: An excellent point: it is also about flexibility and under-valued time. Certain spaces are available at peripheral times, like over the weekend or at night. So in China's crowded cities, a bus shelter becomes public space once the bus stops running at night. It would be great if we could formulate a general proposition that the informal economy is opportunistic and operates in peripheral time and space. But we can't, because centrality is also important to informal economies. We are inclined to think of it in terms of the actors being there, trying to survive and operating—that's all part of it, but the ecology within which it all happens and its complexity are also important to capture.

CHANGE TO SELF-EMPLOYMENT

PO: The cultural sphere has become increasingly informal-ized since the early 1990s, and more and more highly educated upper -middle-class people have taken up informal modes of work and production. This was not the case in the 1980s.

SS: Not to this extent, though it was more so in the arts scene. But yes, there have been major changes since the late 1980s. I completely agree with your description.

PO: You may have heard of the German discussions about "*Generation Praktikum*," the generation of interns. It has become quite normal for university graduates to do unpaid or nearly unpaid work, either as employees or as marginally self-employed. You can see that in the profession of the archi-tect—where the phenomenon took hold in the 1990s, with the crisis of the profession.

SS: You have some of that self-employment in the field of new media and new technology, where there is a roving set of opportunities for people. My son, Hilary Koob-Sassen (www.TheErrorists.com), was like that too, and he made a vast amount of money just because he was very good with tech-nology. Now he is in London, squatting galleries, buildings; they do a big show in a squatted gallery, it will get reviewed, and then they move on. Because legally they can have it for three months—so they play within the interstices of the law. The phenomenon has moved beyond the narrower notion of the informal economy and immigrant communities and has expanded to the middle class, to the professionals.

The self-employed professional—typically, the accountant, lawyer, or doctor—is of course an old type. But what began to emerge in the 1980s as a really significant category is different—there are more artistic types, designers, performers. What has changed today is the "thickness" of the arts and cultural sector. There is a broad range of opportunities, and talent counts for a lot. It's not like being a civil servant where you have to fit the mold. It's a new way of inhabiting the category "professional." You see it in Mumbai, in Shanghai—though it's pretty regulated in its own way there—and also in Buenos Aires, when, during Argentina's major economic crisis, the fallback position became the world of culture and making art on the street.

> PO: Another big shift since the early 1990s is that informality has become fashionable. One example is marketing: companies such as Adidas and Nike are branding themselves by organizing informal street sports events, sometimes even illegally, to market their products. Or there's Comme des Garçons' notion of "guerrilla" shopping. The commercial world of the big corporate firms is adopting these strategies. But you also see the fashionableness of informality in the architectural sphere—for instance, Rem Koolhaas's fascination with Lagos. A series of urbanistic studies of informality have emerged in the last ten years.

SS: One idea has lost some of its power: the centripetal logic that the nation-state is able to keep it all in one container—like a kind of "sausage"—through a regulatory framework. Today there are multiple centrifugal forces which shape all these new different worlds. In addition, there is a lot of romanticizing. Architects have a way of bringing in images from other fields of knowledge and using them for their own purposes, which is fine as a source of inspiration for the architect, but it is quite subjective.

To some extent, these cultural formations are subjective, which in itself is interesting. The middle-class professionals in this informal space have produced narratives about it that the immigrants would not have used. The immigrant would tell you, "I'm a hard worker. This is necessary work. I want to feed my family. I want to be a good American." If the informal earners are middle class and in a creative profession, they are going to use a totally different narrative. Chaos theory, for instance, is a fashionable narrative. This aspect is also part of the subjectivity associated with globalization; it is an assembling, disassembling, and reassembling of a set of images that are very powerful and that sometimes capture a truth. What was lodged in an objective and subjective national "sausage" gets redeployed and constitutes new types of assemblages. These assemblages can be very specialized, they can be global, they can be happening inside the city. And they restructure the situation, condition, space, system of authority—even the provision of rights. Thus, what gets assembled for the informal immigrant worker or the enterprise to exist is quite different from what is required for the informal creative sector to exist.

FORMALIZING THE INFORMAL

PO: At the end of your article you write about the need for us to reevaluate our rules according to the observation of informalities, arguing that informalities can be understood, that they are not chaotic but have clear patterns, which can be formalized. Our research at Urban Catalyst shows that we need to tackle this question from two ends: we need to informalize and adjust our rules, and we sometimes need to formalize the informal.

SS: The concept that I use in my article is regulatory fractures, and by that I mean it isn't a question of violation or of compliance. These are new realities that exist in interstices, so I mean fractures in the sense that quite a lot of the informal economy is entirely licit. Saying it's the underground, or the black economy, or criminal—that doesn't help us understand what it is. What I am trying to do is to understand what is happening. So let's not just think in terms of the violation and compliance of existing rules. These are new developments, and the law does not quite fit in. We need new rules. There is also a large framing for much of this and many other emergent conditions, which has to do with the weakening power of the state to hold things together under one normative frame. Global finance is also an example here. The formation of all these multiple assemblages—from good ones to bad ones, some local and some global—which are very specialized, de-centers what used to be centralized around the *project* that is the making of the nation-state. In many ways, the fragmenting that you describe with respect to urban space occurs also at greater institutional levels. It's a mess out there … adorable, no?

One outcome has been the production of more and more private law systems which are neither national nor international. So you have *lex constructiones*, *lex digitales*, and so on. The actors in the informal world lack the kind of power and resources needed to create these systems, but they often are the source for new formalizations; they capture the making of new worlds, of new politics, of new practices, and new logics. (These types of ideas are developed in my new book *Territory, Authority, Rights*—in German, *Das Paradox des Nationalen*.) Let me add quickly that what I am describing is a larger, partly systemic process or dynamic. In the immediacy of daily survival, many actors in the informal sector do not have the time or interest to create new formalizations for the reality that they are making or experiencing; they would like certain protections in certain situations, but otherwise often do not want to be bothered with that kind of thing.

What we are dealing with is a whole new agenda for thinking about the question of rules. Informality involves good things, bad things, complex things, elementary things. The center doesn't hold here; the existing legal systems don't hold. Adding more rules can serve for certain things—working standards, for instance: here we can use the existing rules just fine. But for other domains, such as the creative domains that you are talking about, part of that can be subjected to existing rules, but part of it is about something completely different.

> PO: If the state just deregulates, there is the danger of the powerful private forces defining the rules for everybody. For us, the interest lies in temporary activities in urban conditions, where you have the shaping of public space being done by people with a very small amount of capital but great creativity and motivation. We have to think not in terms of deregulating but in terms of adapting rules, which empowers processes of self-organization not just in informal economies but also in the middle class, enabling it once more to gain a relevant position.

SS: I agree with that. The bundle of things we include under informality is just one element. In the United States, the private and public domains are being recast: the executive branch of government is privatizing itself and withdrawing from the public domain, and at the same time it is invading the private domain of citizens. That represents a dramatic inversion of what the doctrine of liberal democracy holds and what has been the case at various times, for instance, in the United States: when the executive branch is subject to public accountability and has to accept the privacy rights of citizens, which were hard won by the earlier bourgeoisie. And then you have the question of war—talk about informality! The asymmetries! Our standard conventional military cannot deal with this kind of asymmetry. That is a whole other bundle, and it is affecting international law, treaty law. I am actually organizing a conference where I am bringing together researchers and activists from many different worlds in order to address the question of cities and the new wars, a subject I am doing research on (see http://www.columbia.edu/~sjs2/). For me, informality is an occasion, a heuristic zone, to understand emergent practices, narratives and other forms of understanding, and social formats in the making.

MAKING

It happens to be a great one when you are thinking of the kind of issues we are discussing: cities, economy, and creativity. That is a critical bundle, and it's more attractive than some of these other instances. One thing that runs across all these different informalities is "making." The making of a new political subject, in the same way that in Max Weber's medieval cities a citizen was made through his practices or his ideas; he wasn't just consuming citizenship as an entitlement or a possession or—what we see today—demonstration of the "making" of illegal immigrants. It's about making a political subject, not just about the master/slave dynamic of "give me more, a better job," and so on. Same with the type of war conducted by Al Qaeda. That is about making, not just about deploying. I'm interested in these periods of change, and change doesn't just mean the French Revolution image of the storming of the Bastille. "Making," in the sense of Greek *poiesis*, has become a much neglected critical variable; making that can produce enormous indeterminacy in overdetermined contexts—informality can be seen as such a kind of making. What you are describing in terms of the middle class and creative informality becomes making. It's about making rather than buying or selling or executing an existing project.

PO: When we consider informal urban development on a global scale, the main topic is not the cultural middle class in the cities of developed countries, but the squatting, informal housing, and informal economies in developing countries. Taking illegal settlements as a given, how can we improve the quality of life and the development of these kinds of settlements?

SS: We can start with the perspective of "making" rather than the issue of compliance. "Making" intersects with an old Roman principle, which remains in law today: *usucapio* (right by possession), which all squatters have. After twenty years' occupation, the piece of land is yours. For me, this points to a critical issue: how temporality or duration can alter the meaning of violation of the law. In certain cases, the longer the violation of the law—whether illegal immigration or squatting—the greater your right. That is an incredibly fruitful tension when violating a law for five years gives you more rights than if you had violated it for only a year. In that mutating meaning-making lies the possibility of altering the formal element. Again, these are the kinds of questions I examine at length in my *Territory* book.

Let me mention two related issues here: one good, one bad. The good side: there are times, far more often than one might think, when the state has to accommodate its formal apparatus to a reality on the ground; and it demonstrates regularly that it can do this, as it has with illegal immigrants and amnesties. On the negative side: real estate developers have learned how to push the state to build infrastructure in degraded or shanty areas. As soon as the infrastructure is in place, the developers move in and the squatters are displaced. Suddenly it's all illegal and the people are thrown out; the water pipes, the lines, roads, and electricity—it's all in, and then they move in and "development" can begin.

PO: And this happens where?

SS: Everywhere. It famously happened in Caracas more than twenty years ago, which created such a scandal that it mobilized people—this is often the next step; new politics come into play, new political actors emerge. There is a trajectory there. It's the same for what I described earlier—about how new laws often arise from efforts to formalize a new informal economic or cultural practice. But, getting back to Venezuela, the abuse by developers was rampant, and it all came very fast, because enormous wealth was coming from people getting rich through the new oil regime, OPEC. This mix really alienated the poor, as well as other groups in society.

When I was writing my first articles on the informal economy, the social scientists didn't know what I was talking about. They said it doesn't exist. Now it is recognized by the media and social scientists. And for some it has become a productive category, rather than a designation—as in, "This is the informal sector, and that is the formal sector." Designation is a form of death for a subject. The subject has come into its own—it can accommodate complexity. My starting point has clearly grown. I think it does indicate that I was onto something. I argued that informal activity is not the failure of regulation or a return to older modes, nor is it regressive or an import through the immigrants; rather, I argued that it is part of advanced capitalism. This opened up the field to research and theorization. This kind of informality is also part of advanced capitalist market economies.

WHICH LEGAL CONDITIONS ARE REQUIRED
FOR TEMPORARY USE?

A conversation between Rudolf Schäfer and Urban Catalyst

Urban Catalyst: When one looks at the phenomenon of urban development in European cities, in many places one discovers a glaring contradiction between the permanent planning laws and building regulations and what actually happens in the cities. On one hand, what is formally planned often fails to happen for years or even decades, while numerous unplanned activities go forward. The legal system lags behind the real development process.

Rudolf Schäfer: The tension between planning and reality is undeniable. But I would be careful about concluding that the legal system is lagging behind the real development process. Precisely in the domain of urban development, the purpose of the legal provisions is to create legitimacy, stability, certainty, and transparency over the long term. It is only natural that tensions should arise again and again when developments—as in the case of temporary uses—are interrupted or pursue a trajectory different from that envisioned by the planners. In this situation, it can become a problem for urban development when positive but unanticipated dynamics are hampered or even blocked.

However, whether or not this constitutes grounds for changing the legal provisions is something we would have to consider very carefully. Where are there areas in which one can preserve the stabilizing function of the law while at the same time building in a higher degree of flexibility, which then also helps to enable temporary use?

UC: Many of the regulations being applied in the realm of urban development today date from the period of the full-fledged social welfare state. They are closely bound up with the notion that urban development can be planned and regulated in detail from the top down. On the other hand, economic and cultural development has brought about a need for greater dynamism and flexibility. Are today's planning and building laws still up-to-date?

RS: The administrative mentality of the postwar social welfare state, in which the public sector articulates its interests and uses planning law to enforce them in a top-down manner—a mentality that is especially pronounced in the German-speaking world—is no longer tenable today. At least with larger projects, many arrangements come about through a consensual approach. Legal production on city planning projects today takes place through a kind of genesis, in which wide-ranging stakeholder interests come together to create a use context and ultimately a development plan. The public sector naturally brings its interests into this process and then endorses it at the end.

In this process, the stabilizing function of the law is repeatedly looked to by the property owners, the residents, as well as the municipality. The problem always arises when the development changes course in a number of years and a greater degree of flexibility is required, for example, because a need begins to materialize that is different from those laid down in the development plan.

UC: Thus, there are the simultaneous and conflicting needs for stability and flexibility. Symptomatic of the ambivalence of the informal is the course things have taken in the postsocialist countries since the collapse of the Eastern bloc, a course that led—in the first years following that collapse—to the emergence of a legal and administrative vacuum, an involuntary deregulation. This has given rise to very problematic developments such as the mafia-like privatization of public property, but at the same time it has also brought about very productive informal developments, including the appropriation of urban spaces and the formation of new cultural milieus.

RS: I have a certain aversion to the widely held view that the instruments of planning law are rigid and can only be made flexible through innovation. The determining factor, in my view, is how they are used. And here we find that—beginning in 1945 and lasting well into the 1970s—the Western European states adopted a very narrow view of the city planning toolkit, which they have applied more and more rigidly over time.

As a rule, the statutory provisions of planning law are actually quite flexible. It has never been prohibited to insert into preparatory land use plans discussions that describe the concrete needs of the individual municipality. It has never been prohibited to modify plans quickly. Nor has it ever been prohibited to formulate purely negative plans, plans that say simply: this you may not do; everything else you may.

> UC: In your view, then, the problem is not the existing regulations but the way they are applied and interpreted by administrations, courts, and other actors...

RS: That's right. Of course, that doesn't mean that everything is possible. But the law itself is more open than is often asserted in debates. Nevertheless, in practice people decide to take the opposite approach. Out of fear of the unknown, they attempt to use positive determinations to define a future condition as completely and comprehensively as possible.

OWNERSHIP AND ACCESS

> UC: Let us now turn to a concrete discussion of the legal questions that users, owners, and administrations confront in the course of a temporary use. The first legal conflicts that arise at the beginning of a temporary use involve the accessibility of spaces. Often, suitable spaces stand empty for years, even decades, without the owner being willing to make them available for temporary use. Sometimes the interested parties simply assert the right to use them and take them over, either hurriedly and without being noticed or aggressively, in the form of a squat. In countries like the Netherlands, there are laws that allow others to use a building if the owner does not. After they have been vacant for one year, properties may legally be occupied. In order to prevent a squat over which they have no control, the owners will organize a controlled "squat" in the form of a temporary use. Do property owners in Germany and many other countries have too strong a legal position vis-à-vis other actors in the realm of urban development? Do you feel it would make sense to limit property rights in order to facilitate access to unused spaces?

RS: There is no denying that in Germany and many other Western industrial countries, property law places owners in a very strong position. In principle, I regard a limitation of property rights in the direction you describe as worth considering. I do not believe, however, that in the German property law tradition the establishment of a statute like that which exists in the Netherlands is politically feasible. An entirely different set of pressing problems would have to exist in order for the legislation to be changed. In Germany, there are only a few situations in which property rights are restricted. Thus far, the property owner's power to dispose of his property has only been restricted in exceptional cases, for example, in serious city planning crises or when there is a shortage of available housing at the same time that a significant quantity of housing is standing empty.

> UC: There are many examples in legal history of ownership being closely linked to use. When the property owner doesn't use his property, his power to dispose of that property as he chooses is called into question. Another example of using legal means to stimulate the use of vacant properties is the utilization of tax law. In New York in the 1970s, as a result of high property taxes, the city came into possession of a large number of transferred properties, which made new developments possible. In Germany, a debate is under way to waive the property tax for parcels that are standing empty. In terms of promoting the use of these properties, it would make more sense for the owners to be required to pay higher property taxes when their properties are not being used.

RS: In Great Britain, there has been a penalty tax on disused inner-city sites for a number of years, in order to move them toward new development more quickly. In Germany, proposals like these were discussed decades ago, but they are not politically feasible. This is even more the case today in view of the weakness of the real estate markets, since the owners are already deprived of the income from their properties, and regulations like this could be seen as a thinly veiled form of expropriation.

> UC: Another way to steer vacant sites toward new uses would be to create positive incentives.

RS: I consider operating with incentives to be much more effective than debating new restrictive laws. A positive example is the city-initiated transfer agreements [German: *Überlassungsverträge]* in which the owner temporarily transfers a parcel that is not currently marketable to a public institution or the city itself for a public-interest-oriented use. With transfer agreements, the legal obligation to safeguard the property against hazards also passes to the city, as does the responsibility for preparatory measures. In Leipzig this has been practiced successfully for years.

UC: The powerful status of property is also a problem for the property owner, because it carries with it liability as well as the legal obligation to safeguard the property against hazards, which often becomes the primary obstacle to temporary use.

RS: This is definitely one of the major legal hurdles for temporary use. However, it can be solved by contractual agreements. In Vienna, for the municipal project einfach-mehrfach [see chapter "Cultivating Temporary Use/ Enable"], a model was developed in which the city assumes liability with its municipal liability insurance—a very successful solution and one from which other cities can also learn.

PLANNING LAW

UC: Once temporary users have gained access to spaces by one means or another, the next legal question is: can they actually realize the intended use? Various legal questions play a role in this. One of them is the use laid down in development plans. The temporary use may contradict both the earlier and now obsolete established use as well as the future established use, which has not yet been realized. In Germany, it has been possible for a number of years to impose a time limit on the right to build, that is, to allow built uses only for a specified period of time. Would this be an appropriate legal instrument for temporary uses?

RS: The preparation of a development plan involves considerable time and effort. It is much easier to arrange for temporary uses by means of city-planning contracts, in which agreements can be reached among the city, the owner, and the potential temporary users regarding the preparation and implementation of city planning measures, but also regarding the temporary use of the site. Thus, it is quite conceivable that one could set a classical development plan procedure in motion for the longer-term planning objectives, while also concluding a city planning contract regarding the duration and type of temporary uses.

UC: What role does the municipality play in this process?

RS: Let us imagine a typical scenario. In drafting a new development for his idle inner-city site, the property owner has his eye on the long-term commercial exploitation of the property, and he would like to use the planning laws and building regulations to establish as profitable a use for it as possible. At the same time, however, everyone involved is aware that it is very uncertain whether and when he will be able to find an investor. Because of the attractive location of the area, it should be a primary urban development concern on the part of the municipality to revitalize it. And precisely here, the city should not sit back passively but should play an initiating role; it should actively approach the owner and propose that he open the area up for temporary uses. Hence the proposal: yes, we will create a new development plan for the long-term use of the site, but at the same time we will also create a framework agreement regarding temporary use. And in this agreement, all important questions are fundamentally addressed, for example, a right of cancellation for the property owner should an investor be found prematurely. At the same time, the contract should be flexible enough to allow a variety of temporary uses, many of which are not even known yet at the time the agreement is concluded.

It is becoming more and more important today to be clear about the individual phases of a development project. When and to what extent do I make the site publicly accessible even before the first ground has been broken? Can preexisting buildings be preserved and used temporarily? What kinds of uses should be considered? All these questions can be answered in a general framework agreement, which then gradually acquires concrete form according to the local status of the development.

UC: But this would require an open development plan, in which the long-term use envisioned by the plan does not exclude the temporary use.

RS: Not necessarily. One could use an urban development contract to deviate from the established use and agree upon a temporary use under certain conditions. Classical planning law formulates a stable framework. Depending on local framework conditions, things that call for a greater degree of flexibility and dynamism—for example, temporary uses—can be settled more quickly and easily with supplementary contracts, which can also contain exceptions and exemptions within the limits of the legally permissible.

UC: Of course, this approach presupposes that the municipality and the property owners are well disposed. Temporary use has no actual legal claim.

RS: That's right. This requires that there be a cooperative and consensual basic philosophy, a willingness on the part of all of the stakeholders to agree upon development measures and framework conditions of a common strategy. Or else the temporary users are so politically powerful that they are able to generate enough public pressure to force the other actors to the table. For this, the temporary users have to be well organized. And it only tends to be an option for larger, more high-profile uses.

In practice, the problem of redesignation is often resolved quite informally. For example, in the case of the former railroad areas, which still stand under the use defined in the original plan, there is often a tacit change of use that is tolerated by the relevant authorities, despite the fact that it actually conflicts with the planning laws and building regulations.

> UC: But how can municipalities be motivated to become more open to an approach like this? In the normal day-to-day operations of an administrative bureaucracy, the employees tend to let things come to them, then review them to determine whether or not they should be approved. Now they are supposed to initiate developments themselves in a change from a culture of reviewing, approving, and controlling to one of enabling and initiating?

RS: I think we need to develop a more nuanced picture of municipal reality. What you are urging is already being done in a large portion of municipal practice. Think of the thousands of redevelopment projects in which the municipalities—together with their supporting organizations and other representatives and in cooperation with the principal actors in the redevelopment areas—take the initiative in precisely the manner you describe. Another example is the many initiatives to develop or stabilize downtown areas, the broad range of efforts to convert inner-city military sites and sites belonging to other sectors, etc.

Nevertheless, more still remains to be done. This is where I see a role for the training of the relevant administrative personnel. Much more than has traditionally been the case, planners in particular must be trained to think in terms of interdisciplinary, process-oriented strategies. That means, however, that they must also learn to see things from an entrepreneurial perspective more than they have traditionally done, or at the very least to incorporate considerations of economic viability and financing into their planning calculations. I am by no means arguing for the abandonment of the public interest, but rather for a public-private partnership in public leadership.

> UC: If we are going to talk about public–private partnership, we have to develop a new understanding of the term. Traditionally, the only private actors who are taken seriously by the city planning officials are those who pull up in a Mercedes and have fat wallets, for whom they roll out the red carpet. But these financially strong investors, who are important for the development of the city, can only cover a particular range of tasks and are usually not in a position to bring about a vibrant urban development all by themselves. Thus it is the city's task to bring an entirely different set of private actors on board, precisely those small-scale private actors who—whether their motivations are cultural, social, or entrepreneurial—are precisely often not financially powerful but play a critical role in the city's cultural development and precisely also in public uses. There are often brutal conflicts between these two groups of actors over such questions as the availability of space and other resources, questions in which the limits of a consensual strategy are very quickly reached. Tools like the British "planning gain" can become important in this context. On the basis of a standing rule, a portion of the profit created by the new right to build is siphoned off by the city and set aside for the benefit of the neighborhood. A round table of neighborhood representatives then distributes the money to local actors.

RS: There is no doubt that models involving the distribution of funds are well -suited as a means for promoting and supporting local structures and civil-society-oriented uses. The British instrument of planning gain is a very effective and flexible tool in this regard. In Germany, however, it would be impossible in this form. In urban development contracts here, the funds siphoned off must be used for a purpose that is causally connected with the investment project in question, a requirement that generally leads to the financing of kindergartens, traffic infrastructure, and athletic facilities. An alternative is offered by nonmonetary agreements. For example, within the context of an exemption, permission for temporary uses can be negotiated in exchange for allowing the owner to develop the site more extensively.

> UC: Imagine that the parties have agreed on a temporary permission within the framework of an urban development contract. Imagine further, however, that the temporary use in question

thrives and develops long-term potential. What might an agreement look like that would assure the use a lasting place within the framework of the city's development?

RS: First of all, I would argue for strict adherence to the terms of the contract. As soon as it becomes apparent that contracts are worthless, the willingness to consider temporary uses on the basis of them will diminish even further. Nonetheless, in cases like these the municipality can play an important role. It can either help to arrange an alternative site for the user (and if necessary for the property owner as well), or—within the framework of a stakeholder round table—it can help to negotiate the terms for establishing the use on a permanent basis. It is also conceivable that in certain cases, portions of the temporary use would be allowed to remain at the site in exchange for permission to develop the site more extensively.

UC: Back once more to the subject of the temporary right to build. What is it good for, if it isn't good for classical temporary uses?

RS: For retail stores, say, on the outskirts of the city or at disused inner-city sites. In recent years, discount chains like Lidl and Aldi have received permissions for very problematic standardized structures in areas where no higher-quality development is currently possible. The big discount chains operate with circumscribed depreciation periods, and if setting a time limit on the right to build is compatible with these, then a temporal restriction is not unreasonable. It is difficult to see why these projects should receive a permanent right to build. One can stipulate that in fifteen years, say, it's all over, and the structures must be demolished again. This is a different kind of temporary use from the usual one but one that is very interesting from an urban development perspective.

BUILDING REGULATIONS AND NORMS

UC: In addition to planning provisions, there are also a large number of building regulations that were originally formulated with permanent uses in mind. Temporary uses often tacitly seek to ignore these, because the permitting procedures involved are much too lengthy and also call for costly measures that they are not initially able to afford. Do we need separate regulations with lower standards for temporary uses?

RS: No. The standards embodied in the building code, the over-whelming majority of which serve to safeguard against hazards, cannot simply be modified according to whether the use in question is permanent or temporary. Full advantage should be taken of the available possibilities, and these are then exceptions, exemptions, or—as they are now termed—deviations. It is also conceivable that there would be contractual accords on the basis of the regulations regarding administrative contracts as defined by the provisions of the [German] Administrative Procedures Act.

> UC: It was an interesting experience for us to plan the temporary use of the Palast der Republik (Palace of the Republic). The fire department demanded that sprinklers be installed, despite the fact that virtually no combustible material was going to be brought into the building. That was absurd and caused the cost of the project to triple. The problem went unsolved until two years later, when a planner who had long had good relations with the Berlin Fire Department was able to negotiate an alternative approach. And this despite the fact that the building authority was actually quite receptive to the project.

RS: Of course, it is always more comfortable to play it safe and insist on compliance with the normal building standards than it is to embark on an objective review and ask whether this or that particular measure is really necessary in this form or whether one could resolve the issue differently. And in doing so there is always the risk of making an error of judgment.

What effect these possibilities actually have on the practice of temporary use is not a question that can be answered in the abstract. In the end, it always comes down not only to the purpose of the regulation in question but also to the local conventions surrounding their application. The path to the granting of a deviation is always dependent on different interpretive cultures, contexts, and margins of discretion. Whether actors involved in the permitting process take full advantage of the legal framework so that many things become possible or tend to behave restrictively is something that can only be affected through advocacy work and intensive dialogue. It is definitely also important whether or not there is a recognition of the relevance of temporary uses for the economy of the city. In individual cases, one can certainly also operate with the institution of tolerance. The problem with tolerances, however, is the aspect of private liability, which is always present. And of course there is always the possibility that one will come up against problems of official liability.

> UC: Administrative officials will generally try to avoid risk. They tend to say, I'm going to do this the same way I always do it—that way I won't get in trouble. Nor do they have any incentive to do it differently, unless they happen to be very idealistic, which is something we have also seen time and again. There are "subversives" in the administrative bureaucracies, who—without an official assignment—devote tremendous commitment and energy to getting projects underway.

RS: Twenty-five years ago, when we began to carry out the first model projects in the realm of ecological construction, the building inspectors refused to allow solar cells to be placed on roofs.

At that time, ecology was still regarded as a hippie concern and was not taken seriously. Since then, the situation has changed completely, and approving solar cells for new constructions is no longer a problem. A lot depends on the public perception of the issue. A high value is always placed on economic aspects—job creation, for example. The view of the protection of historic monuments has also changed dramatically. Previously, one avoided the subject of costs, except perhaps in connection with compensation. Today, monuments are discussed as especially suitable locations for certain investments. The public debate on this issue has shifted one hundred eighty degrees. And that has meant a corresponding change in legal practice.

> UC: But if legal practice is so dependent on public opinion, different actors will be treated very differently. For example, when Pink Floyd organizes a concert at Potsdamer Platz, the permitting procedures run like clockwork. But when some African used car dealer wants something, he can easily tear his hair out.

RS: Of course. But that isn't something you are going to be able to solve with regulations.

> UC: As an actor, the public sector is becoming less and less capable of acting, because the government bureaucracy is increasingly being reduced. But everything you are suggesting is very time-consuming and personnel-intensive. How do you see this contradiction?

RS: The shortage of staff is not going to decrease. And it does little to encourage a willingness to tackle complex projects or enter into risky evaluation processes. In Germany in recent years, considerable deregulation has already taken place in the area of building permitting procedures. Whether or not further steps are in the offing—toward outsourcing, for example—is something we will have to wait and see. There is the model of the "technical notary," in which certified private firms take over certain official tasks connected with the building permitting process and discharge them on the government's behalf. One can imagine that there might be certified firms that would be allowed to issue certain kinds of permissions. The individual application or permission would involve certain costs that would have to be borne by the applicant.

UC: The outsourcing of such activity to entities outside the administrative bureaucracy also addresses another problem. Thus far, whenever temporary uses have been managed by the municipal administration, they have generally failed. As a rule, it works substantially better when a private agency concerns itself with that function on the government's behalf—as for example in the case of neighborhood management. That tends to give rise to a completely different dynamic and type of communication. A certain distance from classical administrative bureaucracy has thus far proved to be essential to the success of projects like these.

RS: If you extend your argument to include not only permitting procedures but also the management of complex projects, there are actually numerous practical examples of this as well. In particular, I would point to the practice of urban renewal and more recently to that of urban redevelopment, in which the municipalities almost regularly outsource important management functions by utilizing supporting organizations and representatives. The use of such structures is not an automatic guarantee of success, but—as can be documented with numerous examples—it does open up new or additional perspectives and opportunities for accomplishing complex tasks.

LEGAL CULTURES

UC: When one compares the various European countries, one finds that there are no fundamental differences among them with respect to temporary use. The area in which fundamental differences do arise is in the application of and cultural approach to the laws. In Helsinki, for example, crossing against the light is practically viewed as a capital offense, while in Germany it is sometimes tolerated and in Italy it doesn't bother anyone. The gulf between a high degree of formalization and spontaneous regulation is immense. For us, it was very interesting to learn that in Italy, it is almost impossible to modify the legal system in any meaningful way, although at first we found the informal character appealing. There is the possibility of spontaneous activity in little things, but behind it all stand unwritten laws. Construction often goes on illegally but within the framework of mafia-like structures and the undermining or even wholesale replacement of state institutions by parallel structures. Making decisions about fundamental changes or engaging in planning activity in this context is actually impossible.

RS: Informal behavior patterns can actually be embodied in mental structures in a very stable manner. Thus, resistance to change is actually stronger in such cultures than in countries like Finland, which seem to be guided by regulations. When the regulations change, people's behavior changes along with them.

UC: In social terms, explicit regulations are more open to negotiation than implicit ones. The unwritten law is, as it were, a cultural tradition that is incredibly difficult to gain access to. Whereas one can argue about explicit formulations and renegotiate them.

RS: From the perspective of legal history, what you are describing is the step from convention and common law to positive law. Common law only changes at very long intervals. In order for a right of way to be created in a common law context, two generations must already have tramped through the meadow. Later, however, when it is time to suspend that right of way—and there is no positive law in place—then things get complicated.

UC: In view of the Italian experience, the traditional view that what is formalized is inflexible while what is not is flexible almost has to be inverted. A certain degree of formalization can actually make possible a more powerful dynamic among the actors.

RS: I find that very interesting in terms of the theory and sociology of law. It also fits very nicely with my argument, since I did suggest earlier that what carries one further in the realm of temporary use is not the question of "formal versus informal" but the relationship of regulatory strategies and instruments to consensual ones. If it should prove to be possible to complement the classical, top-down planning instruments with legally resilient consensual ones, a broad range of possibilities for action and flexibility can be achieved.

CULTURAL GENERATORS

Arnold Reijndorp

In almost every city, in Europe as well in other parts of the world, spontaneous activities develop in many locations waiting for redevelopment. Abandoned industrial and harbor sites, vacant office space, and other empty buildings provide space for the development of all kind of entrepreneurial and cultural activities. In most cases, these activities are removed when redevelopment actually starts.

The activities that develop spontaneously in the central periphery of the city might provide an answer to the economic, social and cultural shifts taking place in cities all over Europe at this very moment, that is far more adequate than the official policy approach of the information society.

THE ATTRACTIVENESS OF CITIES

In former decades, especially in the 1970s and 1980s, temporary users have also played this role, but in a different context. "Squatters," "krakers," "Hausbesetzer" were crucial in the development of alternative strategies for official planning aimed at the revaluation of city life, democratization of planning procedures, creation of sustainable architecture and a new meaning of public space. Together with inhabitants fighting the demolition of their inner-city neighborhoods, critical professionals gave birth to the reassessment of city life as an alternative for suburban living. So far we can observe continuities, but at the same moment we have to consider that times have changed and European cities are in a different situation now. In the 1970s, cities were still dominated by an economy that was based on industrial production, and urban development policies were aimed at the modernization of the industrial or harbor city. The development of a modern central business district and the demolition of slums were two sides of the same strategy. The reassessment of urban living as a result of the protest movements heralded the rediscovery of urbanity as the main characteristic of cities. This renewed focus on urbanity became part of a more cultural strategy of urban revitalization.

In policies aimed at the revitalization of cities in the 1980s and 1990s the attractiveness of the city became more and more understood as literally attracting people and companies to the city. Culture became an important means to turn cities into a favorable place for companies and employees in the so-called service industries—mainly bankers, accountants, lawyers and other financial and juridical consultants. A whole new culture of dining, clubbing, and shopping developed alongside new museums, theaters and concert halls.[1] The strategy of the attractive city was aimed at attracting not only companies and their employees, but also a large crowd of visitors. A lively city was seen primarily in quantitative terms—as a space crowded with people. Tourism and leisure became important features of this strategy. Redevelopment of former industrial and harbor sites took the form of *Rousification*, named after its most prominent protagonist, the American developer James Rouse, in which leisure activities, fun shopping, and festivals played a crucial role.[2] A lively public space became the aim of a policy of "cultural animation."[3] In the context of this policy of urban revitalization, culture was understood as consumption—the consumers being "young urban professionals" moving to the city, as well as visitors, as both were looking for entertainment.

THE INNOVATIVE CITY

Recently we have witnessed an interesting shift in the discussion of city economics and city culture and what is essential to it. Slogans are now "The Creative City," "The Innovative City," or "The Knowledgeable City".[4] These slogans are the expressions of a growing awareness that the true kind of capital that cities flourish on is social and cultural capital, in other words: human capital.

At the turn of the century the debate about cities was dominated by the concept of the network society, based on flows of information. The places to be were defined as nodes as the places best connected to the informational network. Nowadays we recognize that the crucial factor is not information, but knowledge combined with innovative and creative skills. As opposed to mere information, knowledge is connected to personal abilities and skills and the way these are organized and facilitated.

The concept of the creative city threatens to downgrade to a concept of the city of the creative class, as invented by Richard Florida.[5] In his view, creative cities are most successful in attracting young, creative people. The strategy is no different from that of the attractive city in former decades: only the personality of the most popular species to attract has changed—from employees of the service industries to the "independents" of the creative sector.[6] But the concept of the creative city is far richer than the city that attracts creative creatures. The creative city is not only a locality for the creative sector: its citizens are con-

1 Sharon Zukin, *The Cultures of Cities* (Cambridge, MA: Blackwell, 1995).

2 John Hannigan, *Fantasy City. Pleasure and Profit in the Postmodern Metropolis* (London and New York: Routledge, 1998).

3 Maarten Hajer and Arnold Reijndorp, *In Search of New Public Domain* (Rotterdam: NAi Publishers, 2001).

4 Charles Landry and Franco Bianchini, *The Creative City* (London: Demos Publications, 1995).

5 Richard Florida, *The Creative Class and How It's Transforming Work, Leisure, Community, and Everyday Life* (New York: Basic Books, 2002).

6 Charles Leadbeater and Kate Oakley, *The Independents. Britain's New Cultural Entrepreneurs* (London: Demos Publications, 1999).

133

stantly inventing new solutions to big city problems. The creative city is the locus and the result of social, economic, and cultural innovation.

The question of how organizations become innovative and creative is thus posed for cities. What is it exactly that makes a city creative? How can a city be transformed into a creative environment? What is the importance of culture, politics, city planning, and architecture in this transformation? The importance of these questions that challenge cities worldwide underlines the significance of places of social innovation as urban catalysts.

The innovative power of cities depends on the differentiation of the local productive environment. As such this differentiation is the result of the availability of many types of entrepreneurs and employees in the knowledge sector and the creative industries, in the proximity of producers and consumers and the multitude of contacts, either spontaneous or organized.[7] Differentiation, proximity, and multitude of contacts are all qualities of urbanity. A city's innovational capacity is in this way directly related to its level of urbanity.[8] The most important characteristics of urbanity are social heterogeneity and tolerance, not just as a condition for the settlement of creative people, as Florida claims, but as a constant challenge for economic and social innovation. In a way the solutions to urban problems, mainly related to the constant flow of people looking for opportunities, can be found—as they have in the past—in the conditions that are causing them. Moreover, the creative city, the city that attracts creative people, is in the first place not an outcome of a revitalization policy, but the creation of a constantly changing population, socially and culturally mixed, looking for opportunities. Which poses the important question of what these opportunities are and how they are created.

CULTURAL PRODUCTION

The new focus on the innovative power of cities comes together with the rise of the so-called cultural industries.[9] The importance of cultural industries for the economy and the culture of cities is not related to the amount of DVDs and computer games it produces (on the contrary, one would say), nor to the amount of public it attracts to the city, but to the opportunities it gives to enterprising, innovative, and creative people. Central in the transformation of the culture of cities—or better, *cultures of cities*[10]—is the shift from the consumption of culture, which was the focus of the concept of the attractive city, to cultural production. Cultural production is more than just the core activity of the cultural industry or media. Cultural production contains the production of all goods the symbolic meaning of which is far higher than their functional

7 Zef Hemel, *Creatieve Steden! Creative Cities!* (The Hague/Amsterdam: VROM, 2002)

8 Jane Jacobs, *The Economy of Cities* (New York: Random House, 1969).

9 David Hesmondhalgh, *The Cultural Industries* (London: Sage, 2002).

10 Zukin 1995 (see note 1).

value. It concerns all fields of design, fashion, architecture, cooking, journalism, entertainment, but also the domains of social relations, politics, and urbanism. These so-called symbolic goods play an important role in the creation of lifestyles, the representation of and reflection on a way of life, which also includes the expression of ethnicity.

In this shift from culture as an important feature in the realm of consumption to culture as a constituting force in the renewal of the economy and the social relations of cities, three important observations are to be made. First of all, the shift from the informational to the creative economy stands for a revaluation of the art of making, concerning arts as well as crafts.[11] Most things, however symbolical they may be, have not only to be designed, but also to be made. That counts in particular for small series, customized design, and prototypes. This shift from cultural consumption to cultural production makes the concept of the creative city less elitist than some critics suggest. The appeal Florida makes for solidarity with the service class (the class of house cleaners, taxi drivers, and pizza delivery boys) is in this sense little more than a moral appeal. A new urban solidarity can develop in the professional networks of each creative field, between entrepreneurs with different skills, designers, craftsmen, and creative financial and organizational experts. This professional "solidarity" expresses itself also in the field of education by the introduction of specific programs in creative crafts, from furniture making and fashion production to theater design.

The second observation is concerned with the path dependency of the creative industry. Cultural production cannot prosper without connection to the local situation. Globalization is not the issue, but localization: the embedding of global processes in local conditions. The innovative city is neither the result of the creation of cycle paths and cultural centers to attract creative people (as Jamie Peck critically suggests[12]), nor of flying in a bunch of talented young experts, facilitating their needs with workspaces, and helping them with grants and interesting commissions. It is the outcome of a permanent interaction between local skills and traditions on the one hand and import of new ideas and talent on the other.[13] These interactions organize a form of so-called "mixed embeddedness."[14] You cannot decide simply to become a city of fashion, architecture or design. Every city has a tradition in certain fields of arts and crafts. If a city wants to become a city of fashion it has to beat a city—such as Paris—that can boast of centuries of reputation but also—and more importantly—of tradition and craftsmanship. This brings to the fore the identity of the city, not as part of a strategy of city marketing but as a way of doing—or of dealing—that characterizes the tradition, the social networks, and the power balance of this specific city.[15]

11 Richard Sennett, *The Craftsman* (London: Penguin 2008).

12 Jamie Peck, *Struggling with the Creative Class*, in: *International Journal of Urban Regional Research*, no. 4 (April 1999), pp. 740-770.

13 Allen Scott, *The Cultural Economy of Cities. Essays on the Geography of Image-Producing Industries* (London: Sage, 2000).

14 Robert Kloosterman et al., *Mixed Embeddedness, Migrant Entrepreneurship and Informal Economic Activities*, in: *International Journal of Urban and Regional Research*, no. 2 (February 1999), pp. 253-267.

15 Janet Abu-Lughod, *New York, Chicago, Los Angeles. America's Global Cities* (Minneapolis/London: University of Minnesota Press, 1999).

The last observation is that cultural production is a networked form of production.[16] Even large cultural enterprises are dependent on talented experts, who are often organized in small offices and networks with friends and colleagues. Cultural industries are not, as the term falsely suggests, industrial in the sense of prediction and routine. Cultural industries are in many ways a risky business. When one has a hit, one can earn an enormous amount of money, but one never knows if and when such an occasion will arise. As is implied, one has to develop a constant flow of new projects. This situation gives chances to young and talented creative professionals. However, what counts in general also counts for these young creative experts. For them as well it is a risky business. They never know if and when they will have a success, and whether this will be long-lasting. Possibilities for temporary use of space are essential to this kind of creative entrepreneurship. This is also the reason for the uncertainty of how "temporary" temporary uses exactly prove to be. Your initiative might become a long-lasting success, but you can also be *in* and *out* nearly overnight.

What to every individual may seem opportunities and niches, appears to be a large pool of overworked and underpaid creative talents from a more objective perspective. Still most people stay for a longer period in this growing pool of creative workers, simply because they are themselves dedicated to creativity and innovation, paid, underpaid, or even unpaid. Free zones, in the sense of affordable space, play a crucial role in facilitating and organizing cultural producers, who have for the moment more ideas and creative expertise than money. That is the importance of an urban development strategy aimed at creative cities. Nevertheless, cultural production cannot flourish without the purchasing power of its potential audience and a structure of private and public commissioning that is open to newcomers, also to different professions, and aimed at innovation and experimentation.

THE CREATIVE CITY AS A CULTURAL GENERATOR

One of the most important conditions for the development of a more knowledge-based and innovative city is to attract creative and innovative people. The creative city profits from people operating at the margins, outsiders to the established order. They do not expect a warm welcome, but they also do not want to be excluded from opportunities.[17] Attracting new talent does not simply depend on the availability of workspace, but also on the broader living conditions that facilitate creativity and innovation. "The conditions that promote development and the conditions that promote efficient production of already existing goods and services are not only different, in most ways they are diametrically opposed."[18]

The innovative city is not the sum of individual artists doing their thing. It is the outcome of professionals working together in networks, meeting each other in intermediate spaces, like galleries, festivals, discussion forums and—last but not least—in certain cafés, restaurants, and clubs. It is at this point that we touch upon the most important contribution of temporary uses as catalysts of the new urbanity, and this is the creation of a new public domain.

The creative city is the result of creativity and innovation in every urban domain.[19] That means the interacting of networks of different professional fields and social groups, aimed at finding new ways in cultural production as well as in education, health care, leisure and tourism, financing of small companies, housing, transport, environment, and governance. In this sense a creative city invents itself over and over again. New public domains make cultural exchanges possible. They consist of places where the parochial domains of different groups overlap and intertwine. Urban catalysts can help a city to become in this way an open, cosmopolitan community, characterized by tolerance but also accepting tension and social turbulence. We have to keep that in mind when we evaluate the role of temporary use as real urban catalyst: Is it mainly creating a sub-cultural niche or organizing connections and overlap with other cultures in the city? That counts equally for cultural production (Is there a connection with old and new local craftsmanship?), for cultural consumption (Are they only producing for the lifestyles of the new cultural class or do they express the cultural diversity of the city?), and for public space (Do they organize just a pleasant parochial realm for "our own kind" or enrich the city with new public domain?). Bonding and bridging are, together, necessary conditions for innovation.

19 Landry and Bianchini 1995 (see note 4); Charles Landry, *The Creative City. A Toolkit for Urban Innovators* (London: Eartscan, 2000).

ART WITHIN THE URBAN REALM:
ON ANALYSIS AND INTERVENTION, TEMPORARY USERS AND CO-CREATORS

Claudia Büttner

Art thematizes spaces, comments on them, and changes them. In the best case, it defines and creates new places. Artists are not only economically dependent on niches in the space of the city; they are also interested in them as subject matter and formal elements for their works. Thus, art not only plays an important role in the reevaluation of urban areas; it also does much to promote awareness and discussion of the situation on site. For with their interest in architectonic spaces, materials and things, historical sites, and social and political structures, artists explore the possibilities of neglected places and point out possible new approaches to the city.

A NEW SELF-CONCEPTION AND POLITICAL SELF-ORGANIZATION OF ART

Around 1960, the art world changed dramatically. In new art forms like neorealism, Fluxus, pop art, conceptual art, and land art, everyday life became the basis of artistic production. The structures and forms of art as well as its presentations changed, dissolved, and merged with forms of theater, music, and everyday life. With the shift from saleable products to actions, processes, and concepts, the artists' own ideas and attitudes became essential elements of art. Artists disputed the right of museum curators and exhibition organizers to exercise sole control and supreme interpretive authority over the objects. They sought to escape both the content and the presentational language of the institutions as well as their narrow focus on traditionally educated, cultured middle-class audiences by organizing events in new and undefined places.

Before artists themselves began to investigate and criticize the content of exhibitions and the political motives and economic power of institutions—including in their artworks—the critique of institutions had already found theoretical expression. After Theodor W. Adorno criticized museums as "family sepulchers"[1] for art in 1955, Herbert

1 Theodor W. Adorno, "Valéry Proust Museum," in *Prisms*, trans. Samuel and Sherry Weber (Cambridge, MA: MIT Press, 1996), 175.

Marcuse and Guy Debord encouraged artists to realize their projects outside of institutions in the realm of everyday life with their ideas regarding art's socially explosive power. If artists wished to become socially engaged and make art genuinely effective, they were going to have to leave the preserves of the art world behind and enter the arena of real life.

This increased the importance of new urban locations where living and working, producing and exhibiting or performing could be combined. The partial politicization of the art scene led to a situation in which—along with demands for antiwar policies, equal rights for women and ethnic minorities, and a general critique of capitalism— the dependencies of the art industry were thematized as well. One form of self-organization was the creation of the Art Workers Coalition in 1969.[2] This organization brought together New York artists and critics who wished to have a say in determining the framework conditions of art and the manner in which their own works were presented at exhibitions and museums, e.g., by demanding to be represented alongside the rich financial backers on the museums' influential boards of trustees. In order to achieve their goals, they organized protest events, sit-ins, and demonstrations.

SPATIAL SELF-ORGANIZATION

Another way to exhibit art independently of the art market, with its galleries and established art museums, was to organize artists' cooperatives, creating producers' galleries and mounting self-juried exhibitions in locations that were not established art venues. In order to do this, artists were dependent on spaces with affordable rents. This is how the economically run-down area south of Houston Street in Manhattan/New York became one of the most influential art neighborhoods in the world.[3] In cafés, private apartments, and vacant stores, in warehouses and factory buildings, Fluxus artists like Allan Kaprow, George Maciunas, Dick Higgins, Al Hanson, and George Brecht, but also pop artists like Claes Oldenburg, George Segal, Jime Dine, Lucas Samaras, and Robert Rauschenberg held their happenings, readings, and exhibitions. With government assistance, the artists created non-commercial, tax-exempt organizations for exhibiting their works and opened their own galleries in so-called "alternative spaces."[4] Beginning in the mid-1960s, minimal and conceptual artists like Richard Serra, Sol LeWitt, Mel Bochner, Robert Smithson, Robert Morris, Dan Graham, and Joseph Kosuth used the new galleries, alternative art spaces, and disused sites for their experimental presentations. Until 1973, the artists usually lived and worked illegally in converted factory

2 Jeanne Siegel, "Carl Andre: Artworker,"*Studio International* 179 (November 1970): 175–179, reprinted in *Artwords. Discourse on the 60s and 70s* (New York: De Capo Press, 1992), 129–140.

3 Comp. René Block et al., eds., *New York—Downtown Manhattan: SoHo* (Berlin: Akademie der Künste and Berliner Festwochen, 1976); Richard Kostelanetz, *SoHo: The Rise and Fall of an Artists' Colony* (New York and London: Routledge, 2003); Julie Ault and Martin Beck, eds., *Alternative Art: New York 1965–1985* (Minneapolis: University of Minnesota Press, 2002).

4 The most important were Holly Solomon's 98 Greene Street Loft, the artist Jeffrey Lew's 112 Workshop Inc., and Steina and Woody Vasulka's The Kitchen. See Stephen Reichard, "Alternative Ausstellungsräume: Eine direkte Politik für die Avantgarde," in René Block et al., eds., *New York—Downtown Manhattan: SoHo* (Berlin, 1976), 238.

buildings and stores. By the time the avant-garde artists of the 1970s exhibited there, the artists had already been joined by galleries, cafés, and restaurants, and later by the art tourists. SoHo had thus become an internationally famous art scene. By 1967, it was already so well established that the artists themselves were leaving, and its history was being presented at exhibitions.

BRINGING ART AND LIFE TOGETHER

The activities of Gordon Matta-Clark combine many of the social and formal motivating factors that preoccupied artists at the time, and they bear witness to the intimate new connection of art and life. In 1971, together with the dancers Caroline Goodden, Suzanne Harris, Tina Girouard, and Rachel Lew, Matta-Clark opened the restaurant FOOD in SoHo as a project for "reconfiguring space to meet the participants' own needs."[5] In doing so, he not only opened one of the area's first restaurants; he also created flexible jobs for artists, with guest chefs on Sundays—including Donald Judd, Robert Rauschenberg, and Keith Sonnier—and a changing menu and calendar of events. The effort to satisfy existential needs like nourishment was symptomatic of the attitude of the time (and it reappears as an important theme in the socially engaged art movements of the 1990s). In the open kitchen, cooking performances were regularly held that included everyone, from the visiting chefs to the dishwashers to the guests.

In setting up the restaurant, Matta-Clark did one of the first architectural "cuts" with which he would cause a worldwide sensation in the years to come. He used a chain saw to saw geometric sections out of the walls of buildings, exposing their structure and providing new pathways for light to enter the spaces. Later he put the sawed-out portions together into new sculptural forms at exhibitions. For this procedure, which he had first employed in his own loft in 1971, he used abandoned buildings that were slated for demolition, like the warehouses on the piers along the Hudson River, or—as in 1975 for the work *Conical Intersect*—apartment blocks that were due to be torn down beside the Centre Georges Pompidou, which was then being built in the Paris neighborhood of Les Halles. Because he turned buildings into formal material, the effect of his spectacular interventions was brutal, but compared to the razing of entire neighborhoods, they seemed almost to be a kind of respectful laying open of what was already there.

George Maciunas and Takako Saito, *Flux-Treadmill*, New York, 1973

5 Comp. Catherine Morris, ed., *FOOD,* White Columns (Cologne: Walther König, 1999); Lori Waxman, *The Banquet Years: FOOD, A SoHo Restaurant in the Early 1970s* (New York University, 2004), www.as-ap.org.

The restaurant FOOD at the corner of Prince and Wooster Streets, New York, 1971

Gordon Matta-Clark, *Conical Intersect*, installation, Paris, 1975

Matta-Clark's works are connected with a movement that was paradigmatic for later artistic production and cultural politics, that of art projects in the urban space. More and more artists created spatial installations for particular situations and went out onto streets, squares, and disused sites in order to do so. They also incorporated preexisting architectonic elements and the viewing situation of the visitors into their works. In addition to an interest in aesthetic categories like form, color, and space design, they also addressed the social, historical, and political conditions of their surroundings. By conducting surveys, collecting evidence, organizing actions, and creating model situations, they sought to point out possibilities for change in the concrete conditions of their environment. In the 1970s, the first art educators and curators began to take an interest in the site-specific methods of particular artists and invited them to do new projects in the public space. In 1971, Gordon Matta-Clark was invited by Alanna Heiss, the former director of the Municipal Art Society, to participate in an art project that she was organizing in the urban space. "It lasted only three days and it was destroyed, but its success proved that the walls of a museum were unnecessary for exhibitions. I wanted an organization that we could move constantly. The only consistent feature would be the name of the institution on the announcement card. So, we organized The Institute for Art and Urban Resources. The word 'urban resources' was added to indicate the intention to use city locations."[6] Later, Heiss sought to obtain the long-term use of three buildings on Eighth Avenue for Matta-Clark's project *Twentieth Century Ruins,* but unfortunately without success.

6 Alanna Heiss, Presentation, Anchorage Museum Art Charrette, October 24, 2003.

INCREASED IMPORTANCE OF CURATORS IN "ALTERNATIVE" SPACES

Alanna Heiss was one of the first curators to offer the artists institutional assistance and to bring them to the attention of broader audiences with professional press and public relations work. Art forms like earth, land, performance, action, installation, and conceptual art called for new spaces, new occasions, and new exhibition formats. Because the execution of the sometimes monumental projects made permits and funding necessary, committed mediators—as exemplified by a smattering of gallery owners and private collectors but especially by the newly emerging curators—were becoming increasingly important. Some of them garnered attention for new movements by mounting sensational exhibitions in unusual places and worked to ensure that they would be viewed in an art-historical context. Thus, Harald Szeeman presented conceptual and minimal art and arte povera in and around the Berner Kunsthalle in 1968 with the exhibition *When Attitudes Became Form*; in *Sonsbeek 71,* Wim Beeren had every conceivable contemporary art form developed and presented in various locations and public places throughout the Netherlands; and in 1973, Achille Benito Olivas organized a kind of arte povera exhibition in Rome in the garage of the Villa Borghese.[7]

7 Contemporanea, Roma, Parcheggio di Villa Borghese, Centro di Firenze 1973.

The reutilized spaces have gone on to become some of today's most important venues for presenting contemporary art, including the Institute for Art and Urban Resources Inc. Directed by Alanna Heiss from 1971 onwards, its first location was the Clocktower Building at 108 Leonard Street; since 1976 it has been housed at P.S.1, the former Public School No. 1 on Long Island. Fueled by an interest in new spaces and materials and a desire to escape the famous "White Cube"[8] of the museums and established galleries, the established art industry has long since caught up with these alternative spaces. Museums in former industrial and transport buildings such as the private Hallen für Neue Kunst in Schaffhausen (1982), the Tate Liverpool (1988), the Deichtorhallen in Hamburg (1989), the Kunstwerke in Berlin (1990/99), the Hamburger Bahnhof in Berlin (1996), MASS Moca in North Adams, Massachusetts (1999), and Tate Modern in London (2000) are examples of this trend, which has turned the appropriation of found spaces into its own popular category of museum architecture.

8 Comp. Brian O'Doherty, *Inside the White Cube: The Ideology of the Gallery Space* (Santa Monica and San Francisco: Lapis Press, 1986).

ARTISTS AS "ETHNOGRAPHERS"

Together with artist friends, Gordon Matta-Clark formed the group Anarchitecture, which used artistic practice to grapple with theoretical discourses and writings as well as with architecture and urban structures themselves. Other artists, such as Vito Acconci, Michael Asher, Dennis Oppenheim, Dan Graham, Hans Haacke, and Martha Rosler, also began to explore their physical surroundings and working and living conditions in the city. In their works, they documented and critically analyzed the space of the city, focusing especially on social, political, and economic structures, and then went on to exhibit their investigations in the art world or intervened on site in various ways. In this way, they marked and emphasized the places or transformed them into something new. The artists acted as "ethnographers,"[9] adding scientific methods such as documentation, typology, and mapping to their already existing repertoire of artistic techniques. In addition to the general interest in design and urban coexistence as well as the living

9 Comp. Hal Foster, "The Artist as Ethnographer," in: *The Return of the Real* (Cambridge MA: MIT Press, 1996), 171–203.

situation in the city, social structures and the problems of particular social groups became the primary focus of artistic works.

These developments were taken up again in the 1990s by artists like Mark Dion, Andrea Fraser, Christian Philipp Müller, Renée Green, and Tom Burr, reinforced by themes and issues from the observation of their surroundings inside and outside the art institutions. In addition to analysis and documentation, their "critical practice"[10] also included interactions in the context of everyday relationships. However, unlike their precursors, they always remained committed to the art world, which they never left, even in remote locations and even when incorporating objects from real life into art institutions.[11] With the establishment of independent project exhibitions, the institutional framework conditions had changed so dramatically that artists could now organize projects together with curators and carry them out using funds raised by institutions, some of which were specifically earmarked for local, socially integrated programs and events.[12] While independent project exhibitions were at first only possible in isolated cases—for example, when financial backers and sponsors could be found for unusual undertakings—project exhibitions in the urban space became an extremely popular presentation format in the 1980s. The one-time character of site-specific installations, which were only on display for a short time in a single place, and the thematization by contemporary art of distinctive local features such as architecture, landscape, and historical monuments, made these art projects attractive to more than art audiences alone. City marketers and the tourism industry also began to take an interest in art on site. More and more cities and towns became organizers of art biennales and triennales. Periodic art events with changing teams of curators such as Manifesta and Going Public began to make appearances in increasingly remote locations. More than this, however, there was hardly a city anniversary year, world's fair, or horticultural show that was willing to pass up the opportunity for an attractive "artistic intervention" by contemporary site-specific art.

With the right kind of press and public relations work, even projects in far-flung locations could remain a part of the art world. They were visited by art audiences, publicized by the media, commented on, and institutionalized as art events. Thus, in 1993, the curator Yves Aupetitallot invited some forty artists and architects to the French town of Firminy, to realize art projects in twenty-eight apartments of Le Corbusier's ambitiously conceived residential complex Unité d'Habitation, which was now run-down and semi-abandoned. For *Project Unité* the artists created spatial installations in which they addressed the standardization of the living spaces, the noise situation in

10 James Meyer, "Was geschah mit der institutionellen Kritik," in Peter Weibel, *Kontext Kunst* (Cologne: DuMont, 1993), 239–256.

11 See also Nina Möntmann, *Kunst als sozialer Raum* (Cologne: Walther König, 2002).

12 For more on this development, see Claudia Büttner, *Art Goes Public. Von der Gruppenausstellung im Freien zum Projekt im nicht-institutionellen Raum* (Munich: Silke Schreiber, 1997).

Jan Dibbets, *Untitled*, temporary floor installation on the street, different views, Monschau, 1970

the poorly soundproofed rooms, and the cramped conditions of the little apartments. They also designed functional spaces, including a café; experimented with living in the complex themselves; and in a few cases sought to enter into a dialogue with the residents by documenting their lifestyles. The project went almost totally unnoticed and was largely seen by art critics as a casualty of its own ambitions.[13] The curator had intended to "provide a group of artists with concrete material that they could use to carry out an experimental research project in a context both real and symbolic that would do justice to a complex reality. At the core of the entire enterprise was a desire to question the role of art and its audience in their relationship to society."[14] While it offered art audiences a voyeuristic glimpse of an alien social situation, artists, visitors, and residents remained strangers to each other. The long-term mutual approach and trust-building measures that would have been necessary to bring about the desired social dialogue were never a component of the curatorial or artistic work.

13 Isabelle Graw, "La Culture. zur Ausstellung *Project Unité* in Firminy (1993)," in Bernard Fibicher, ed., *L'art exposé* (Sion: Musée Cantonal des Beaux Arts, 1995), 107–123.

14 Yves Aupetitallot, "Relatives Scheitern? Ein Gespräch mit dem französischen Kurator Yves Aupetitallot," in *springer* III, no. 3 (1997).

ARTISTS AS CO-CREATORS OF SOCIAL REALITY

Precisely this, however, was the explicit aim of the so-called "public art" movement, which emerged in the 1990s at the same time and sought to pay attention not only to the subjects and locations involved but also to the residents and their living situations, which it attempted to view as more than mere occasions for raising predetermined issues.[15] The public art movement combined a variety of approaches, all of which were specifically designed to create an engaged dialogue with the social situation. Problems and issues were often taken up and dealt with together with the people on site. Once again, space and living conditions in run-down, inner-city residential areas with vacant stores and disused sites provided both the space and the impulse for communal artistic activities.

Stephen Willats, An Island within an Island, A Postmodern Lifestyle, Berlin, 1992–1993

This art had its precursors not only in the critical and analytical conceptual art of the 1960s but also in certain exponents of engaged social art who had already worked with participatory approaches. As early as the 1960s, artists like Stephen Willats had already gone beyond the critical inventory of social conditions to involve the residents actually affected by economic changes and structural transformation in their projects. Moreover, in writings such as *Art and Social Function,*[16] Willats defines a new relationship between author and audience, one that does not grant supreme design authority to the artist but enables him or her to play an active role in the shaping of social life. In "interactive" works like the *West London Social Resource Project* (1972) and *Contained Living* (1975) in the Friars

15 For more on this, see the following anthologies: Arlene Raven, ed., *Art in the Public Interest* (New York: Da Capo Press, 1993); Suzanne Lacy, ed., *Mapping the Terrain* (Seattle: Bay Press, 1995).

16 Stephen Willats, *Art and Social Function* (London: Latimer New Dimensions, 1976).

145

17 Stephen Willats, "Contained Living. Second Problem Display. Thinking about our present way of life, 1978," in Horst Kurnitzky, ed., *Notizbuch 3. Kunst. Gesellschaft. Museum* (Berlin: Medusa, 1980), 116.

Wharf housing development near Oxford, Willats developed survey and documentation techniques that gave people the opportunity to comment on their living conditions and discuss them publicly. In addition, he used photographs, interviews, and other means to document their living situation and formulated issues that were put up for public discussion on exhibition panels in the complex with questions like, "In which way can each of us contribute something towards improving the identity of this modern environment?"[17] The residents' responses on specially provided sheets of paper were also presented publicly, in this case in the neighboring Museum of Modern Art. The result was a complex inventory of the social situation and existential condition of the neighborhood. More important to Willats, however, were the communicative structures that the project had initiated in the neighborhood itself. The discussion he sparked brought the residents together for the first time and also made them visible within the larger context of the city.

PUBLIC ART AS CREATIVE TEMPORARY USE

Decades after Willats, who continued to pursue similar projects, the idea of participation and self-organization was newly taken up by various artists in the United States and Europe. One of the most prominent artists currently reflecting on urban life and actively dealing with social problems in her projects is the Dutch artist Jeanne van Heeswijk. Invited by the municipality of Vlaardingen and a property management company to develop a master plan for art in the public space, Heeswijk proposed a long-term project with various cultural activities in 1995. In addition, she transformed an empty shopping arcade in the neighborhood of Westwijk into an active cultural center from May 2002 to 2004 with her project *De Strip*. With 319 participants and 102 events in two years, she succeeded not only in initiating active life in a run-down part of the city and thus in giving people a new social center; through her stubborn "interference," she also succeeded in becoming a contact person for the planning of the area's future design and use. In the empty stores of the shopping arcade, the artist initiated art exhibitions, cultural and social events, educational offerings, a café, an open video magazine, and a studio program. Artists and artisans were able to live and work there for three-month periods, provided that they opened up their studios to visitors or offered workshops in return. As a temporary annex, the Rotterdam Boijmans Van Beuningen Museum exhibited arts and crafts in addition to modern art. MAMA, an event organizer for media and kinetic art, organized video workshops for young people. A video magazine and an events -magazine

Event within the scope of Jeanne van Heeswijk, *De Strip*, Vlaardingen Westwijk, 2002–04

in comic-book format that was published every two months covered topics of current interest, especially future plans for the site. Jeanne van Heeswijk describes her approach as "urban curating": "Urban curating to me means maximizing the potential for open dialogue, communication and acting communally within communities. The key to this is creating and implementing an infrastructure or network which can maintain such a dialogue and can establish the conditions for a critical discourse that clarifies the possibilities for social change. To achieve this you constantly need to go back, need to listen time and time again and make it clear that public space in essence means shared space, where everyone's contribution is important."[18] Based on her analysis of the existing situation, van Heeswijk develops offerings for communication and attempts to spark new activity and engagement.

A similar strategy of instigating communication and independent activity was pursued by Cora Hegewald and Benjamin Foerster-Baldenius in 2003 when they initiated a project for the Thalia Theater Halle in Halle-Neustadt, a tower apartment block complex on the outskirts of the city, which at this time was highly depopulated. Basing their approach on theater rather than the visual arts, the businesswoman and architect developed a project for the urban space, especially, however, for the young people in the precarious living conditions of the shrinking city. Together with some one hundred young people, they transformed an eighteen-story high-rise in the satellite city into the "Hotel Neustadt" for a period of two weeks. They worked for months to turn the rooms of the abandoned building into eighty-four themed rooms, some of them quite odd; reinstalled basic equipment such as water connections, toilets, and kitchens; and organized services like reception, laundry, and bar, as well as an outdoor sauna and other wellness offerings for the hotel. It took enormous motivation and staying power on the part of the untrained young people and the organizers to do the renovations; furnish and decorate the rooms using paint, papier-mâché, original design creations, and donated fittings and furnishings; and organize the staff and hotel management and run the hotel's day-to-day operations. In order to motivate people to make the required commitment of time and effort, the organizers put on a fourteen-day festival called "Hotel Neustadt." Ten teams from various artistic disciplines realized and presented projects at the hotel that had been selected by an expert review panel from ideas submitted by artists and performers in a public competition. The projects ranged from performances, actions, service offerings, spatial installations, and video and photographic works to participatory projects involving the young people. While this "festivalization" did much to improve the neighborhood's public image, the longer-term collective

18 Comp. Mirjam Westen and Jeanne van Heeswijk, "The Artist as Versatile Infiltrator of Public Space: 'Urban Curating' in the 21st Century," *n. paradoxa,* no. 12 (2003), 24–32.

„Balcony Tuning" by Peanutz Architekten within the scope of „Hotel Neustadt", Halle Neustadt, 2003

commitment to a creative approach to the dismal situation on site was more important for the project itself. Follow-up facilities and projects underscored the significance of the cultural commitment to preserving social life at the location.

FROM ARTISTIC TEMPORARY USE TO ACTIVELY DESIGNING THE CITY

Some artists commit themselves to more than short-term projects and the temporary use of empty buildings and disused urban sites, especially when, as residents of a redevelopment area, they themselves are affected by a region's structural transformation. Instead, they wish to have a hand in determining the future and take a political stand for the modification of planned projects. They occupy sites, mobilize residents, and work together to develop new plans for future uses that often intervene less radically in the existing social fabric.

Thus, as early as 1983, the artists' initiative Political Art Documentation Distribution (PADD) mobilized against the buying up of apartments in New York's East Village. They designated the walls of the buildings surrounding Tompkins Square as fictional "street galleries" and proceeded to put up anti-gentrification posters, specially designed by artists for the purpose, there and in the surrounding neighborhood streets.[19] Similarly, Cathy Skene, Margit Czenki, and other artists participated in a long-term initiative effort in the Hamburg neighborhood of St. Pauli, where beginning in the mid-1990s, citizens' initiatives worked together with various groups to demand the construction of a park on the Hamburg waterfront instead of the luxury apartments envisioned by a real estate investor. They too characterized their political activism as an art project, found support and financial backing for their actions from the Ministry of Culture, and framed "Park Fiction" as a phenomenon of the art world (see the essay on Park Fiction by Wanda Wieczorek in this volume, p. 282). By contrast with what tends to take place in pure art projects, the artists made long-term commitments of time and energy and participated in educational work in the neighborhood that drew little public attention, as well as in local politics, initiatives, and the district. In 2003, with a great deal of energy and effort, they succeeded in realizing a portion of the—albeit much reduced—communal design for the public park.

Unlike the Park Fiction project, which was partially successful and also received international attention and recognition thanks to its participation in documenta 11 in 2002, the outcome of a similar project in Milan is still uncertain. The Luxemburg artist Bert Theis has lived in the northern Italian city for twelve years and is fighting to create an art

19 See Lucy R. Lippard, *Get the Message: A Decade of Art for Social Change* (New York: E.P. Dutton, 1984).

and community center on the grounds of an abandoned factory in the neighborhood of Isola, the "Stecca degli Artigiani." In 2001, he drew attention to the situation and the need to have a place for community and art-related activities with the Isola Art Project, which began by putting on a number of outdoor art actions: "We had a wooden fence of one hundred meters painted white, like a symbolic barrier against the street. Of course a symbolic barrier can stop nothing. So we had to build a social barrier and a political barrier around it. So in 2002 we entered this building owned by the city and we squatted the upper floor—it's 1,500 square meters."[20] In 2003, Theis joined together with artists, curators, a philosopher, and other residents to form the Isola dell'Arte Association, which organized numerous events. In 2005, they were able to officially open the Isola Art Center in the factory building against the plans of the city, which wanted to develop a four-teen-story shopping center on the site. Now longer-term exhibitions and programs could also be held there. The neighborhood's interest went further, and in 2006 the facility was expanded into the Isola Art & Community Center, which also houses a café as well as other cultural actors. However, at the instigation of the property owners, in April 2007 the building was cleared by the police on suspicion of drug dealing, and steps were taken to proceed with its destruction. The ensuing community protests won initial validation in the form of a court decision withdrawing the permit for the shopping center.

In addition to a practical interest in the temporary artistic use of niches and disused sites in the urban space, the goal of these and similar projects is a changed view of the contemporary city as a place to live. Thus, artists like Christoph Schäfer see "the urban as a completely different category, a practice and way of thinking that stand opposed to the political and the state and are not identical with the democratic, and that also stand opposed to any unified artistic vision. ... Any city worth living in is a place of contradictions that live side by side, pile up, and potentially continue to grow indefinitely."[21] Thanks to the variety of its methods and aesthetic forms, but also by dint of its status and institutional connections, art—understood as a wide-ranging cultural practice—has the chance to play a role in shaping urban life in a new, more open sense. Thus far, however, there have been very few exam-ples of independent projects that have succeeded in combining the concrete objectives of artists with years of commitment to the struggle for a vision of the future and its realization.

Much more frequently, the potential of artistic forms and interventi-onist projects is exploited for predictable interim programs and events with the aim of enhancing the economic status of places. Construction sites, disused areas, and unrented stores are temporarily used by attrac-

20 Bert Theis, in Yasif Kortun, "Walking Discussion with Bert Theis," Cuma, Haziran 15, 2007, Istanbul Biennale 2007.

21 Christoph Schäfer, "Urbane Erfahrungen und Gedanken, durch Park Fiction gesehen," in Ralph Lindner, Christiane Mennicke, and Silke Wagler, *Kunst im Stadtraum—Hegemonie und Öffentlichkeit* (Dresden: B-Books, 2004), 285.

tive cultural projects, especially popular light installations and musical events. Real estate developers and property management firms, but also municipalities, have long since discovered the long-term advantage of media attention to unusual artistic productions for the places that serve as venues, and above and beyond the spaces themselves, they now also offer funding and commissions for new projects. Thus, not only have the institutions of the art industry followed the artists onto the street, "museumifying" the alternative spaces and turning project work into a common museum practice; city planners too, the guiding political and economic forces of the city, stand ready to appropriate these successful artistic strategies for revitalizing the city.

EVERYDAY URBANISM

Margaret Crawford

A multiplicity of simultaneous public activities in Los Angeles is continually redefining both "public" and "space" through lived experience. In vacant lots, on sidewalks, in parks, and parking lots, these activities are restructuring urban space, opening new political arenas, and producing new forms of insurgent citizenship.

Looking beyond the culturally defined physical realms of home, workplace, and institution, we can identify "everyday space." Everyday space is the connective tissue that binds daily lives together, amorphous and so persuasive that it is difficult even to perceive. In spite of its ubiquity, everyday space is nearly invisible in the professional discourses of the city. Everyday space is like everyday life, the "screen on which society projects is light and shadow, its hollows and its planes, its power and its weakness."[1]

Events like the urban disturbances in Los Angeles in 1992 can be seen as a form of public expression that produces an alternative discourse of "public" and "space." During the riots spaces formerly devoted to the automobile—streets, parking lots, flea markets, and strip malls—were temporarily transformed into sites of protest and rage, into new zones of public expression. The riots underlined the potent ability of everyday spaces to become, however briefly, places where lived experience and political expression come together. This realm of public life lies outside the domain of electoral politics or professional design, representing a bottom-up rather than top-down restructuring of urban space. Unlike normative public spaces, which produce the existing ideology, these spaces help to overturn the status quo. In different areas of the city, many generic spaces have become specific and serve as public arenas where debates and struggles over economic participation, democracy, and the public assertion of identity take place. Without claiming to represent the totality of public space, these multiple, temporary, and simultaneous activities construct and reveal an alternative logic of public space.

Woven into the patterns of everyday life, it is difficult even to discern these places as public space. Trivial and commonplace, vacant lots, sidewalks, front yards, parks, and parking lots are being claimed for new uses and meanings by the poor, the recently immigrated, the

1 Henri Lefebvre, *Critique of Everyday Life* (London and New York: Verso, 1991).

homeless, and even the middle class. These spaces exist physically somewhere in the junctures between private, commercial, and domestic. Ambiguous and unstable, they blur our established understandings of these categories in often paradoxical ways. They contain multiple and constantly shifting meanings rather than clarity of function. In the absence of a distinct identity of their own, these spaces can be shaped and redefined by the transitory activities they accommodate. Unrestricted by the dictates of built form, they become venues for the expression of new meanings through the individuals and groups who appropriate the spaces for their own purposes. Apparently empty of meaning, they acquire constantly changing meanings—social, aesthetic, political, economic—as users reorganize and reinterpret them. Temporally, everyday spaces exist in between past and future uses, often with a no-longer-but-not-yet status, in a holding pattern of real-estate values that might one day rise. The temporary activities that take place there also follow distinct temporal patterns. Without fixed schedules, they produce their own cycles, appearing, reappearing, or disappearing within the rhythms of everyday life. Use and activity vary according to the seasons, vanishing in winter, born again in spring. They are subject to changes in the weather, days of the week, and even time of day. Since they are usually perceived in states of distraction, their meanings are not immediately evident but unfold through the repetitious acts of everyday life.

Conceptually, these spaces can be identified as what Edward Soja, following Henri Lefebvre, called the "thirdspace," a category that is neither the material space that we experience nor a representation of space.[2] Thirdspace is instead a space of representation, a space bearing the possibility of new meanings, a space activated through social action and the social imagination. A number of public activities are currently transforming Los Angeles everyday spaces, among them the garage sale and street vending.

THE GARAGE SALE

An unexpected outcome of the recession of the 1980s and the collapse of the real-estate market in Southern California was the proliferation of garage sales, even in the city's wealthiest areas. As an increasing number of people found themselves un- or underemployed, the struggle for supplemental income turned garage sales into semi-permanent events. The front yard, an already ambiguous territory, serves as a buffer between residential privacy and the public street. Primarily an honorific space, the lawn is activated as the garage sale turns the house inside out, displaying the interior on the exterior. The same economic

2 Edward Soja, *Thirdspace: Journeys to Los Angeles and Other Real and Imagined Places* (Cambridge, MA: Blackwell, 1996).

forces that caused the proliferation of garage sales also produced their mobile clientele, shoppers who drive through the city in search of sales or who discover them accidentally on the way to somewhere else.

In the Mexican American barrio East Los Angeles, with its less affluent population of homeowners and low real-estate values, commerce and domesticity have coexisted for a long time. A more permanent physical restructuring has already taken place, generated by a distinct set of social and economic needs: the front yard is marked by a fence, delineating an enclosure. The fence structures a more complex relationship between home and street. Different configurations of house, yard, and fence offer flexible spaces that can easily be adapted for commercial purposes. The fence itself becomes a display for ads or goods. Paving over the lawn, a widespread practice, creates an outdoor shop. For Latino women who do not work outside the house, the garage sale has become a permanent business. Many move beyond recycling used items to buying and reselling clothes from nearby garment factories. Garages are simultaneously closets and shops, further linking the commercial and the domestic and producing a public place for neighborhood women. Men use the paved yards differently, as spaces for auto repair or car customizing. This attracts other neighborhood men, establishing a gathering place that is similarly domestic and commercial.

STREET VENDORS

All over the city, informal vendors appropriate marginal and overlooked sites chosen for their accessibility to passing motorists and pedestrians: street corners, sidewalks, and parking lots and vacant lots that are often surrounded by chain-link fences. Exchanges both commercial and social, including that of the messages transmitted by T-shirts and posters, take place. The vendors' temporary use hijacks these spaces, changing their meaning. Publicly owned spaces are briefly inhabited by citizens; private spaces undergo an ephemeral decommodification.[3] Temporarily removed from the marketplace, these spaces now represent more than potential real-estate value.

Vending on public property, streets, and sidewalks is illegal in both the city and county of Los Angeles. When enough vendors congregate in a single place regularly enough, however, they can muster the political power to change the nature of urban space. Chanting "We are vendors, not criminals," Central American vendors demonstrated at the Rampart police station, demanding the right to pursue their economic activities without police harassment. Since many of the vendors are undocumented, this makes them doubly illegal. Central American vendors have organized themselves, acquired legal representation, and pressured the

3 The term decommodification refers to a process that removes grids from the system of the market. In its literal sense it means measures that have been institutionalized by the welfare state and that cushion the commodity character of the "commodity of labor" and the pressure to secure one's livelihood through wage labor/gainful employment. While commodification is connected to reinforcing the market principle and directly linking social security to employment, the term decommodification refers to a reduction in employees' dependence on the market. (Editor's note)

city to change its laws to permit limited vending. Through the defense of their livelihood, vendors are becoming a political and economic force in the city.

DEMOCRACY AND PUBLIC SPACE

This brings us back to the question that started this investigation: how can public space be connected with democracy? Individual garage sales might not in themselves generate new urban politics, but the juxtapositions, combinations, and collisions of people, places, and activities that I've described create a new condition of social fluidity that begins to break down the separate, specialized, and hierarchical structures of everyday life in Los Angeles. Local yet also directed to anyone driving or passing by, these unexpected intersections may possess the liberatory potential that Henri Lefebvre attributes to urban life. As chance encounters multiply and proliferate, activities of everyday space may begin to dissolve some of the predictable boundaries of race and class, revealing previously hidden social possibilities that suggest how the trivial and marginal might be transformed into a kind of micro politics.

Global and local processes, migration, industrial restructuring, and other economic shifts produce social re-territorialization at all levels. Residents with new histories, cultures, and demands appear in the city and disrupt the given categories of social life and urban space. Expressed through the specific needs of everyday life, their urban experiences increasingly become the focus of their struggle to redefine the conditions belonging to society. Once mobilized, social identities become political demands, spaces and sites for political transformation, with the potential to reshape cities. In everyday space, differences between the domestic and the economic, the private and the public, and the economic and the political are blurring. Rather than constituting the failure of public space, change, multiplicity, and contestation may in fact constitute its very nature. In Los Angeles, the materialization of these new public spaces and activities, shaped by lived experience rather than built space, raises complex political questions about the meaning of economic participation and citizenship. By recognizing these struggles as the germ of an alternative development of democracy, we can begin to frame a new discourse of public space, one no longer preoccupied with loss but instead filled with possibility.

"DON'T OBSESS ABOUT PERMANENCE…"

A conversation between Margaret Crawford and Tobias Armborst

Tobias Armborst: In 1999 you published, together with John Case and John Kaliski, the book *Everyday Urbanism*. From 2001 to 2009 you taught a class at the Harvard Graduate School of Design called "Temporary Urbanisms" that dealt with temporary events and the ways in which they transform urban life and urban space. What brought you to this topic at that time?

Margaret Crawford: In the book *Everyday Urbanism* we talked a lot about time being as important as space. Once you start looking at time, it immediately becomes obvious how important temporary uses and occupation are and how little architects and urbanists deploy them. In the class, students examined practices ranging from tailgating at Harvard football games to taking over the freeway in Manila to force a change in government. There are important lessons to be learnt from these vernacular practices about how to understand, structure, and manipulate time in space. We also tried to assemble a body of theory that would support this.

Working with students on this topic turned into an extremely productive form of research. Their work has energized all the concepts, fleshing them out with real projects and real places and bringing them to life. These collaborations, including your own thesis which dealt with time in a very innovative way, have been very important.

TA: A very significant transformation of urban space resulting from temporary use is a phenomenon you call "social decommodification." How can temporary use actually redefine the status of a piece of land as a commodity?

MC: Building on Arjun Appadurai's idea that objects can move in at least two directions, becoming commodified but also decommodified, I proposed that land can also become decommodified, losing its market value. As different individuals and social groups use and appropriate urban space, they emphasize its use value rather than its exchange value. A former student, landscape architect Takako Tajima expanded on this with the concept of "weak land tenure." She argues that under different conditions—neglect, contamination, etc.—various types of land as power corridors or left-over sites exist in a condition of weakened ownership that makes them available for other uses. She applied this to Orange County, California, finding enough available land in this category to re-introduce agriculture into the northern part of the county. In her project "Agricultural Revolution" she completely redefined what "farm" and "farmer" mean. She identified many different groups who could take on agricultural activities. It's a brilliant project and it's a very realistic thesis, because it combines a number of existing parcels with weak tenure—the potential farms—with ongoing agricultural projects undertaken by ex-cons, schools, immigrant farmers, or people who pick up fallen fruit—the potential farmers.

> TA: Does this imply a permanently weakened tenure, or is there a slow take-over?

MC: The ownership is there, but you could say it is bracketed. Clearly, in legal terms the land is still owned by someone, but their ownership is weaker, it's not absolute. At the end of the day, who knows what will happen, but there is a lot of play in the system and there is a lot of slippage in terms of use that doesn't have to do with ownership. That's where use-value prevails over exchange-value. In many situations vacant lots have been used for all kinds of things: People turn vacant lots into parks, and since there is no other function for that place, it's tolerated. It's relatively easy to "borrow" land and sometimes you don't have to return it.

> TA: Right, like the people in Detroit, who just take over the neighboring city-owned lots to expand their property and create these large and sometimes oddly-shaped "blots." The land value doesn't really matter there, because it's almost zero.

MC: Yes, that land is entirely decommodified. In Detroit the situation of weak land tenure is very prevalent.

> TA: But then there are these other examples, say in Berlin, where it's more like landbanking, and the temporary use in some cases even increases the exchange value after a given time.

MC: What's interesting is that the two things can happen at the same time: The land is being held in order to increase its real-estate value, but at the same time it can be used for some other purpose, it is temporarily out of the market. So use-value prevails for a little while.

TA: So it goes from exchange value to use value to exchange value…

MC: If you add time to the equation it dramatically changes the circumstances. As long as you don't obsess about permanence, there are lots of things available to you!

TA: The temporary uses you describe in *Everyday Urbanism* are informal practices that don't take place so much on vacant land, but in the middle of busy streets, sidewalks or parking lots. Residents or vendors turn these places temporarily into entirely different spaces, giving them a new use and a new meaning. What is the short- and long-term transformative potential of these informal practices?

MC: These spaces are public. And in certain ways public spaces are even more available for appropriation, because a member of the public is claiming them. The whole message of public owner-ship is that everyone owns these public spaces. So in a sense it makes a space genuinely public when someone actually tries to enact that ownership. This is different than the "for everybody" public space, which usually means "for nobody." It's very para-doxical, but if you are able to manipulate time in the city it gives you a lot of room to maneuver.

TA: So someone turns public space temporarily into something else by using it. But at the same time there are other people with very different interpretations of that same space.
What is the significance of the mixture, contamination or con-tention that results from this co-presence?

MC: It makes it even more interesting! In many cases the appro-priation of public space can of course be contested. But in a sense it is exactly that contestation which creates a public sphere, where questions about all kinds of things are being enacted under these spatial circumstances.

TA: You also say that these practices "refamiliarize" the urban environment. What do you mean by that?

MC: Human occupation of inhospitable urban spaces transforms these places into more home-like environments. Vendors are a good example, selling products along the streets of Los Angeles. The physical qualities of their goods are connected more with domestic environments than with the harsh landscape of the street. By hanging cheap rugs on chain-link fences around vacant lots, for example, vendors create a soft space, more like an interior. The multiple patterns of the rugs evoke a multiplicity of domestic settings, reminding us of home. Tamale vendors wear aprons and cover their stands with tablecloths. This evokes the warmth of the kitchen, cooking, eating and domestic life. Refamiliarization is on the one hand the opposite of "defamiliarization" the modernist cultural practice of "making strange" since it makes the strange more familiar. But at the same time, it is also a type of defamiliarization, because you don't expect to find the domestic in the no-man's-land of the street.

TA: Since 2004 you have been researching the Pearl River Delta, which is one of the most rapidly urbanizing regions of the world.
Did you observe ways in which people there are starting to refamiliarize this largely new environment through temporary or informal practices? What could Everyday Urbanism be or add in those specific circumstances?

MC: This project is challenging because obviously it's very hard to understand what's going on in Chinese cities. Initially I wasn't so convinced but I think now that Everyday Urbanism could make a real contribution in China. When you look at China, the new cities are alienating in the most extreme fashion possible: the scale, the repetition, the complete indifference to the quality of daily existence. But in many places in China, people, left to their own devices, come up with amazing things that address these issues. For example, there's the great photo of pool tables under the freeway in Guangzhou.
I think that by investigating some of these environments, especially villages, there are a lot of interesting clues about what life could be like, about what you could do.
The village environment is the most de-valued in China, yet in a way it's one of the most flexible forms of urbanism. The villages actually take care of a lot of urban needs.

159

Entrance to Dutchess Mall in Fishkill, New York, whose owner opted for a strategy of "landbanking"—keeping the shopping mall closed until rising real estate values make rentals more profitable. In the meantime, semi-illicit activities have developed around the mall, including prostitution, flea markets, stalls, car owner meets, or a driving school. Based on a speculative scenario, the architectural and urban research group Interboro (Tobias Armborst, Daniel D'Oca, Georgeen Theodore) investigated how landbanking could lead to new opportunities for developing the site: the existing informal uses in situ could be reinforced by a series of small-scale, low-budget interventions, such as a fitness center, day care facilities, a sculpture park, or a stage. The period of waiting for better times is thus transformed into a period of opportunity for the endogenous evolution of a new bottom-up urbanism. ("In the Meantime, Life with Landbanking," Interboro, 2003–2007)

For example for the migrants who come to the cities to work but don't have work permits—the so-called floating population—often end up living in villages.

TA: Those are migrants within China?

MC: Yes, they come from all over China to work in the Pearl River Delta, the most intensive manufacturing environment in the world. Many live in dormitories attached to their factories but for others, the only way they can legally live and also afford to live is to rent rooms in the villages. Because the villages existed partially outside of the communist system of control, they had a certain autonomy, even though this autonomy is often challenged. That's why they are very promising places to investigate. I remember reading this interesting critique of Rem Koolhaas who went to Shenzhen and said: "There was nothing here and now it's a completely new place." But he didn't really pay attention, because there were all these villages before, and they are still there, but now engulfed by the city. The city just grew around them.

TA: And the villagers still live there?

MC: Yes, and they become small-scale entrepreneurs within the city. In a sense they have more mobility and possibility in the current circumstances of top-down planning and large-scale real-estate development that exists in China. The only exception is the village: small, contained, and much more flexible.

It's funny, because when we went to the Pearl River Delta with students, our charge was to design a new city, but the only thing the students could relate to was the villages.

On the other hand the people who are designing the new cities don't even see the villages. They are invisible to them.

But the villages provide many useful services for the new cities: They have places where you can get your hair cut, you can buy food, and they have open-air restaurants with tables out in the street. They have all of the things that the new urban developments lack completely. So there is a relationship with the villages, but it's not official.

TA: I would like to ask you about a different place that you have studied recently for a couple of years, namely a small town in Massachusetts. Chelsea is a working class town that has served as a zone of transition for generations of immigrants.

Acknowledging the fact that cities are ultimately unknowable, you and your students set out to accumulate a wide array of local knowledge of this town through a number of methods and experiments, taking on different roles and perspectives. At the same time you applied this accumulated local knowledge by trying to implement a number of temporary interventions that developed out of the sometimes hidden local dynamics. To me this project is particularly interesting for the way in which architectural projects are not brought to a given site but emerge out of an understanding of the city's everyday life. What are the approaches to implementation that have come out of that work?

Building on the Dutchess Mall project, in 2009 Interboro developed a public park with an exhibition space and nursery on a temporary brownfield site in New York.

MC: This project was amazing in terms of the ways the students interacted with this real place with all its complexities, and also in terms of the human dimensions of the city. This project identified something very important, which is another form of temporariness or temporality, namely human relationships: It all became about meeting people at restaurants, parties, city offices, and other local activities. The relationships develop over time.

One of the students, Dan Adams, became obsessed with Chelsea's salt-pile. In the city there is an enormous salt-pile where they store all the road salt that is used in Eastern Massachusetts. In the winter it's a very big pile and in the summer it gets much smaller. Cargo ships—these gigantic Panamax freighters—come through Chelsea Creek and unload the salt, which comes from different places all over the world and has different colors according to where it comes from. So the salt-pile changes color, it changes size: it is in constant flux.

Dan started out by doing some light projections on the salt-pile. In one of the classes we had a party and we met a guy who is a lighting designer and a long-time Chelsea resident, so he and Dan started collaborating on the projections, funded by the salt-pile's owners.

In the beginning he had a more Barbara Kruger-like approach, where he came up with an enigmatic phrase and planned to project it on the salt-pile. But about a week before he was ready to do it—they had worked on it for a long time—the people from the salt-pile called him up—this was when the Boston Red Sox won the world series—and said: "Look, can you project 'Go Sox!' on the pile?" And so he did, and it completely changed his idea about how he could have a dialog with the city through the salt-pile and the projections: it became much more ordinary but in many ways much more communicative.

Aerial photograph of the salt-pile in Chelsea, Massachusetts.

"GO SOX" projection
In 2004, Dan Adams and David Rusolf projected GO SOX over the surface of the salt-pile as the Boston Red Sox entered the World Series.

TA: So the interaction with the people there changed his way of working?

MC: Yes, and the whole thing actually led to him being employed by the salt-pile—very nicely employed I might add. He now has been working as a consultant to the salt industry for several years and he recently curated a museum exhibition on salt. He got a fellowship from Harvard that let him follow the salt back to its sources, in Mexico and Ireland and other places. So the salt also connected him globally. It's a wonderful testament to obsession.

TA: Through this temporary project he defined the future job that he would hold at the salt company? He created his own job?

MC: You should see his business card! He became a kind of facilitator for all kinds of people. His new project is an incredible kind of temporary urbanism: Next to the salt-pile there is a tank farm that is going to be eliminated. And Dan has designed a park for this site that is based on the fact that in the winter the pile occupies the space but in the summer the pile retreats. Dan has designed this summer space as a flexible location allowing all kinds of community activities and access to the water. It's a park that changes according to the salt-pile's changes. It's based on the idea of oscillation. You can coexist with an industrial environment; it doesn't have to be eliminated to allow a recreational environment. These two seemingly oppositional activities can actually share the same space just not at the same time. In the winter when the salt-pile is there nobody is actually out and about. In the summer the pile shrinks and they cover it with a tarp, leaving an open space for a farmers market and other community uses. The project came out of an intense engagement with this real place.

The other interesting thing about working in a real place is politics: Adams spent more than a year working with different groups in the community to make this park happen, to explain the idea, to meet with city government, with the environmentalists who hated the salt-pile and wanted to get it eliminated, to get all of them on board with this idea.

The people who own the salt-pile have ships and cranes and all this heavy equipment. At some point they said: "Dan, we are going to Baja California and the place where we get the salt is also where a lot of whales come to die, so there are huge whale carcasses on the beach. Should we just bring a couple of them back to put into the park?" This underlines the park's surreal quality; but at the same time it also operates on an everyday level.

Also, right across the street from the salt-pile are several nice Greek Revival homes, and the people who live there have become his greatest supporters. So in a way all the expectations that you might have about what the managers of the company would be like or what these neighbors would be like turn out to be more complicated than you would imagine.

Snow Spectacle projection, Christmas 2004

> TA: It seems to me that in this project the role of the designer is very much that of a tactician in de Certeau's sense: he works with the constantly changing conditions of time and space and tries to use them to his advantage. An unpredictable event—such as the Red Sox winning the World Series for the first time in 86 years and the salt company wanting to celebrate this fact—would have easily derailed a more traditional, "strategic" approach, but here it is harnessed as an opportunity to give a new dimension to the project.
>
> If the question would be, how such a temporal or tactical approach could inform planning practice in general, one could say that tactical planning is always inextricably tied to the specific conditions, people, and—if you will—anecdotes of a particular place at a given time.

The *To Spring V* projection followed in spring 2005. The projection successively dissolved as the material was removed.

MC: I am convinced that specificity is important. What you learn from seeing examples like this is that every place is completely different, and you get your ideas from the circumstances and the situation.

To me, this is an important point about temporary projects. You can't just go somewhere and say: "There is going to be a temporary thing here, because temporary things are good." Every place is different.

> TA: So there is no point in generalizing?

Maritime Festival, 2007
In 2007, the salt-piles that had been removed during the summer prompted Dan Adams to initiate public events on the industrial port areas that were becoming available in collaboration with the Eastern Salt Company.

MC: This is an important issue. I am totally against generalizing from examples and then applying these "rules" or "models" to other situations. The idea of generalizing and than applying the generalization to other circumstances is very much of a modernist project. This logic is no longer convincing. It is particularly inappropriate for temporary urbanisms, which must be rooted in specific circumstances to succeed.

163

I support a different logic, which is one of accumulating knowledge through specific cases. You can learn a lot, but you can't generalize from them. You need to understand your specific case. It's great to see other examples, because it shows that a lot of things can happen, so it gives you a sense of the possibilities.

OPEN PLANNING

Urban Catalyst with Jesko Fezer

The integration of temporary uses in processes of planning is characterized by a fundamental contradiction: temporary uses rely on the principle of spontaneous action by a group of participants and develop their vitality precisely through their renunciation of determining and ensuring a long-term ideal plan. Classic planning, on the contrary, is based on designing a desired final state for a client who has the means to also attain this condition.

The ideal of absoluteness and permanence has forever dominated architecture and planning. In 1452, Leon Battista Alberti defined architecture as "harmony and concord of all the parts achieved in such a manner that nothing could be added or taken away or altered except for the worse." Determinism, previously formulated on an aesthetic basis, was programmatically constituted anew by the functionalist approach of twentieth-century Modernism: for their optimization, uses and functional processes were henceforth fixed in every detail.

All thought relating to the goal of long-lasting perfection is always connected with an authoritarian gesture as well. Vernacular building, on the contrary, is always characterized by the possibilities of adaptation, change, and further development. Since the beginning of Modernism at the latest, such ideas have also penetrated design attitudes and planning methods, although mostly just as a peripheral exception in a profession characterized by a top-down decision-making approach. It is not a consistent line of tradition though, but a multitude of parallel approaches that are followed for various reasons.

Some positions seek to integrate the user into the planning and the construction process; others strive towards the potential of expanding and changing built structures for yet-unknown growth; a third group is concerned with the instability of lifestyles and everyday practices, or seeks changeable building types. Common to all approaches is the attempt to combine openness to unknown development with a degree—considered indispensable—of stability and continuity in spatial, aesthetic, and structural terms.

In the following synopsis, the first six approaches are concerned with various forms of the bottom-up, while the last four operate by loosening the rigidity of the top-down. All of the presented methods are based, however, on the linkage of both process directions, each with varying emphases and procedures. In the context of this book, the ten illustrated methods are meant to demonstrate traditional lines of work that have proven capable of integrating temporary uses in longer-term developments.

STEP BY STEP

The Swiss sociologist and urban researcher Lucius Burckhardt spoke out at the beginning of the 1970s emphatically for the deferment of planning decisions: "This purposeful postponement of decisions is an art that is still barely mastered by those who plan the planning. Even so, no fame can be swiftly earned" (Fig. 1). For planners, Burckhardt's almost counterproductive stipulation fundamentally violated the modernist planning ethos of feasibility and bold decisions. For Burckhardt, all planning—inasmuch as it is not concerned exclusively with current, short-term needs—was based on an extrapolated future with a fixed final state. He regarded this position, however, as unrealistic, "because time must elapse and represents a development; we only initiate a process—we may institute its development—but not conclude it."

Burckhardt called for restricting planning stipulations, formulating and approaching goals only in stages. In contrast to the pictorial representation of a guiding concept, decisions should rather be deferred than anticipated. With his plea for the non-programmed or the indistinctly programmed, he did not mean, however, the absence of planning, but a new form of open planning, which allows for the freedom of alternative use. His question was: "How little may be planned and, how little could be planned at all?" He proposed postponing as many decisions as possible in order to allow for the possibility of collective influence on decision-making processes.

A similar concept of planning procedures was already advanced in 1959 by the American economist and political scientist Charles E. Lindblom. He introduced the term "muddling through" (Fig. 2). Lindblom summarized his approach therein, which forgoes every form of centralized planning and draws instead upon mutual coordination of those involved. In opposition to the predominant form of comprehensive planning, he juxtaposed regulation in small, manageable, easily revisable steps, because he assumed that complex societal problems cannot be rationally formulated and judged in their entirety. Only by means of incremental adaptation and an approach using concrete compromises, can one define and reach practical goals. For Lindblom however, this was no departure from the principle of planning. For him, in fact, "the iterative method of limited comparisons is, in fact, also a method or system; it is in no way the failure of all methods, for which the administration should feel guilty."

The notion that planning should proceed step by step has found expression in architectural projects that attempted, not to create finished buildings, but to integrate the process of use into the designs as a phase of continued building. Herman Hertzberger's term "semi-finished products" or Jaap Bakema's project "Growing House" created architectural freedom for subsequent decisions. Nicolaas John Habraken, director of the architectural research institute SAR in the Netherlands, worked in the 1960s on design and construction methods that—by differentiating between "support" and "infill"—enabled small-scale, individual adaptations (see the chapter "Open Framework", p. 186). For this purpose, Habraken developed dimensioning grids, zoning of buildings, and decision-making procedures intended to make it possible for buildings to have the capacity for subsequent fit-out and renovation.

3

The "Park Fiction" project in Hamburg, paid for by residents and an artist initiative, was able to open a small, self-designed park at the harbor's edge in St. Pauli in 2005, after ten years of debate (Fig. 3). The goal of the citizens' action group, established in 1994, was to prevent construction on the last remaining open areas and instead push through creation of a collectively designed open space. The basis for this was not a landscape architecture design, but the organization of a process determined by the aspirations and desires of the residents.

DO-IT-YOURSELF CONSTRUCTION

In large parts of the world houses are built, not only without architects but also without construction firms and tradesmen, by the inhabitants themselves. In his book *Planet of Slums*, Mike Davis predicted that a dramatically greater proportion of the growing world population will live in slums, favelas or bidonvilles. He presumes that across the Earth today, a quarter of a million such areas already exist (Fig. 4).

4

But also in some suburban zones of industrially developed regions, the inhabitants erect their houses to a large extent by themselves and unregulated. The low standard of the accommodations, with mostly bad natural lighting, ventilation and facilities as well as a lack of public infrastructure often allow nothing more than mere survival. The absence of all planning, which is what makes these forms of living at all possible in the first place, is likewise the cause of their extremely poor quality of living conditions. For some time, attempts have been

made to address this problem with limited planning interventions (see "Building Onward" below, p. 174).

In the mid-1950s, the British architect John F. C. Turner already concerned himself with the practice, widespread in Peru, of illegal settlement and do-it-yourself construction—also known as self-build. For him, this self-organized practice was superior to mass residential construction in terms of the full utilization of limited resources, the integration of social networks, and the possibility for adaption to changing family and/or occupational circumstances. Turner's research shifted the perspective from the built object onto the social and economic relationships (Fig. 5). His studies commanded attention throughout the world and prompted a new, more positive image of informal construction, which until then was only perceived as a problem to be solved.

In a completely different respect, do-it-yourself construction, autonomous action, and the resourcefulness of amateur craftsmen formed an important point of reference for Charles Jencks' and Nathan Silver's manifesto *Adhocism* from 1972 (Fig. 6). The later theorist of the Postmodern era enthusiastically collected examples of spontaneous inventions in design and building activity. Invited by the socialistic government of Salvador Allende, in the same year—1972—Martin Pawley proposed using refuse and by-products of the growing Chilean consumption industry for do-it-yourself construction (Fig. 7). Packaging, for instance, should be produced from materials that can be of further use in building houses. And for a Chilean Citroën factory that was no longer receiving deliveries of motors, Pawley developed a concept for how car body parts from the Citroën Fourgonnette system could be incorporated in house construction.

Whereas these ideas remain unrealized, with the hippie movement in the USA of the 1960s and 1970s, a do-it-yourself construction culture developed that even more fundamentally combined technical innovation with do-it-yourself construction methods. These initiatives reached their culmination with the projects of "dropouts." With the *Whole Earth Catalog*, the dropouts supplied themselves with plans, products, and ideas that made this alternative viable (Fig. 8). Richard Buckminster Fuller and his geodesic domes, which were at first primarily conceived for military use, served nevertheless for a while as guiding examples (Fig. 9). Based on Fuller's concepts, over two hundred thousand bizarre abodes out of cardboard, plastic, bamboo or textiles were produced.

More recently, the Japanese architect Shigeru Ban attempted to design light buildings for disaster areas from simple materials that could be quickly assembled. The projects are based on principles of prefabrication and do-it-yourself construction (Fig. 10). For instance, in 1995 Ban developed emergency shelters made of cardboard tubes for the victims of the earthquake in Kobe. The constructions, made from glued layers of recycled paper, are also used in other countries as an interim solution for emergency situations.

Another tradition of do-it-yourself construction—also known as self-build—arose through the inclusion of do-it-yourself concepts in the predominant building culture of developed industrialized countries. To enable home ownership for low-income population groups, planners had already experimented with do-it-yourself building settlements in the crisis-ridden 1920s and 1930s—in the context of the Deutscher Werkbund (German Work Federation) and the reform, cooperative society or Garden City movements (Düsseldorf Kleinsiedlungshaus, 1931, Fig. 11). Generally supplemented through subsistence farming, a low standard of habitation fit for human beings could thus be enabled through the use of family labor.

The British architect Walter Segal conceived something fundamentally new in the field of do-it-yourself construction in the 1970s. Simple rules, a rigorous grid, the use of products from the building industry, manageable size of building parts, simple assembly, ease of maintenance, flexibility for alterations and technical guidance—all this enabled the do-it-yourself construction of high-quality residential buildings. Segal's method was applied for the first time in the mid-1970s in the development of a small housing estate in the London suburb of Lewisham, in this case applied to wood frame construction (Fig. 12). Projects such as the Bauhäusle student residence in Stuttgart by Peter Hübner and Peter Sulzer picked up on these construction principles in Germany in the 1980s; the dormitory was planned and built by sthe students.

Eilfried Huth, Otto Steidle, Ottokar Uhl, Lucien Kroll, and Herman Hertzberger also integrated varying forms and degrees of do-it-yourself construction into their participative projects. As part of the 1987 International Building Exhibition (IBA) in Berlin, the *Selbstbauterrassen* (self-built terraces), the *Wohnregal* (literally "residential shelving") and Frei Otto's *Ökohaus* (ecological house), in which certain building elements or the interior finishings were rendered by do-it-yourself means, were created. The goal was to engage the users in the fundamental building decisions, to make better living conditions possible through cost savings, and, furthermore, enable the user to make subsequent, further constructive adaptations.

The Rural Studio and many other community design centers in the USA are currently intensively concerned with building for the underprivileged, who are not accommodated by the housing market. Together with students, communal facilities and residential buildings are thus constructed with do-it-yourself effort—complementing other forms of planning and political engagement. To do this, simple, donated and re-used building materials are employed to a great extent.

DO-IT-YOURSELF PLANNING

Whereas concepts of participation developed in the attempts to democratize planning in the 1970s and 1980s, in which self-planning was connected with self-production, self-planning has in the meantime freed itself from this connection. Self-planning is today a matter that is also pursued by commercial providers as part of their product innovation strategies.

Based on new, digital techniques of planning and production, the concept of "mass customization" arose in the 1990s to refer to processes in which the consumer is involved in the design of the goods he or she purchases. In this way, the object is individualized to a certain extent. Ideally, one doesn't buy a finished product, but a manufacturing service geared to meeting personal needs. In practice, this means individual customization of a desikgned product with regard to size, color, and other properties. The use becomes a "co-designer"

A few architects have attempted to transfer this concept, successful in particular in the garment industry, to residential buildings. Admittedly, the projects thus far aren't for the most part convincing in terms of their architectural quality; they also haven't been realized. Worth mentioning here is, in particular, Kas Oosterhuis's project *Variomatic* (Fig. 13) as well as the now defunct Internet platform etekt.com.

Such procedures are also practiced in the building industry, although without aspiration for the architecture. For some time now, it has been possible for prefabricated houses to be individually tailored. For instance, a basic type can be expanded by means of various styles of roofs and bay windows as well as by adding another floor or an extension (Fig. 14, Streif Company). Not only materials, color, and details can be freely selected and combined with each other; the floor plans can also be adjusted to individual preferences.

Another means of self-planning is offered by planning software for laypeople. With such help, clients can design their dream house single-handedly—in two- and three-dimensional views—and hand over almost-finished plans to the architect to make the building permit application. The software offers a so-called "floor plan assistant." Furthermore, it permits the simulation of light, calculation of the costs, and the use of construction details. Lastly, it offers extensive tools for visualization, including the possibility of embedding personal digital photos. The software Virtual Architecture / ArCon, now marketed in

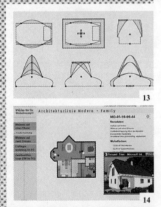

13

14

over ninety countries, is a good example of this type of self-planning. Such amateur planning, though, is not new; previously it was simply a rare exception. For example, in the eighteen and nineteen centuries the Prussian kings drew sketches for new buildings, which were then implemented by the commissioned architects—among them, Georg Wenzeslaus von Knobelsdorff and Ludwig Persius.

More strongly linked to the emancipatory tradition of participatory building are *Baugruppen* (building collectives, literally "building groups"), which have become popular in recent years in Germany and Austria with a middle-class clientele who find the conventional offerings on the real estate market either too expensive or too unspecific. The *Baugruppen* develop multi-family housing through collective planning, often with very individual designs. During this process, the users, who are also the owners, formulate and talk through their individual desires in countless discussions with the architect. The residential buildings' designs emerge from cooperation between the future occupants and the architect, in Vienna, with BKK-3; Berlin-Oderberger Strasse housing project, with BAR Architects (Fig. 15).

15

Unlike with house construction, participation in the field of urban planning always entailed taking part in the planning process without helping to build. The possibility for influence is generally limited, since the decision-making power is not ceded to the participating citizens. For this reason, such procedures frequently run the risk of being pro forma events, in which the residents are communicatively integrated, but without the ability to exert perceptible influence on the respective project. Legally regulated and bureaucratically organized, participation processes are often perceived merely as instruments of obstruction by planners and politicians, where positive impulses and innovative proposals can only unfold in the rarest cases.

Nevertheless, here there are also innovative methods. Almost analogous to the working method of *Baugruppen*, the concept of *Planungszellen* (planning cells) is based on the combination of amateur and expert knowledge. On a random basis, approximately twenty-five citizens are selected and—exempted from their other duties—work together in groups for a week in order to develop solution proposals for a given planning problem (Fig. 16). The process is conducted and assisted by a moderator. Any needed expertise is obtained by asking professionals from the respective interest groups.

16

The possibility of growth by means of additive forms of construction has always been an essential characteristic of vernacular building. As part of the informal process of urbanization, this principle is continued today with modern construction methods. Daily building practices in southern Europe and the developing countries show what role deliberation and preparation plays in future growth (Fig. 17). To a large extent without the assistance of architects or engineers, owners go about the horizontal and vertical expansion of their houses, which takes place over the course of years according to the needs of their growing families and their own financial resources. Tax regulations often benefit unfinished houses. Reinforced concrete frame construction offers ideal possibilities for the growth of houses; the stubs of columns for future expansion and their protruding reinforcing rods are a symbol of the rapidly growing cities, which resemble perpetual building sites.

Despite the dominant interest many architects have in absolute, ideal objects, concepts for developable buildings have been part of Modernism's agenda from the beginning. A familiar example is that of the designs for a *wachsende Haus* (growing house) in the 1932 Berlin exhibition of the same name, conceived by Martin Wagner (Fig. 18). In light of the Great Depression, the city's planning director proposed designing a small core house, which, according to the needs of its inhabitants and their capabilities, would be constructed and expanded step by step. The mode of expansion was part of the architects' designs, whereas the users were to determine the individual steps and the time-table themselves.

The *wachsende Häuser* exhibited by Wagner were to be industrially prefabricated to the greatest extent possible. The concurrent experiments of the architect Konrad Wachsmann went one step further in this regard. That's because Wachsmann used the technical potential of prefabricating building components for the development of entire modular systems for wood and steel construction. By freely adding together a large quantity of a few different elements, almost every construction task could be solved. The structures could be enlarged or made smaller as required.

Today, one can hardly imagine everyday life without industrially fabricated structures. On almost every construction site, modular scaffolding is employed; meanwhile, they are also used for temporary architecture (*Add on* art project, 20 meters high, Vienna, 2005, Fig. 19). Modular systems are indispensable, especially in industrial and commercial construction. They guarantee short times for assembly, modification and disassembly. Above all, they contribute to amortizing an investment more quickly.

A particularly successful example—along with Norman Foster's Renault automobile factory in Swindon, Great Britain, constructed between 1981 and 1983 (Fig. 20)—is the Thomson electronic factory in Guyancourt, France, completed in 1991 (Fig. 21). The building is meant to be able to grow in multiple stages that are not yet determined at the beginning. Renzo Piano and Michel Desvigne thus created a concept for the gradual transformation from landscape to built structure. Initially, the landscape predominated; but drainage channels, trees, and parking lots anticipate the striped grid of the future factory halls.

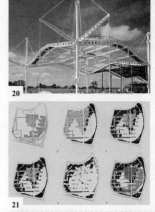
20

21

The infrastructure for a growing sector like aviation was also confronted with lasting expansion barely capable of being planned in advance. It is precisely the spatial and construction chaos of giant airports such as Frankfurt am Main or London-Heathrow that show, however, that in most cases the terminals are planned as final projects, without serious thought about expansion, although a design approach based on growth is entirely possible, as the example of Terminal 2 at Paris-Roissy airport from Paul Andreu makes explicit. With this departure hall an infrastructure band meant to be continued linearly was begun in 1982 and has meanwhile been extended twice, so modifying the module (Fig. 22).

22

Alfred Mansfeld was thinking more in conceptual rather than technical terms with his design for a growing Israel Museum in Jerusalem (Fig. 23). For this project the architect also coopted the contemporary structuralistic discourse. Since at the beginning of the planning phase in 1959 the museum possessed neither an art collection nor a construction budget, Mansfeld developed a design strategy that was founded on the basic principles of "growth, change, uncertainty." The basic module was a concrete mushroom-shaped structure, an umbrella supported by a central pillar, which spanned more than 100 square meters and could be used for various programs. Growth was structured by a grid that permitted manifold variations of the same module. In fact, the museum was expanded, piece by piece, from 1962 to 2000—over a period of almost forty years—according to Mansfeld's strategy, even though the design of some modules was altered by subsequently commissioned architects.

23

Although unrealized, Le Corbusier's 1928 design for a growing museum is still architecturally interesting. The "Mundaneum" bears evidence of a unique fascination and the enthusiasm that architects have always felt for the spiral, because in its form, nature, and growth it always attains visual unity (Fig. 24). This approach was further

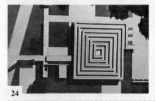
24

developed in the parametric design practices that emerged in the 1990s (see "(De)Regulation", p. 80). Another source of inspiration in this area was the book *On Growth and Form*, published in 1917, by the Scottish mathematician and biologist D'Arcy Wentworth Thompson.

BUILDING ONWARD

Even though architects and planners usually presume that they design the final configuration of ultimate significance for a building, it often doesn't take long before the original built structures are reshaped. Now and again, potentials and qualities that no one expected unfold in the built structures. Informal processes of appropriation are often what overlay initially planned structures. But, conversely, self-organized housing settlements can also be reshaped afterwards through planned interventions.

25

A classic example of the former is the Pessac workers' housing complex, constructed in 1925 according to plans by Le Corbusier (Fig. 25). As depicted in 1966 by the French sociologist Philippe Boudon in his influential study, after just a few years it had already been radically changed by the inhabitants with regard to program, forms, and colors. Boudon saw this extensive transformation as originating in, among other things, Le Corbusier's open spatial concept.

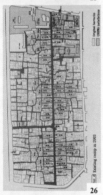

26

Change of use and lack of space can encourage reshaping, as the example of the Neirab Palestinian refugee camp in northern Syria demonstrates (Fig. 26). In 1948, the Syrian government made the site, formerly used by the French military, available to the Palestinian refugees. The barracks were divided inside by partition walls and then assigned to families. In an informal process during the next sixty years, the occupants expanded the buildings at first horizontally, until only a few public access paths remained. Subsequently, additional floors were added, such that the barracks are meanwhile completely overgrown by the expansions. Today, just under 20,000 people live here in the tightest of quarters.

27

One finds the reshaping of planned structures in countless new building developments within Central and Eastern Europe, for example in Wolfen-Nord, a *Plattenbau* housing estate from the 1960s and 1970s (Fig. 27). Along with the do-it-yourself alterations, from wood paneling to mural paintings on the balconies—as was almost commonplace in the *Plattenbauten* of the GDR—the residents there created copiously designed front gardens. With their gravel paths, fishponds, windmills, decorative *Fliegenpilze* or toadstools, shelters, hillocks, and fences, they corresponded to the front gardens of rural single-family houses. The people in Wolfen-Nord were moved here from a village that fell victim to brown coal surface mining. They were skilled craftsmen with an interest in recreating their old neighborhoods. After 1989, these structures of appropriation were completely eliminated in the context of refurbishment and demolition, whereas they were often intensely developed further in other eastern, formerly socialist, countries.

Reshapings can apply to various types of architecture. In Germany, squatters, for example, often take possession of *Gründerzeit* buildings or even older ones (Fig. 28). At first they barricade off a residence, then they share out the rooms, define common spaces, and add missing utility services and facilities. Thus a "tenement" constructed by a purely capitalistic economy is transformed into a residence belonging to an often politically and culturally active collective.

Such changes to existent architecture do not only take place informally, but also formally, as the history of urban renewal since the nineteenth century shows. A familiar example of the further development of a postwar, large-scale housing estate is the remodeling of the Perseigne housing estate in Alençon, France, built for low-income social groups by the Belgian architect Lucien Kroll (Fig. 29). To revitalize the uniform, indeed monotone district, and in close coordination with the residents, Kroll appended various buildings with gabled roofs to the cubic building blocks. He had parts of buildings demolished, retrofitted balconies and stairs, and changed the appearance of the facades. He even sought to make the flat terrain more varied—by creating a "visage pluraliste" as the expression of a complex, democratic society. For Kroll, these interventions were a reaction to the shortcomings of modern architecture: "As long as architecture adheres to the rules of homogeneity, to the repetition of identical elements, to the discipline of materials and to symmetry, as well as to its self-imposed inflexible and unchangeable character, . . . it will remain militaristic. It will not be able to express the values of a complex, creative, dynamic and democratic society."

In projects mostly conceived for developing countries, other architects plan from the start so that the facilities can be built further after initial completion. They accept that—unlike with growing structures, which remain faithful to the original concept (see previous section, "Growing Structures")—further development of their projects takes place unconnected with their planning, thus in new mode. The 1967 PREVI international competition for low cost housing in Lima attempted to put this practice into effect in an architecturally exemplary manner. Many of the participants—among them such renowned offices as those of Christopher Alexander, Atelier 5, Georges Candilis / Alexis Josic / Shadrach Woods, Charles Correa, Aldo van Eyck, Kisho Kurokawa,

30

31

32

Fumihiko Maki, Herbert Ohl, and James Stirling—concerned themselves, within the framework of a UN housing construction program, with the new build of 1,500 low-cost houses and with strategies to formalize and upgrade spontaneous housing settlements. Aldo van Eyck, for example, designed clusters of courtyard houses with a structure that could be expanded both horizontally and vertically using do-it-yourself means; van Eyck's only half-designed residential buildings were intensively altered and upgraded immediately after completion of their construction (Fig. 30).

In 1975, Steven Holl planned a housing estate for do-it-yourself construction in Manila, Philippines (Fig. 31). The design dictated solely the parceling of lots, the road system and the technical infrastructure. The state furnished only the water supply with centralized water distribution points, the sewer system, the electricity and the main roads. The gradual development of the parcels was meant to be left to the financial capabilities and needs of the residents; they turned to conventional construction methods and in part also used found and recycled building material. Similar projects have been realized elsewhere, if only as an exception, as for example, by a cooperative in São Paulo (Fig. 32). Here the attempt was made to enhance informal building through, among other things, joint construction of an upwardly expandable basic module for each housing unit.

The reverse procedure, in which informally developed housing settlements later experience revaluation through partial interventions, achieved greater acceptance. Due to its scope and success, Rio de Janeiro's Favela-Bairro program is particularly well known. Since 1980, districts have been modernized by nearly one million residents (Jorge Mario Jáuregui, Favela Salgueiro, Fig. 33). Along with construction of the streets and laying of water pipes, continued building in the favelas also comprises the establishment of nursery and elementary schools, provision of sports fields and green spaces as well as legalization of real estate ownership.

33

ACUPUNCTURE

Acupuncture is a balancing and regulating therapy in traditional Chinese medicine that is also prevalent in the Western world as part of the practices of complementary and alternative medicine. With a few pinpricks, the energy flow of the whole body is meant to be put back into balance. Analogous to this, architects and artists understand small interventions as acupuncture when their effect reaches far beyond the local intervention. That which exists is not ignored, let alone eliminated, but transformed through skillful diversion of existing energies. The city is meant to regenerate itself solely through slight external interventions. In the process, the time factor plays an essential role: "acupuncture" on the city's "body" counts on a time lag between the intervention and its effect. Since the interventions, which are themselves often minimal, can be of a temporary or permanent character, temporality as such becomes a variable of the strategy.

Temporary interventions were propagandized, for example, by the British architectural group Archigram. Their *Instant City* project of 1968 to 1970 was intended to revitalize cities beyond the metropolises by means of a kind of migratory idea-circus (Fig. 34). Using mobile equipment, local events were to be stimulated; ideas and concepts brought along were to be incorporated. The cities along the route were to be networked; it was hoped that a virtual metropolis would develop.

34

At the same time, groups of Austrian architects and artists experimented with related performances and installations. For instance, Haus-Rucker-Co. introduced themselves to the public in 1970 with the *Giant Billiard* project as part of an exhibition in Düsseldorf (Fig. 35). A 225-square-meter air mattress and three plastic balls gave museum visitors the opportunity for physical activity with games and exercise, and, in the process, the chance to blur the borders between city and museum, on the one hand, and useful object and pure artwork on the other hand.

35

Today there is a broad praxis of performance-related interventions initiated by architects and artists. For example, the Mexican Betsabe Romero introduced missing greenery into the poor suburbs of Mexico City with a bus that was converted into a garden (Fig. 36). The garden bus became the center of events that encouraged the residents to add greenery to their domestic surroundings. With other temporary installations—including *Kitchen Monument*, erected in various European cities by Raumlabor Berlin with Plastique Fantastique (Fig. 37), or the mini-architecture of *Mobile Porch* from the artist group Public Works (Fig. 38)—the installations lasted just a few days or weeks. Here it was a matter of the transformation of ordinary urban spaces into new meeting places, ateliers, and spaces for exhibitions and performances.

36

37

The initiators of such interventions always hope that an event gives an impulse to a longer lasting development. They want to put unused spaces into the public consciousness and establish local contacts, indeed entire networks. Their goal is for citizens to have greater participation in urban development. That is why a social event is at the center of such interventions; it is meant to give a certain clarity and aesthetic presence to the artistic creation.

38

Many projects were conceived primarily as symbolic interventions, such as the campaign *Liebe deine Stadt* (Love Your City) by

39

40

the Cologne artist Merlin Bauer in cooperation with the architectural group BeL, which encouraged debates on the use of neglected buildings from the 1950s and 1960s that were threatened with closure, demolition or privatization, through temporary actions. For a few months each, specific buildings were marked with giant letters proclaiming "Liebe deine Stadt" (Fig. 39). Public events referred to as "awards ceremonies" and a series of lectures accompanied the actions.

An even more streamlined approach was pursued by the Austrian artist Karl-Heinz Klopf with his project *Mind the Steps* at the 9th Istanbul Biennale in 2005. Klopf's interest was to expand the Biennale route, which concentrated solely on the city center; he wanted to unveil the everyday spaces in the dilapidated and impoverished neighborhoods of Istanbul. The artist mounted ordinary spotlights above various staircases and asked residents to organize a public event for each (Fig. 40). Seemingly banal places of social interaction were turned into "stages" that illuminated the local physical and social surroundings for one hour every evening and drew attention to their problems and potentials.

The spectrum of temporary interventions also includes the entire range of political protest with which long-term changes are sought through urban actions. Bernard Tschumi's manifesto *The Environmental Trigger* of 1974 in fact declared temporary "rhetorical actions" to be the only effective means at architecture's disposal. Tschumi, also active today as a practicing architect, polemicized at that time against the mere planning of buildings and organization of spaces, because both only apparently change the structure of the community whereas in reality they serve conformity. Instead, Tschumi called for radical actions. He invoked, among other things, the artistic experiments of the Situationists, whose socio-critical approach have influenced western European protest movements since the 1960s. The Situationists' involvement with the monotone, functional, capitalistic urban machine was not aimed at mere "animation"; instead, they encouraged "disturbances," sometimes even anarchistic "destructions," in order to provoke societal changes.

The idea of urban acupuncture is in no way restricted to interventions limited in duration. Isolated permanent interventions can also pursue strategic goals. In this regard, the plea made in 1981 by planning theoretician and sociologist Lucius Burckhardt for the "smallest possible intervention" is interesting. Whereas large urban schemes generally aspire to reorder the city, the smallest possible interventions could establish a superior order that is more socially stable. A rather playful example of this approach was the *City Magnets* project by Cedric Price (Fig. 41). In 1996, Price proposed to erect "magnets"

41

at ten sites in the center of London that he considered to be flawed or underutilized. Placed on flexible, technical structures such as cranes, hydraulic platforms, and pontoons, the "magnets," according to Price, would not be functionally determinate and would stimulate previously unknown activities (see also chapter Cultivating Temporary Use). As early as 1969, David Greene, a member of Archigram, had proposed creating a portion of technical infrastructure in the outdoors with the *Logplug* project: tree trunks with electrical outlets and additional utility connections were to provide travelers with urban comforts in an undisturbed natural setting.

Besides such unrealized concepts, there are a large number of smallest possible interventions for urban development of districts that have been realized. On several occasions since the middle of the 1990s, for example, the London borough of Southwark gave young architects and artists the task of enhancing the district through micro-interventions on bridges, streets, intersections, and other nodes as part of the "Future Southwark Urban Design Initiative." This is exempli-fied by the application of lettering at underpasses and the use of street signs and manhole covers as wayfinding systems by Caruso St John Architects (Fig. 42); the same holds true for the work of the group East, which enhanced dreary sidewalks by using colorful paving slabs with lettering.

42

The municipality of Medellín, Colombia, has pursued a related approach at a larger scale since 2004 with a program for slums (Fig. 43). Architects designed small urban plazas that became focal points for the neighborhoods; furthermore, they planned district centers, cultural centers, and libraries. By means of ambitious design and new

43

ideas for the use of public spaces, the municipality and the architects were also concerned with encouraging the residents to use their own initiative to enhance the neglected areas.

The *10x10* project in South Africa relies even more on imitation. To explore the possibilities for constructing functionally and aestheti-cally high-quality, environmentally friendly living space that is nev-ertheless affordable for the poorest segments of the population, the initiative Design Indaba commissioned ten local and international architectural teams to develop prototypes. The first of this program's housing types, designed by Luyunda Mpahlwa of Cape Town-based mmp architects, was realized in 2008 as part of a development plan for the Freedom Park informal settlement (Fig. 44). By distributing the execution plans and construction specifications, including proposals for adaptation, it was hoped to stimulate wide-scale imitation.

44

Although the long-term goals as well as the concrete strategies are often different, all these acupunctures pursue something similar in principle: they investigate how the greatest possible effectiveness can be achieved with the least possible financial investment, something formulated more poetically by the French landscape architect Michel Desvigne: "How can one paint a large apartment building when you only have one can of paint?"

(DE)REGULATION

45

For the sake of open planning, some urban planning concepts forgo all spatial planning and provide at most a series of rules that, due to various external and internal factors, can lead to quite varied results and thus remain open for the future. Most radical in this regard was the "Non-Plan" manifesto by Reyner Banham, Paul Barker, Peter Hall and Cedric Price, published in 1969 in the magazine *New Society* (Fig. 45). The four proposed a "precise and carefully observed experiment in non-planning." In place of the paternalism of an overly regulated social welfare state, the citizens should be able, within specific, special zones, to make autonomous decisions about the design of their built environment. As part of this experiment of controlled planning withdrawal, planners were to gain insights about the real tastes and needs of the inhabitants of Great Britain.

Non-Plan, however, made the ambivalence toward deregulation strategies blatantly obvious: was it a matter of an anarchistic-libertarian proposal for the emancipatory self-empowerment of the residents or an early example of the neoliberal policy of governmental withdrawal for the benefit of private investors? Barely a decade later, the Non-Plan co-author Peter Hall became a mastermind of the neoliberal politics of the Thatcher government by introducing the concept of special economic zones for the increasingly deindustrialized and impoverished centers of major British cities, which was implemented shortly thereafter. Through restrictions in taxes and duties, and the abolition of governmental regulation and planning, ideal conditions for business were to be established. As the development of the London Docklands demonstrates, instead of greater citizen involvement as demanded in Non-Plan, entrepreneurs and developers became almost the sole actors in the urban development process. Out of the demand "more power for citizens" came "more power for investors." The British "enterprise zones" of the 1980s thus established were and are the inspiration for neoliberal urban planning politics, today spreading exponentially worldwide, in which the role of the state is increasingly restricted to creating ideal parameters for investors.

In contrast, a number of different approaches can be identified that in no way pursue deregulation as a primary goal, but rather replace classic spatial planning techniques with rules of various types. Precise form is not defined for the site, but the regulations determine a specific character and precise qualities, which unfold incrementally in interaction with other factors. Thereby, the spatial composition opens up to the unforeseeable; it favorably incorporates developments that are not controllable by the architects.

A good example of this is the concept of the *Industriewald* (Industrial Forest) in the Ruhr region, developed as part of the Emscher Park International Building Exhibition and realized in 1996 (Fig. 46). Inner-city industrial wastelands became public green space, without being designed in terms of landscape architecture. Instead, rules for the care of the terrain were defined, whose vegetation emerged from ecological succession.

46

In 1996, the American architect and theorist Michael Sorkin "designed" an entire city with a similar method. In place of a spatial master plan, Sorkin's pamphlet *Local Code: The Constitution of a City at 42 North Latitude* states nothing more than the written description of individual elements of a future city, such as its gates, party walls, public spaces, et cetera. The urban design becomes a text; the translation from text into space and built form leaves room—intentionally—for interpretation.

The urban design plan from Kees Christiaanse Architects & Planners (KCAP) for Wijnhaven Rotterdam is also fundamentally based on rules instead of spatial determinants (Fig. 47). In this way, greater formal diversity and improved marketability are to be achieved at the same time on the site of the old harbor. The planning from 2001/02

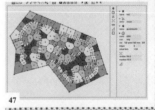

47

fixed a road system with parking spaces, the parceling of lots and important public spaces. Instead of the typical regulations for building volumes, heights and alignments, there are merely a few rules. For example, the building volume for a lot is not permitted to exceed 22 cubic meters per square meter of ground surface. Consequently, investors can determine for themselves whether they would prefer to build wider and more cost-effectively or higher, more slender and more expensively. Neighbors can cooperate to their mutual advantage; buildings with shared party walls are permitted to be higher. Further rules—for example, regarding lots and neighborhoods or for ensuring good natural lighting and ventilation—have an impact on the buildings without determining their forms in advance.

Based on this project, in the following years the office KCAP, together with the University of Kaiserslautern and the Swiss Federal Institute of Technology (ETH) in Zurich, developed the urban design planning software KaisersRot, which in the meantime has been used in several projects. It enables the direct involvement of future residents in the design of a housing settlement. From the preferences of the homeowners, a multifaceted overall plan with individualized lots emerges. The project illustrates of the use of parametric design in contemporary planning: decisions are made individually; from them, an overall plan is generated. The final form is not what is designed, but the generation form on the basis of various parameters.

CIRCUMVENTION

Modern planning ideology is characterized by high expectations of the state as a planning and regulating entity. In most of the industrialized countries, this attitude led to spatial planning with blanket coverage throughout multiple levels of scale. With the end of the Fordist state, the fundamental paradigms for modern planning—universalism, the notion of equality, positivism—have been put into question. The state increasingly relinquishes its function as a planning entity to private investors and project developers; the extant instruments of planning policy have gotten into a tense relationship with the reality of planning.

Alongside the criticism by investors and industry representatives of the planning system's lack of adaptability, even architects and planners polemicize against the regulatory thicket and demand reforms. But in reality, all the players have long since found a pragmatic way of dealing with the body of rules: "What is useful is used, and what disturbs is circumvented or forgotten. The planning system is, however, thereby more and more reduced to reconstructing in formal legal terms what has emerged in preceding negotiation processes" (Karl Ganser, 2006). According to Ganser, plans are no longer used as instruments for the regulation of future developments; rather, they are adapted to the brisk changes of reality and thereby establish a certain legal certainty. Breaking the rules appears to have become a societal holy grail. Architects and planners themselves supply pragmatic strategies for doing so.

Outside of the leading industrialized countries, it is already daily practice to ignore governmental planning and statutory regulations, inasmuch as they are existent at all. People build illegally. The rapidly growing Latin American, African and Asian megacities, whose urbanization takes place in large part on the basis of illegal land occupation, exemplify this. The absence of effective planning, governmental provision of housing, and legal supervision leads to illegal construction at a large scale, such as the urbanization of Istanbul or Mexico City

48

illustrates (Fig. 48). The do-it-yourself builders can often rely on mid- or long-term legalization, because local politicians are courting the voters' approval before every election with the promise of legalization and investment in the construction of streets, schools, or technical infrastructure.

Also in Western Europe, calculated breaking of the rules is common tactics. Those who build like this accept small penalties or gamble on the susceptibility of the authorities to bribery. As the heavily over-developed Spanish and Italian Mediterranean coast demonstrates, now and again those responsible within the local authorities accept a bribe and earn a bit with illegal planning and construction. In this manner, giant hotel complexes, golf facilities and entire streets of houses developed, for instance in Benidorm in southern Spain (Fig. 49).

Another form of circumventing planning law is the making of demands on the municipalities by companies and investors. When it is a matter of deciding for or against a location, the players know how to cleverly exploit competition between cities. The aircraft manufacturer EADS, for instance, successfully threatened in 2004 to relocate jobs if the controversial expansion—in Mühlenberger Loch, a protected nature conservation area—of their Hamburg Airbus factory was not given approval (Fig. 50). Through attractive offers of exceptions and circumvention and on their own initiative, many municipalities are meanwhile attracting investors to their cities. Justified by the primacy of securing jobs, larger projects are often pushed through "contrary to the plan."

However, the tug of war amongst administration, investors and residents regarding investment terms and conditions can also be more shrewdly instrumentalized, indeed institutionalized, by municipalities. In 1961, a horse-trading principle was already established in New York City for the mutual benefit of investors and the city: project developers are allowed to exceed the building height or floor area ratio permissible by planning law if they invest in publicly accessible atriums, public usable spaces or the upgrading of subway stations. For creating 1 square meter of public usable area, investors can, for instance, be permitted 3 square meters of additional usable area in buildings, up to a maximum of 20 percent of the permissible total floor area. The Citigroup Center (formerly Citicorp Center) from 1977, raised up 35 meters above its plaza at street level, is a good example of this bonus principle, which lay behind an entire generation of high-rise office buildings (Fig. 51). Other cities in the USA established similar regulations in conjunction with the linkage programs that emerged in the 1980s. Higher construction on lots was permitted upon payment for urban planning measures, for residential construction, for landmark preservation et cetera.

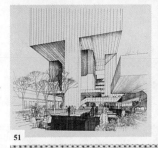

Architects also succeeded, through intelligent interpretation of existing laws, in erecting built structures that were never intended

by the lawmakers. The architect Benjamin Förster-Baldenius, for example, skillfully exhausted the full potential of the possibilities of German building law in his project *Hausgarten – Bauen ohne Genehmigung* (Garden—building without a permit) (Berlin, 2000, Fig. 52). For a typical Berlin allotment garden colony, he designed an additive structure from three components: a "sculpture," an "arbor," and a "greenhouse," each of which just barely still falls under the category *"genehmigungsfreie Vorhaben"* (approval-free projects) according to paragraph 56 of the *Landesbauordnung* (State Building Regulations). A habitable building with a total of almost 50 square meters was thus erected.

VAGUENESS

Based on the experience that future developments are not foreseeable, a number of planners thus intentionally leave many things in their projects vague and only determine a framework that relates to forms, dimensions and functions. Although the projects in their entirety remain descriptive, the planning requirements do not go beyond approximations, so that the freedom needed for later extension and adaptation of the project can develop. With a vague project, the planner proposes a procedure of fuzziness, without the process being open to anything and everything. Vagueness is an approach that uses planning requirements to start a preferably open controversy, in order to integrate the results into the project. Vagueness is an approach, on the basis of which potential variants can be explored.

Fumihiko Maki, a member of the Japanese Metabolist group that declared their technical-utopian manifesto of the organic-changeable city at the World Design Conference in Tokyo in 1960, worked at that time on the subject of "collective forms" (Fig. 53). Together with Masato Otaka, he presented a concept for the development of a district in Tokyo whose guiding notion was called "group form." With that, they meant a collection of built structures whose quantity could arbitrarily increase or diminish, because the composition as a whole was not subject to the laws of classic harmony. In contrast to the approaches of the usual "compositional form" or the newer "mega-form," group form was characterized by an inner structure in which the individual parts, although individually independent, were still linked by relationships to each other. Maki spoke of an additive system in which one could remove or add parts within a structural frame without jeopardizing the planning approach as a whole. His first built project, the Hillside Terrace apartments in Tokyo, was designed on this basis in 1966.

In his competition entry for the new Center for Art and Media (ZKM) in Karlsruhe, the Austrian architect Ottokar Uhl proposed in 1986 leaving "to themselves" the planning of the ZKM and its surroundings. Uhl wanted to make possible a process-oriented, open type of planning by using hardware and software. His plans thus showed not so much buildings, but rather procedures. The drawings simply determined vague areas, spaces, and limits, and indicated possibilities for development. Almost all the specifications are furnished with either the abbreviation "min." or "max." or the adjective "possible." The structure was thus to be established for an "electronic agora in the form of a construction site office." In it, all interested laymen and specialists were to receive a console with suitable programs and be connected via telephone with the project's nerve center. As many people as possible were to partake in the planning process and have an influence on the built result.

The British architect Cedric Price pursued such an idea of vagueness in his entire oeuvre. He wanted to determine nothing with his designs—and thus not restrict any leeway—but wanted much more to create new possibilities. In his drawings, one sees mostly lines that only consist of small dashes or dots. They vividly demonstrate potentials, without specifying them (Fig. 54).

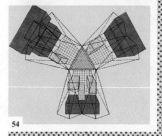

54

In the 1990s, the concept of "fuzzy logic", also relevant to architectural discourse, played a certain role in formal experiments. This theory for dealing with so-called fuzzy quantities in programming assumed that, in contrast to traditional quantities—in which a certain element of a given set can only be contained fully or not at all—with a fuzzy, or indistinct, quantity, such an element can also be contained in partial quantities. On this basis, washing machines can be programmed, for example, so that they control the amount of detergent according to how dirty the laundry is, even though the amount of soiling can't be determined precisely. This fragmenting principle in programming logic, with its paradigm of 0 or 1, poses fundamental questions for the common architectural and planning practice of functional assignment and spatial determination.

An innovative project that experiments with vagueness comes from the office of LIN / Finn Geipel and Giulia Andi. It is a design from 2004 for the transformation of unused railroad yards in Munich (Fig. 55). By means of landscape interventions—the reshaping into circular islands— is intended to form a "pioneer trailis," which refers more to the current state and potential for development of the site than finished solutions would have offered. Geipel and Andi thereby aimed at the possibility of an initial orientation in the direction of a constellation that, at the time of planning, could still not be discernable at all.

55

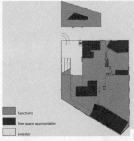

functions
free space appropriate
exterior

56

57

With the next steps, programmatic detail, connections, and expansions follow. An urban park will not emerge until the end of the process.

Even in building projects that could be realized, concepts of vagueness have been pursued time and again. The Quinta da Malagueira housing estate in Évora, Portugal was designed by Álvaro Siza in 1977 as an open, developable structure (Fig. 56). Between the individual ensembles of buildings, he conceived free "gaps" that were intended to be used differently or built upon in the long term. During construction of the École Nationale Supérieure d'Architecture (ENSA) in Nantes from 2006 to 2009, a highly economic frame construction enabled the architects Anne Lacaton and Jean-Philippe Vassal to offer—in addition to 12,500 square meters of programmed space—an additional 5,500 square meters of "extra space" that the school's users could freely appropriate (Fig. 57). For Albert Dietz and Anett-Maud Joppien, in the case of the 2004 UFO commercial building in Frankfurt am Main, it was a matter of incorporating programmatic vagueness by means of an overly dimensioned structure as well as an excess of means of access and technical equipment. As a result, the building can accommodate a wide variety of uses. That profusion in architecture enables openness was already articulated by Ludwig Mies van der Rohe in a pithy conversation with Hugo Häring in the 1920s: "Make your spaces big enough, man, so that you can walk around in them freely, and not just in one predetermined direction!"

The principle of vagueness found its way into the urban planning mainstream during the 1980s under the term "strategic planning," for example in Barcelona. Following the concept of the same name in business management, the gap between the determinism of master planning and the limited effectiveness of individual projects was overcome by combining a vague future scenario with precise, short-term projects.

OPEN FRAMEWORK

In the architecture as well as the urban design of the modern era, concepts were repeatedly developed in which the determination by means of a design or plan intentionally remained restricted and incomplete in order to make room for the undefined, for future developments, and for individual appropriation. For this—whether in architecture or urban design—a framework of overriding importance is defined in such a way that it guarantees spatial stability, coherence of the whole, formal consistency, and functional ability. Not more, however; because at the same time, large areas are offered—within the framework—which can be developed as desired and of which the architects and planners are divested of control.

In this regard, the frame construction method developed in the late nineteenth century opened up previously unimagined possibilities, as shown by Le Corbusier with his Domino House (1914/15, Fig. 58) and Ludwig Mies van der Rohe with his apartment building in the Stuttgart Weissenhofsiedlung (1926/27). But otherwise, a functionalistic-deterministic understanding of architecture dominated in classic Modernism. Opposing standpoints first began to emerge with the influential Metabolist and Structuralist movements in the 1960s.

58

For the Japanese Metabolists—who, as the name suggests, viewed urban processes as metabolism—cities were subjected to constant change and growth, which is why they sought to replace master planning with a systematic planning that would permit further development. They differentiated between primary and secondary structures. Permanent infrastructures were to form a stable framework within which elements—similar to the now renowned space capsules—could be shifted, replaced, and added (Kiyonori Kikutake, Mova Blocks, Tokyo 1959, Fig. 59).

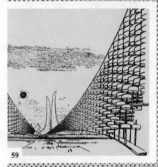

59

Whereas the Metabolists pursued a concept of technological-architectonic changeability, the European Structuralists were interested instead in social interaction. They wanted to provoke new forms of use by encouraging users to make structural changes to buildings. Herman Hertzberger's Diagoon houses in Delft (1967-1971, Fig. 60), for instance, are principally incomplete and likewise spatially varied in order to encourage the residents to reappropriate them repeatedly. In 1959, Georges Candilis, Alexis Josic, and Shadrach Woods had already planned unobstructed spaces with the technical basis for appropriation by their users in their *Proposition pour un habitat évolutif* (Proposal for an evolutionary habitat) (Fig. 61). The apartments were however missing every spatial-architectonic specificity that was essential for Hertzberger. For the new building of the Freie Universität Berlin (1963-1973) meant to unite multiple institutes and seminars, Candilis / Josic / Woods developed their approach further.

60

61

In his book *De Dragers en de Mensen* (trans: *Supports: An Alternative to Mass Housing*), in 1962 Nicolas John Habraken proposed to relinquish the design of residential floor plans to the inhabitants themselves. In 1965 he was named Director of the Foundation for Architectural Research (SAR), which was founded by ten architecture offices. This research group developed a concept of separation between support and infill. The support comprises all massive, site-specific building elements; it provides an open primary structure elaborated through grids and zones. The infill, on the contrary, can be personalized with the help of light, industrially manufactured non-location-specific elements (Fig. 62).

62

187

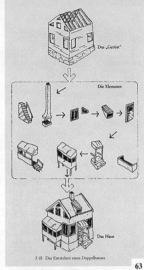

3.10 Das Entstehen eines Doppelhauses

63

64

Bands

65

In more conceptual rather than concrete terms, Lars Lerup demonstrated in his 1977 book *Building the Unfinished* (Fig. 63) that architecture is nothing permanent and emerges fully only through creative appropriation. He thus demanded acknowledgement of the experienced reality that cities and architecture always remain unfinished, and that precisely this incompleteness would enable the necessary appropriation. He placed the activist, who thinks and plans "interactionistically," in opposition to the prevalent manager-type of planner. In an architectural framework that necessarily acts restrictively—a "framework for living"—the residents could also become activists and take part in the negotiation of space, and thus gradually form a community. Lerup illuminated this process colorfully with an example of the incremental construction of a backyard garden in Berkeley, California, which the owner, Mrs. Ivy, built piece by piece and rented out. She controlled the process but also involved the tenants.

Even though some of the aforementioned projects make their arguments urbanistically, the principle of a developable framework was in all cases equivalent to an architectural strategy. Admittedly, the same principle existed in urban design well before these projects were conceived. At the beginning of the enormous urban growth of the late nineteenth century following industrialization, it was actually the basic principle of urban planning par excellence: one defined the street grid and with it, a spatial framework (Fig. 64); for the rest, the formation of the cities was relinquished to private investors and speculators who merely made accommodations for public safety. This form of sub-regulation led to overly concentrated, often heavily polluted cities with countless slums. High rates of illness and death were the consequence.

While investigating Manhattan's grid system in *Delirious New York*— published in 1978 at the beginning of the postmodern era— Rem Koolhaas rediscovered the advantages of "programmatic instability" and later transferred this concept to urban design schemes, such as the 1987 competition project for the new Paris suburb of Melun-Sénart (Fig. 65). The project defined programmatic bands with collective functions and zones kept free of buildings and left in their natural state, which—irrespective of the architecture to come—were to guarantee identity and even beauty. The islands between the bands have different circulation patterns, but otherwise remain undefined at first. Over the course of the twenty-year-long construction process, they can develop varying characters depending on the site, the architect and the program. Rem Koolhaas / O.M.A. attempted here, as in some other projects, to combine architectural specificity with programmatic indeterminacy.

The architect Florian Beigel took up this concept in order to concretize it in some of his own projects. For the former Witznitz coal briquette factory located south of Leipzig, from 1996 to 1999 he developed a strategy for situations of economic and social uncertainty. The landscape, or rather the "architectural infrastructure," defines spaces and materials but not uses, thus remaining open for the still unknown future development of the site. Experienceable, palpable qualities of spaces are meant to stimulate new uses; new activities not further defined are meant to be encouraged in a region that has been dominated by economic crisis and shrinking for a long time. The planning doesn't stipulate; it encourages and enables.

Operating with the concept of an open framework in urban design shifts the focus of design from built elements to landscape structures. Architects such as Florian Beigel and Charles Waldheim turned to landscape architecture, and more and more landscape architects are developing flexible urban design concepts. The list of offices that work in this manner includes, for example, Adriaan Geuze / West 8 in Rotterdam, James Corner / Field Operations in New York, Michel Desvigne in Paris, Lukas Schweingruber and Rainer Zulauf in Zurich, as well as Klaus Overmeyer in Berlin. These innovative strategies are exemplified by the Fresh Kills project (2001–, Fig. 66)—in which James Corner transformed the largest landfill in the world, on Staten Island in New York, into a people's park—and the Oerliker Park in Zurich (1996–2001, Fig. 67), designed by Lukas Schweingruber and Rainer Zulauf.

66

67

DIGITAL URBANITY

A conversation between Aram Bartholl and Philipp Oswalt

Philipp Oswalt: Fifty years ago, media theorists believed that with the advent of new media, cities would disintegrate and physical locations would lose their relevance; the category of space would no longer play a role. Yet in recent years we've experienced a boom in location-based media and information—be it satellite navigation, services such as Google Maps or Google Street View, or Geo Tags. In theory, one therefore speaks of enhanced or augmented urbanism and makes reference to the fact that new media are not causing the local to disintegrate, but, on the contrary, are strengthening it. How have new media changed the way we use the city?

Aram Bartholl: The classic notion is much like that in the movie *Matrix:* we are swimming in a liquid and everything is acted out in a virtual world. Yet today, it's the other way around, that is, we slip digital space over real space. What was initially a placeless network is now location-based. This becomes apparent in services by Google, Microsoft, or others that recreate the earth digitally, down to the last detail, integrating site-specific information. In the future, we'll no longer have to consult Google Maps for information, but will be able to summon them into everyday life, into public space via augmented reality,

PO: How does this change the way we perceive space?

AB: First and foremost with respect to the social benefit, our networking among one another. Among other things, with the result that the first thing that happens is: "Ah, I noticed that you were there yesterday, at that event." And we begin to journey digitally into town. For example, before I patronize a store, I view pictures of and comments made by others about it on the Internet. Without having been there, you already know a great deal about your destination and can form an opinion. And then when you're actually there, you discover that the store doesn't even exist anymore or has moved. It's interesting to note that this is how a big discrepancy develops between digital information and the reality in situ.

PO: But it gets interesting when it goes beyond being purely an aid—how do I find the place I wanted to visit? You say that virtual space is now being projected into real space. Virtual space is organized differently. You talked about social things, social media, and so on. What's projected into it that was previously not specific to urban space? Where's the difference?

AB: The relationship between public and private has changed radically in digital space. In particular for people who use services such as Facebook and the like and handle their personal information very publicly. In contrast, real public space in cultural circles is assigned fixed rules and codes of conduct. These are traditional social conventions that don't change quickly and differ from cultural circle to cultural circle. What I find interesting are the interfaces between real and digital space, for instance the question of how you get to know other people—in an online chat or in the conventional way in public space or at an event.

RadioBallet Leipzig, an event by the performance group Ligna in Leipzig's main train station, 2003

PO: An early example for the penetration of social interaction out of the virtual into urban space are flash and smart mobs. There are computer games in the meantime in which real urban space is the setting for the game. In your view, what are the other developmental trends looming ahead in the next few years or decades?

Flashmob pillow fight, Frankfurt, 2010

AB: An important area is personalized advertising in urban space. Companies such as Google will sooner or later introduce user-related, interactive advertising into public urban space, will place ads on screens in urban space. People who are actually standing in front of the advertising panel will be addressed with target marketing. Google uses information for this which it collects via services such as Facebook. Information obtained digitally will be used to be able to interact in urban space. This will certainly be one of the first phenomena to surface. In addition, there are numerous site-related projects and services, such as Foursquare or Gowalla. These are a mixture of a game and a location-based social network: Where was I? Where am I? Do I log in here?

The first stickers for certain services are meanwhile cropping up in urban space, be they Qype or Stickybits, that provide information about certain places. The stickers have codes you can use to log into digital space in situ. This is comparable to traffic signs in public space that control physical traffic. I can very well imagine that in future there will be a level of signs or visual icons in urban space with the aid of which you can explore digital space and navigate through it based on your location.

> PO: Where there would be a cross-reference to digital space in physical space? This has been around for several years now in the form of audio guides that can be retrieved by cell phone using location-based telephone numbers.

Map, Berlin Sculpture Park, 2008

AB: Yes, except that the technology has advanced. Square QR codes have established themselves in the meantime, which aren't only used in the area of logistics, by the postal service, or when booking tickets for events. They've long since begun appearing in urban space, for example on billboards. I can retrieve information anywhere in town by means of wireless Internet connections. And these tags contain references to the respective digital content.

> PO: Physical space thus becomes a navigation level for digital space; I discover references to a range of information being offered in digital space. Conversely, it can also happen that I navigate differently in physical space with digital navigation aids than I was accustomed to doing previously. And so I suspect that this also changes the way I use space. In historical terms, centrality always played a role in urban planning: Main Street was also where I found certain key functions—the church, the post office, the city government, the most important businesses, and so on. This is less relevant today, because navigation aids and selection mechanisms can deliberately find things that, although they might be located off the beaten path, correspond exactly to what I need.

AB: Sure, due to specific filters and precision in the Net you can of course navigate more selectively through town, get your bearings, and pick out special things as well. The question hanging in the air is: how does a city itself actually change? This question shows that the digital is so ubiquitous and so flexible that the city as such isn't cancelled out so quickly. The home as an enclosure structured around man will naturally continue to be necessary. What changes, for instance, are working situations or the dynamics of products or buying. There will be more delivery service, for example, and less shopping in stores; spatial centers will shift, and so on.

PO: There probably isn't any pressure for structures to change, but the way they're used will change significantly, because you can also more quickly reorganize them by means of additional information. It's now easier to change the information than to change physical structures.

AB: That's true in any case.

PO: Linking virtual with physical space can also enable or strengthen the coexistence of different readings of the same physical space. In that the one uses the space with this digital information background and the other with that, different parallel perspectives of the same space become possible.

Advertisement with a quick response code that can be read by passers-by with the use of their cellphone, Tokyo, 2009

AB: Yes, that's hardly physically tangible, but involves social space. With services such as Foursquare, the game principle is that I log in at certain places as often as possible, which means that I'm also actually at that place. Then I get points and batches are unlocked. He or she who's there most often is then the "mayor." And some people frequent certain places in order to stay at the top of the list. Some bars and localities give the "mayor" a free drink or other extras. A game develops around the location that is strongly influenced by the digital social network. And the same thing happens with photographs of places and geo tags. These can also be read locally or filtered. It's chiefly this social aspect that plays a role here.

The multiperspectivity and the erosion of one-time centrality also show themselves in a quite different respect. A fine example of this is citizen journalism: countless people are physically present at places in a variety of situations and document them by taking photographs or shooting a video. And according to how relevant they are, these images immediately land in the mainstream media, generating a powerful social impact. These are currently pivotal developments. And all of this will continue to evolve—we're still in a start-up phase.

PO: Much more specific forms of publicness are being produced nowadays due to the development of new social networks, because specific preferences can come together via networks, via filter functions, something that was previously not possible in this way. Traditional social networks are family, neighborhood, institutional bonds, employers, school, stores. Today, social networks are being created via completely different parameters, for example, based on certain lifestyle parameters, certain ideals, even isolated from established everyday practices and contexts. The Dutch photographer Bas Princen, for example, has documented new recreational activities that organize themselves via these kinds of digital networks.

AB: It used to be the chat room in which hackers met who were scattered across the globe. In the meantime, however, digital space has more and more become a reflection of the classic social space you just described. Today, if I'm a student and have schoolmates, then they're naturally online at the same time. As adults we can't imagine what's happening today in this phase of adolescence, in which social structures are radically changing. "Who is my friend? Who is my best friend?" Services such as Facebook and StudiVZ have a very strong influence on this.

PO: You're in New York right now, for example, and by communicating online, your chances of meeting someone who interests you professionally increase, because you can also be more specifically located. We're having this conversation for a book on temporary use. How can these processes impact phenomena of temporary use? Our assumption is that new media enable new forms of spatial appropriation, in particular spontaneous and momentary spatial organization.

The new media facilitate dealing actively with the city. They enable editing the city. Temporary uses are concerned less with construing new spaces than with locating existing urban spaces in order to edit and curate them; with forming networks and activating others. This is all more an issue of social organization and not one of physical change, and this—as you have described—is precisely the potential of the new media.

AB: Yes, you've already mentioned the classic examples—flash mobs or spontaneous parties. These are certainly signs for this. In the meantime, however, there's the Serendipity iPhone application by Marc Sheppard, which while displaying the route from A to B, generates a detour via various hot spots and islands. In this way, the coincidence is again introduced that you used to have when you lost your way in town.

I'm currently working here in New York on the project *Dead Drops*, classically a place where spies handed over items or information. I plant USB sticks on the walls of buildings in the city so that only the plug is sticking out, and people can dock on to the stick with their laptops, that is, link up directly to the building, in order to leave behind or record data. And they're offline, not connected to the Internet. The Internet is virtually ubiquitous with wireless access, but this also makes it arbitrary. Now, if I have a friend who releases an album on a dead drop, then anyone who wants to have it actually has to travel to Brooklyn in order to retrieve it. In this way, there's a very concrete connection to an urban site.

> PO: You've also projected processes and elements from virtual into urban space in other projects. In the "Map" project, you produced the Google Map pins as meter-tall sculptures in urban space. Is there also a counterdevelopment—the increased projection of physical into virtual space?

AB: This is exactly what's happening now with all these maps and 3D world services such as Google Earth or Bing Maps. Everything is emulated digitally and enhanced with photographs from private individuals, who can likewise be located.

> PO: Can you then say that digital space, which was originally construed as being something very different, is changing due to this reciprocal penetration of the physical and the digital? That, as there are no longer any opposing organizational principles, it results in a fusion?

Dead Drops, New York, 2010

AB: At the moment, services such as Facebook are becoming relevant, which also include depictions of physical space—in concrete terms, Facebook Places—even if this continues to use conventional 2D Web sites. You can enter your current location in order to more effectively exchange information in the social network. However, lots of people have misgivings about revealing their own physical location.

There are various Web 2.0 services that deal with locations on the basis of which they specifically organize their social network. It began with the travel network Doppler, in which I indicate the city I'm currently in and the one I'll be in, and then I can see who among my circle of friends and colleagues will also be there for a conference. And then there are services such as Foursquare, where you can log in and leave comments, your GPS coordinates are displayed, and the whole thing becomes a kind of game. The whole point of Foursquare is that you log in as often as possible at certain locations and see who was already there, who did something there, or who wrote comments. Finally, there are auxiliary modules such as Facebook Places.

Even the older concepts of augmented reality, Second Life and numerous computer games, for example, precisely take aim at the fusion of the physical with the digital world—an interpenetrating and mutually reinforcing nexus of digital and physical space.

culti
vating

Urban development through temporary use has long been a reality. But can it be planned? How can city planners learn from temporary users and integrate informal practices into their planning? In open-source city planning, the planner's task is less to establish facts than

tempo rary use

to create new possibilities. The users themselves become producers of the urban environment. On the basis of such experimental projects, six different strategies can be described. These approaches highlight a new field of possibilities in dealing with city planning and temporary use.

WHAT IS TO BE DONE?

With temporary uses more and more often playing a strategic role in urban development, the question arises what city planning can learn from them. How can the potential of unanticipated developments and the energy of spontaneous uses be incorporated into planning processes? Can temporary users do more than serve as stopgaps until the return of economic demand? How can their potential be harnessed for long-term developments? Are alternative models conceivable for a brand of urban development that does not dictate or define but rather enables?

With the subject of temporary use, fundamental parameters of classical urban development are called into question. Traditionally, planning begins by formulating an end result and then proceeds to consider how that result can be achieved. With temporary use, this relationship is reversed: one begins by asking how a dynamic can be engendered, without defining an ideal final state. In this scenario, planning is restricted to a time-limited intervention that does not seek to dictate the total development. Such a minimalist approach to planning acquires strategic significance particularly in phases of transition: through targeted interventions, it is possible to instigate, accelerate, or facilitate the transition from one state to another. For long periods of time, no planning intervention whatsoever is undertaken. Development is largely left to pursue its own trajectory.

In this way, planning acquires the character of "enabling," a notion first introduced in the 1960s by the British architect Cedric Price.[1] According to Price, the primary aim of planning is not to specify an ideal state but to open up new possibilities for the participants. In the context of temporary use, this amounts to a kind of "weak planning," in which resources and energies are activated by the removal of development obstacles and inhibitions, by de- and reformalization, and by the reinterpretation and conversion of existing structures. With this approach, a minimum of effort achieves maximum effect.

This entails a shift in the role of the planner. The heroic and visionary designer is replaced by an agent working on others' behalf. He or she is not a "decider" but rather an enabler who brings the various actors together. The users themselves become producers of space. The planner's role is that of a strategist, agent, or curator. He or she mediates among the disparate worlds of the users, owners, and governmental bodies. With the abandonment of the grand final plan, the instruments of planning change as well. Instead of a situation dominated by an architectural and city-planning design whose realization requires that all other actions be subordinated to it, there are multiple different actions that take place in parallel. In addition to spatial and constructional interventions, which continue to be important, these actions primarily consist of economic, legal, communicative, and organizational measures. They may include payment guarantees, loans, and rental agreements, as well as press campaigns and the formation of interest groups or round tables. The change in the nature of the instruments reflects the change in the content of planning. For rather than the question of built form, the dominating issue is that of the program.

OPEN SOURCE CITY PLANNING

When applied to city planning, the idea of enabling may be compared to the open source principle. On analogy with the open source principle in software programming, whose recipe for success is "open source = many ideas," urban development can also benefit from this fundamental idea by involving a broad range of social initiatives in the genesis of the city, by allowing citizens, not just to inspect plans, but to design the urban landscape themselves.

But what is the difference between open source city planning and classical planning models? There are three key aspects.

1. Planning Becomes Dynamic

Unlike traditional master planning, dynamic planning only defines rough objectives at the outset; this is done on the basis of possible use programs, built and unbuilt spaces, and webs of spatial relations and densities. The "source code" of the existing structures of a disused site represents the principal foundation for open source urbanism; the latter's goal is to define as little as possible and as much as necessary.

The principle of dynamic development turns classical planning mechanisms upside down. Instead of first achieving an accumulation of building volumes and then renting space to users, open source urbanism seeks to bring about a gradually increasing concentration of activities, programs, and networks, which little by little begin to express themselves in constructional terms as well.

In the first phase, the emphasis is on the informal activation of the area— securing usable constructional resources, stimulating public awareness, and cultivating temporary uses. Directly interacting with spaces produces an idea of a site's potential, above all a notion of how it might be used. The result is an initial activation without a large investment of capital. The period that separates the existing state of the site from its desired condition (the realization of the planning goal) is more effectively utilized; valuable stimuli are provided for long-term development. If the process of informal revitalization is successful, the site comes back into use. A specific public identity comes into being. What were originally temporary users may even become renters or owners later on.

Examples of this approach are the planning of the Revaler Viereck (a former railroad repair works in Berlin), the NT area in Basel, and the KDAG factory grounds in Vienna, where many of the preexisting buildings were preserved. All of these projects began with small-scale measures that might be compared to "acupuncture treatments," in which access points were created, infrastructure was reactivated, buildings were converted, and surfaces were modified. In this way, the planning effort supported a lively appropriation of the area even before the construction of any new buildings, and that process of appropriation has gone on to serve as an important catalyst for all subsequent development.

Thus, in open source city planning, the planning of buildings and open space is less important at the beginning of a project than it is in its later stages, once clear uses have developed and can be planned for with the long term in mind. As the process goes forward, the plan is checked against reality and continuously adapted.

2. Shared Control

To play, as it were, with a site's possibilities in the opening phase of a project by exploring a variety of uses without any prior investment in construction—this is a method that involves surrendering a fair amount of the control, design, and utilization of the site to its active users. However, this supposed loss of "supreme planning authority" can lead to the minimization of risk and to a win-win situation for all involved. In difficult economic and city planning situations, new developments can be sparked when owners, municipalities, and active citizens overcome existing barriers and release synergies. Precisely what role the principle of shared control actually plays in particular open source planning projects depends on the ownership structure and the constellations of actors. The prospects for user participation are more favorable when the public sector leases an area to a group for a low price, or when the chances for successfully marketing a site are so poor that the owner is happy to have users of any kind and is more than willing to hand it over to these particular users for a period of time.

An innovative example is the borough of Amsterdam Noord. Here the city held a competition for the temporary use of a shipyard hall and, in this way, incorporated local initiatives into the urban development process. In the best-case scenario, the users themselves become owners—for example, thanks to temporary financing provided by sympathizers or foundations—and can freely decide what to do with the site. In the case of projects with private owners, the likelihood that the development process will be left entirely in the users' hands is slim. In practice, where a site is privately owned, the creation of "open source islands" is a more realistic prospect. Either the owner allows a limited period of time for broad involvement by multiple users, or else he or she limits the open source approach to a portion of the overall area in hopes that the rest of the site will benefit from it as well. Here too there are positive real-world examples: with the help of its municipal Broedplaatsfonds (or "breeding ground fund"), the city of Amsterdam creates financial incentives for private project developers who are willing to enter into an organic development process involving temporary uses.

3. Sampling

In open source processes, site designs and use concepts do not come about as the result of architectural competitions and approval planning efforts. Instead, they come about as the result of action. The existing planning instruments, however, are not intended to facilitate the direct appropriation of space but are focused instead on the establishment of permanent structures. They must therefore be supplemented by new management tools that, on the one hand, make it easier to work with unfinished states and transitory situations and, on the other, lower the entry bar for active involvement on the part of a broad range of participants. In the same way that sampling is used in music to create carpets of sound with distinctive sonic patterns, city planning seeks to expand the latitude for action, to integrate short- and long-term action, and to devise planning strategies that combine hard and soft tools. Calls for ideas that invite applications for pioneering uses, the cultural activation of public sites, the manipulation of access points, the recoding of preexisting structures, and the creation of networks of actors supplement the provision of infrastructure and the design of public spaces, that is, construction activity.

THE ENABLING STATE

For several decades now, the notion of the social welfare state has increasingly been replaced by that of the economically oriented "lean" state. The resulting increase in social problems is supposed to be addressed by the concept of the "activating state" (to use the new buzzword). The state spurs civil society to assume social welfare tasks itself. Thus, this notion implies the existence of a passive population that must be activated by the state. Despite this note of paternalism, however, the state is also determined to carry out former social welfare tasks in a cost-effective manner.

By contrast, the notion of the "enabling state" is based on the initiative of the citizens themselves. It sees the potential for significant social impulses precisely in the actors' ability to organize without external control. From this perspective, it is the task of the state to support actors who are innovative but lack sufficient capital, to stand by them as cooperation partners and allies in cases where their activity has positive consequences for development and social cohesion. This concept counteracts the antisocial consequences of neoliberal conceptions of policymaking and politics—as expressed in such slogans as "strengthen the strong"—without, however, falling back into the paternalistic mold of the classical welfare state. In terms of open source urban planning, this means enabling financially weak actors to actively design the city.

This approach is expressly not a matter of multimillion-euro support programs but rather of making intelligent use of governmental authority and available resources as well as activating untapped potentials. The reformulation of legal regulations (planning law, property law, neighborhood law) can make it easier to find innovative solutions and reduce the hurdles faced by weaker actors. Accelerated permitting procedures for temporary uses, the possibility of short-term licenses, and reduced legal standards for plans involving minimal construction can make it considerably easier to activate disused urban areas. Another approach that has great potential is the reform of property law. Thus, in the Netherlands, property owners' rights are restricted in order to make buildings that stand empty for a long time available to the public. In return, the owner's liability or level of property taxes can be reduced, something that is already being done in Leipzig, for example, through the use of license agreements. The situation is even simpler when the government makes state-owned buildings available. In this case, short-term, purely fiscal calculations must give way to long-term cost-benefit analyses that take the entire society into account.

The state can also play an important role as mediator between the various private actors. By providing a payment guarantee for the initial phase of the project, the borough of Friedrichshain-Kreuzberg actually made it possible for temporary use of the Revaler Viereck railroad area to proceed. For in this way the borough created the conditions in which the private owner was willing to offer a rental agreement to the temporary users. As a mediating agent, the state helps to eliminate obstacles and inhibitions and brings together space providers and interested users into temporary use pools.

PARADOXES OF MANAGEMENT

As enablers and supporters of informal uses, municipalities frequently find themselves faced with a twofold dilemma: the existing management and planning instruments are designed to maximize control and definition, while the fostering of user-oriented projects calls for openness, autonomous momentum, and the surrender of control. City governments are often afraid of this contradiction and refuse to even consider taking on the role of enabler.

An additional paradox is that attempts both to integrate financially weak actors by organizing programs to eliminate vacancy and to encourage business creation or neighborhood initiatives sometimes have the opposite effect, especially in inner-city areas. New identities and scenes attract additional investment; established firms and solvent renters materialize. The primary beneficiaries of rising rents and real estate prices are property owners and investors. The original initiators of the transformation, however—provided they have not become owners themselves—are excluded from the value creation chain. Certainly the upgrading of urban neighborhoods leads to an improvement of living conditions for their residents. When it is the users themselves, however, who have driven the development in question by their own efforts, it may reasonably be asked to what extent they themselves benefit from the "upgrade," be it through secure lease agreements, options to buy, or financial compensation.

The paradoxes of management cannot be resolved. Their contradictions, however, make it necessary for urban developers—a group that includes private actors and users in addition to cities and towns—to grapple more intensively with the intersection of informal activation and formal planning, control and autonomous momentum, profit and non-profit, professional design and design through use.

STRATEGIES FOR URBAN DEVELOPMENT THROUGH TEMPORARY USE

It goes without saying that these principles do not pretend to be a magic remedy for unmarketable disused sites and the absence of investment. They do, however, open up new avenues toward an alternative form of urban development. The focus of this approach is the designing of space by users with little capital who become active in their own right. The open source method offers them the opportunity to be more than mere temporary stopgaps. On the contrary, they are given the opportunity to become serious partners and catalysts of a use- and process-oriented form of urban development. The latter should not be restricted to strategies of recycling like beach cafés and pony rides. Its goal must be to synchronize the stages of formal planning (competition, outline plan, development plan) with the phases of informal activation (establishment and cultivation of temporary uses). In the best-case scenario, the formal planning process is so open that, as in the case of the Revaler Viereck, the informal development of uses becomes part of the forward projection and realization of the plan. Thus, actor- and program-focused conceptions of development do not by any means exclude traditional city planning. But it is an outrage when city planning excludes actors.

The six strategies presented below are all based on different intentions and constellations of actors. Each model influences and modifies the character of temporary uses in its own particular way. Whereas the strategy of "enabling" is the one that most fully accommodates the unpredictable character of possible uses and is wedded to the perspective of the users, in the case of the strategy of "exploitation" priority is given to the interests of the owner or municipality, to which the range of possible uses is subordinated. Each of these models is incomplete, since each one only corresponds to a limited stage of development, so that in the course of a project multiple strategies may be employed. Strategies like "enabling" and "initiating" stand at the beginning of temporary uses, while interventions that employ the strategy of "formalization" cannot take place until much later on.

This overview of strategies is based on the study and conceptualization of a practice— still quite young—in which architects, planners, agents, owners, investors, municipalities, and users incorporate the practice of temporary uses, which has always existed, into classical forms of city planning and real estate development. It was only once the shortcomings, indeed the crisis of the model of the "entrepreneurial city," which was introduced in the 1970s, had been recognized that the subject of temporary use began to spark interest beyond the subcultures. With the growing importance of the "cultural industries" on the one hand and the critical shrinking of so many locations on the other, efforts to incorporate temporary uses into urban development will increase.

When informal uses are combined with classical planning, both are transformed; something different from both of them arises. This fusion initially has a paradoxical character, for in many respects it attempts to combine what are actually polar opposites: one term is based on small, short-term steps without a long-term goal, the other on a grand final vision. One of them essentially operates from the bottom up, the other from the top down. One of them attempts to enable development without capital, while the purpose of the other is in most cases capital growth. The new hybrid of open source urbanism will not be able to preserve the authentic anarchistic character of informal uses; nor will it be able to achieve the security, stability, and singleness of purpose associated with classical planning. Nor will it exhibit the "one true face" of an alternative city planning. Instead, it will give rise to a variety of hybrids: short-term and long-lasting ones, goal-oriented and open-ended ones, spatially compact and fragmented ones. There is one thing, however, that all the heterogeneous forms of open source urbanism have in common: they all incorporate spaces, actors, and developments into the process of city planning that classical city planning has long since ceased to reach.

NOTES

1 Royston Landau, "A Philosophy of Enabling: The Work of Cedric Price," in: Cedric Price, *Works II* (London: Architectural Association, 1984), 9ff. See also "Das Ungewisse, Die Freude am Unbekannten, Philipp Oswalt im Gespräch mit Cedric Price," *Arch Plus,* No. 109/110 (1991): 51ff.

STRATEGIES FOR ACTION

ENABLE

The inhibition thresholds for temporary uses are broken down: possibilities for using derelict spaces are pointed out and publicized, access to these spaces is made easier, communication between property owners and potential users is improved, and legal problems are solved. The initiative for all this is taken by the city, property owner, or agent, whose goal is to revive a sizeable urban area with many little-used properties and make it dynamic. Programmatically unspecific, the intervention is open to the as yet unknown ideas of prospective users.

A typical example of this strategy is the placement agency: as an intermediary between property owners and users, it generally has access to a pool of available properties. In addition to direct mediation it also takes care of legal issues such as liability, designing the contract (license agreement), and obtaining a permit. This function is usually assumed by the city—or sometimes a nonprofit association—which is able to assist with the process in important ways, whether by cosigning leases, providing municipal liability insurance, or radically simplifying the process of obtaining permits and communicating with the authorities through the creation of one-stop offices.

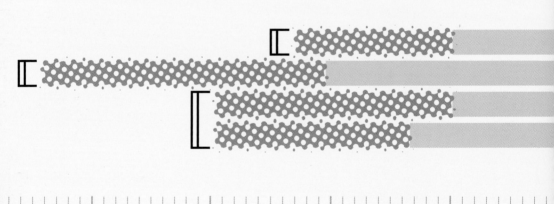

INITIATE

Agents initiate a cluster of temporary uses for a sizeable unused area—an agreement with the property owner and the resolution of legal questions creates a foundation for users. The starting point is sizeable derelict inner-city sites for which there are no commercial development opportunities in the short or medium term and that are also too big for individual temporary users. Planners, associations, or alternative real estate developers act as agents to develop a short- to midterm strategy for the location and interact with the property owner and licensing authorities to negotiate a concept with possibilities for the activities of a wide variety of users. Within this framework, there then arises a cluster of extremely diverse activities, whose profile and programmatic orientation bear the stamp of the self-conception of the initiators, their networks and motivations.

Users fight for contested spaces and spaces for contested activities. Their efforts are based on a programmatic idea that generally stands in conflict with the objectives of the property owner and city planning authorities. The intention is to create new public spaces that generate new cultural and social impulses and are protected from commercial development, a social platform in which many different groups participate, some of which are marginalized in the formal city. Central to success is a public debate, which the initiators generate by means of actions in the public space and reporting in the media. The illustration of alternative use scenarios and their potential also arouses the interest of the public.

COACH

Users and interested parties are given support and linked together into a network. This leads to the creation of joint platforms, which increase the network's public presence and lend its members greater weight for carrying out their objectives. Support of this kind may be self-organized (as in the case of the Clubkommission, or Club Commission, in Berlin), or it may be provided by sympathizing agents (as with Stalker: Ararat, Rome) or by the government (as in the case of neighborhood management). Whereas self-organization, stabilization, and further development promote uses that originated on their own, government intervention within the framework of a crisis management effort often seeks to eliminate local deficits by stimulating civil society activities. When taken to an extreme, this leads to the simulation of use and urban life—autonomous and independent activities are replaced by the artificially generated and short-lived animation of areas.

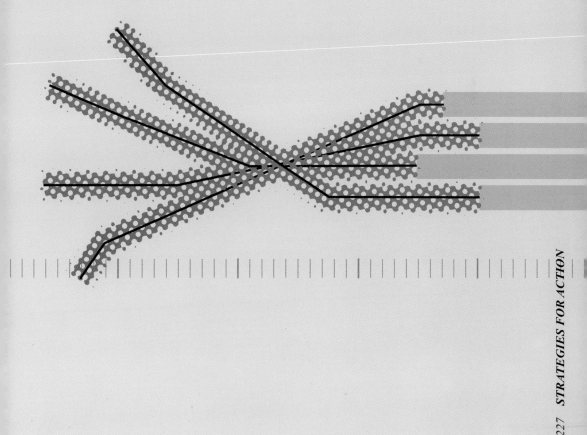

FORMALIZE

Successful temporary uses have generated a critical mass, and there is now a desire to use their potential for the long term. Improvised, informal solutions give way to lasting structures such as open-ended leases and permits, consolidated legal structures, and professionalized management. The goals of such consolidation and perpetuation vary depending on the actors involved. Solid business models are developed in the service of an economic interest (as in the case of Arena in Berlin), associations work to enhance their neighborhoods (RAW-Tempel e.V., Berlin), and cultural politicians champion new programs (Tempodrom, Berlin). When a use becomes formalized, its profile changes, and these transformations sometimes fail, as shown by the example of the Tempodrom in Berlin. The impetus for formalization may come from external pressure and the endangerment of the use, for example by the threat of eviction; or it may be based on a potential for development, for example long-term rental income or an option to purchase the building.

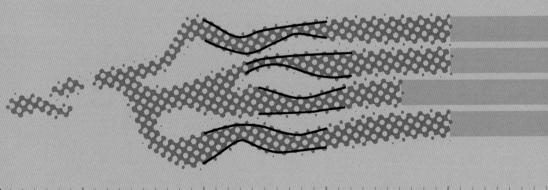

EXPLOIT

Temporary uses are employed by third parties as a way of pursuing interests of their own. Property owners initiate temporary uses in order to win public awareness for their sites and build up use milieus that attract commercial users. In doing so, they benefit from the fact that today's temporary users organize important programs for the life of the city and are able to attract a great deal of attention with their public events, whether in art, culture, entertainment, recreation, or other areas. In this way, the temporary users also generate the cultural milieus that are so important in today's knowledge society and whose proximity is increasingly being sought by commercial developers. Through targeted interventions such as selecting the users or defining framework conditions, the property owners are able to influence the profile of the temporary use in accordance with their plans. Despite such exploitation, collaborations like these can be beneficial for both sides. Such models also receive support from town planning authorities, which see them as a way to promote a vital mixture of uses and urban diversity in the city's neighborhoods.

By contrast, when fashion labels adopt temporary use models as a way of marketing their products and brands, the result is a one-sided exploitation with no productive spin-offs. Whether it be Adidas, Nike, or Comme des Garçons, the imitation of subcultural activities attracts young target groups and helps lend the brand in question a hip profile.

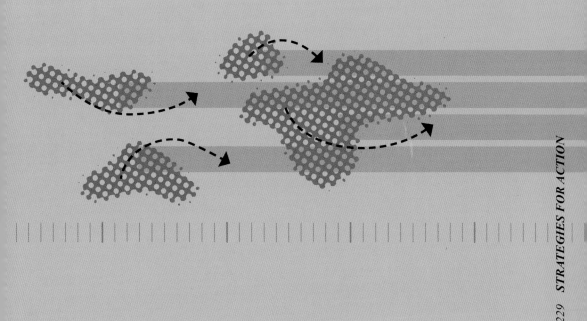

ENABLE

The strategy of enabling seeks to facilitate the creation of temporary uses by lowering initial hurdles and removing obstacles. A key role in this process is played by a neutral mediator between owner and user whose position is usually funded or supported by the city. Generally speaking, no attempt is made to influence the profile of the use or the makeup of the user group directly—the decisive impulses regarding the content of the use come from the users themselves. The motivating factor is rather an overarching concept of urban development that goes beyond individual temporary uses, a desire to revitalize urban spaces and create opportunities for a broader range of actors.

The mediator is a kind of agent who, in part through his or her own considerable competence and commitment, wins the trust of the various actors and, as a moderator, manages communication among them, negotiating, making connections, and overseeing the implementation of agreements. These agents are either part of the city government or else private individuals or people from civil society groups, working on behalf of the city or on their own initiative.

Those agents who do form part of the city administration sometimes have no official assignment but operate under the radar out of a sense of their own commitment, making use of their room for maneuver in a kind of micropolitics. In this way, for example, Jutta Weitz played a central role as a leader in the city's leasing of commercial space in Berlin-Mitte in the 1990s. Similarly, the original impulse for the extremely successful project einfach-mehrfach in Vienna came from individual city government employees, who succeeded in having their concept for the temporary use of particular public spaces established as a long-term official project of the city of Vienna (see p. 238). A liaison office was created as a one-stop office. As a mediating entity within the administration, this office shortens the participants' path through the thicket of official agencies, radically simplifies the process of getting permits, and also helps in other ways to facilitate communication among the participants.

The assignment of spaces to temporary users through the public sector can, however, prove to be problematic, which has less to do with the agency itself than with general municipal conditions. This is shown by, among others, the Neuland project in Berlin. In the vicinity of to the huge residential slabs and tower blocks built in the borough of Marzahn-Hellersdorf on the eastern edge of Berlin in the 1970s and 1980s, due to the massive decline in the birthrate in the past decade, far more than 100 schools and preschools became superfluous and were consequently demolished. Because Marzahn-Hellersdorf has no further use for the fallow land, it has been transferred by legislation into a municipal property fund with the aim of the yield-oriented marketing of the properties. Thus, a large part of the properties have reached a dead end: due to a lack of demand and of potential buyers, on one hand; and on the other hand, because the borough no longer has the open spaces at its disposal.

The goal of the Neuland space and communication strategy, initiated in 2006, was to find users for the idle properties in cooperation with a local coordination office for temporary usage. This was meant to encourage neighborly commitment, improve public offers, promote entrepreneurial action, and attract new investments in the long term.

Selected idle sites were marked with arrows, flags, ground and tree markings, and made

known with the aid of flyers as well as a web site. Interestingly enough, it was primarily social fringe groups, such as the Russian-Germans, who showed interest in using the idle sites. After initial successes in the start-up phase, for various reasons, the process faltered and ultimately failed completely. The main problem was that while the initiative experienced a broad spectrum of ideas largely related to the public good, such as vegetable production, youth camps, field preschools, or sculpture parks, the potential users could not afford the leasing prices of the property fund, which is oriented toward marketing.

Subsequent to this experience, in strategic partnerships with the housing associations, the municipal actors concentrated more strongly on activating selected sites with the aid of the immediate residents and through more closely controlled projects structured according to content. The sites are owned by building societies that also promote "unprofitable" uses in order to keep tenants in the long term by means of a stabilization of the residential environment.

Compared to city governments, private agencies and associations are usually more flexible. For example, in Leipzig-West the idea of regenerating and thus rescuing *Gründerzeit* neighborhoods threatened by vacancy and decay—an idea born in the context of the city's neighborhood management effort—nearly failed because of obstacles and objections within the city administration. It wasn't until the independent nonprofit association HausHalten e.V. was created as a mediator between private owners and temporary users that the project could be realized successfully. The city is cooperating with the association.

As a result of the increasing spread and popularity of temporary use as a tool for city and neighborhood development, professional service providers have begun to spring up in the field. In Berlin in 2005 the Zwischennutzungsagentur (Temporary Use Agency) was created in order to reactivate 100 vacant salesrooms through temporary use in the

Prediction of day care center and school vacancies by the year 2020 in Marzahn-Hellersdorf

Reuterkiez area of the Neukölln borough of Berlin within the framework of the program Soziale Stadt (Social City). In the two years that followed, of the 100 salesrooms, more than 56 could be rented and roughly 200 new jobs created. The rental contracts were very short-term, and at € 1 and 1.5 per square meter, the rents were very low without being subsidized. In the associated Lokale Kooperationsnetze Eigentümer und Nutzer (Local Cooperation Networks Owners and Users) project, the temporary use agency promoted the further development of successfully begun approaches to action and the networking of small businesses. In the meantime, the project chiefly concentrates on the owners in the neighborhood and attempts to actively include them in the development of the district.

TOOLS

The central task of agents and agencies is to help temporary users find suitable spaces and help owners find suitable users. In the simplest cases it is sufficient to arrange for a participant to receive information or help them make the necessary contacts, that is, to provide some initial help with communication between the actors. For this purpose, web-based databases with pools of spaces and users are increasingly under discussion, for example in the case of the Leipzig association HausHalten e.V. and the Zwischennutzungsagentur in Berlin. However, such databases do not replace but only supplement actual face-to-face consultation. In order to lower the entry bar for users even further, financial support can

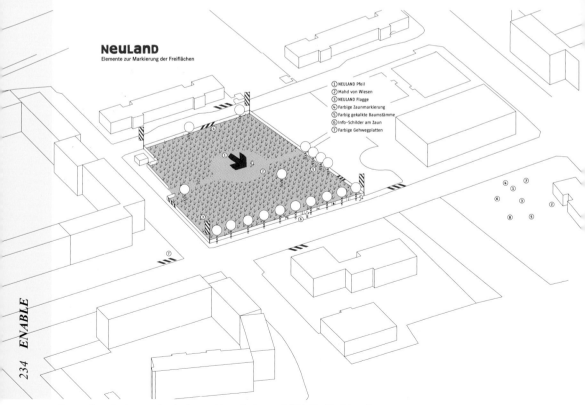

Suggestions for intervening in the marking of a brownfield in Berlin-Marzahn

also be helpful in the form of donations, rent subsidies, loans, and microcredits (which are more familiar in the context of developing and newly industrializing countries). Direct material and personal support can be helpful as well, including helping participants locate or procure construction materials, used furniture, and technical infrastructure as well as making efforts in the framework of job creation programs and social welfare projects.

For the owner, the determining factor is the existence of a reliable contractual partner. In the case of the project RAW-Tempel in Berlin, for example, it was possible to persuade the owner, Vivico, to accept the temporary use of its buildings for cultural activities by means of a kind of guarantee model. During the initial phase of the project, tensions were eased when the borough administration of Friedrichshain-Kreuzberg took charge of the buildings and then sublet them to the temporary users. This guaranteed the owners that the rent would be paid and also gave them legal indemnity. Similarly, in Leipzig the association HausHalten e.V. functions as a dependable contractual partner for the owners. The association then rents the spaces to the temporary users. In doing so it reduces the owners' risk as well as the effort and expense that would otherwise be involved in supervising the properties. In the case of the project einfach-mehrfach in Vienna, the deciding factor for both private and public property owners was the fact that the city of Vienna used its municipal liability insurance to cover the risk arising from the grant of use for the owners with respect to the safety of the properties involved.

All of this once again demonstrates the great potential of enabling strategies. By operating intelligently, making use of existing resources, and using only a small amount of government funds, impressive results can be achieved. Of special interest to cities is the possibility of tying the awarding of new construction rights—a change of use, for example, or an increase in building density—to concessions for temporary use on the part of the owner, a practice formally engaged in Great Britain and informally in Germany and Austria.

CONCLUSIONS

In contrast to the regulating role of the social welfare state and the paternalistic role of the activating state, the strategy of enabling stands for a state that does not dictate but rather creates opportunities, in the consciousness that responsibility is shared by society as a whole. This approach demands a certain restraint on the part of government entities or a willingness to pull back when the time is right, in order to ensure that temporary uses have independence and the ability to develop freely and to keep a relationship of dependency— for example in the form of permanent supervision—from even arising. The concept of enabling is the strategy that is most in a position to preserve and promote the originary qualities of temporary use.

FURTHER INFORMATION
www.neuland-berlin.org
www.einfach-mehrfach.wien.at
www.kreativgesellschaft.org
www.haushalten.org
www.zwischennutzungsagentur.de

Search, communicate, facilitate, develop, store
Core tasks of municipal coordination offices for temporary use

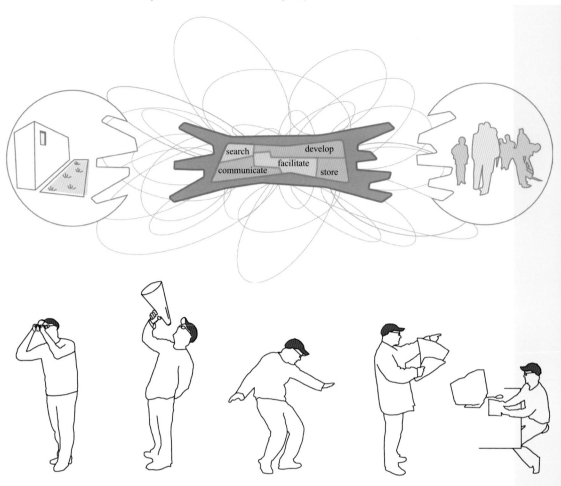

Michl
Mellauner

OBJECTIVE: To enable alternative cultural and recreational
offerings through dual use of
available open spaces

PROTAGONIST: Kommunale
Koordinationsstelle für Mehr-
fachnutzung der Stadt Wien
(Municipal Liaison Office for
Multiple Use of the City of
Vienna)

USE: Sports, culture, recreational activities for children
and young people, urban
gardens

STATUS: Municipal program

PLACES: Vacant lots, school
playgrounds, underpasses,
other public and private lots in
Vienna

TRAJECTORY: 1997 develop-
ment of the concept by the
Magistrat der Stadt Wien
(Municipality of Vienna), 1998
creation of the Kommunale
Koordinierungsstelle, ongoing

COST: Cost of individual
projects is borne by the
districts; Kommunale
Koordinierungsstelle is
financed by the municipality

In Vienna there is a shortage of open spaces, while those
that exist are strictly regulated and sometimes inadequately
equipped. Especially in areas of the city that are densely built-
up, the result is that open spaces near houses and apartments
are overused by children and young people. Because of these
deficiencies, in 1997 a small group of Viennese municipal
government employees and institutions close to the city,
under the leadership of Jutta Kleedorfer, began to look at the
possibility of the dual use of lots that at certain times are used
very little or not at all. These include school playgrounds and
school athletic facilities, vacant lots, construction sites that
are temporarily idle, and pedestrian tunnels. The goal was to
offer the population more, and more diverse, open spaces by
activating these areas.

In the same year, the Wiener Bodenbereitstellungs- und
Stadterneuerungsfonds (Vienna Land Procurement and Urban
Renewal Fund) held an event called "Wenig Platz–Mehr(fach)
nutzung" (Little Space–Multiple Use). The topics under discussion included international examples and possible strategies for improving the supply of open space and facilitating
communication among the various groups of users in Vienna.
Out of this event came the working group einfach–mehrfach
("simply multiple," a play on words implying that the "simple"
solution to the city's open space problem is "multiple" use)
under the auspices of Municipal Department 18 (Urban Planning, Group for Open and Green Space). The working group's
immediate objective was to make open spaces at Vienna's
schools, which are primarily used when schools are open,
accessible to the public during the times when they are not,
that is, in the afternoons, on weekends, and during school
vacations. The obvious course of action was to work to bring
about a situation in which these sites, appropriately equipped,
could be used for movement and play by neighborhood children and young people after school hours. The group com-
posed a set of dual-use guidelines describing the framework
conditions, the types of support available for realizing projects, and the projects actually realized.

ONE-STOP OFFICE
The working group assembled materials on designing, maintaining, and organizing the spaces, the costs involved, the
legal basis, and a checklist. In late 1997 its findings were
presented to an audience of interested experts and discussed.

After its opening in May 2002, the local project space "Fluc" in Vienna's North Train Station building developed into a well known club and cultural event venue. The operators were given notice when the train station was renovated.

A demand was made for the creation of a liaison office for multiple use. In 1998 Jutta Kleedorfer was appointed project coordinator—she reported directly to the Magistrats-direktor (Chief Executive Director) and thus had cross-departmental authority. This decision was an important step. However, although the city had said yes to temporary use, the lack of staff and financing stood in the way. There was a coordinator but no clear financing for her position. Nevertheless, the group succeeded in launching projects. These projects are still in existence today, and their contribution to improving the supply of public space in Vienna has been such that it is hard to imagine the city of Vienna without them. The group was especially successful with open spaces at city-administered schools. Jutta Kleedorfer's conviction and her power to motivate others were initially a necessary catalyst for achieving these successes.

An important factor in gaining the acceptance of the responsible politicians and administrators was the fact that the schools themselves do not have to supervise the use—that job is done by park supervisors and local youth workers organized in associations. They guarantee that the spaces are handled with care. The districts finance any necessary construction, the additional cost of maintaining the facilities, and the supervision of the children and young people. The districts may propose candidates for supervisory positions—the task of interviewing candidates to assess their child care credentials is carried out by the municipality.

LIABILITY

For legal reasons, it was often necessary for the city of Vienna to extend its blanket liability insurance to the open spaces being temporarily used. This way, the owners of the lots are relieved of the legal risk associated with the grant of use. An important requirement for this was that the lots be made available to the people free of charge. The spaces must be under the control of a municipal property management office. When necessary, therefore, contracts to this effect must be drafted between different offices. Ms. Kleedorfer acted as a catalyst in this process. She is usually the one who brings people together when the process stalls. But by now the offices have mastered the formalities. Together with municipal departments, district administrations have been quietly setting up access to open spaces like these for years. Provided they are suitable, all spaces owned by the city of Vienna are available to be mobilized for temporary use. At this point the einfach-mehrfach project often runs by itself.

For example, open spaces at schools are easily available. Whether and how they become part of the einfach-mehrfach project depends entirely on the engagement and initiative of the district mayor. Savvy district mayors use their position and authority to link investments to the opening of these spaces. Where obstacles do arise, they tend to have more to do with personal animosities, which does nothing to alter the fact of the strategy's success. What has proved to be more difficult, however, is the process of activating spaces not owned by the city of Vienna. In these cases too, a property management division must take formal control of the area so that the city's blanket liability insurance can take effect. A characteristic phenomenon of life in Vienna is the often considerable reticence of its citizens—independent initiative is often lacking. Ms. Kleedorfer supports engaged citizens and interested politicians. But the program itself is not promoted among the population.

Just ten years ago the focus was on providing additional open spaces for children and young people to move and play. Today, cultural aspects increasingly form an important part of the picture. In this way, residents of the city become cultural producers, who establish forms of everyday culture in public—albeit temporary—open spaces. Indoor uses have also joined the list, for example a space for young people at the Tröpferlbad and the use of old pedestrian underpasses. By contrast, in other locations it's the altered rather than the alternative use of spaces that predominates, as in the case of the *Mädchengärten,* or girls' parks, where only girls and young women are allowed. Today the temporary use of open space is an integral part of life in Vienna. The additional supply is urgently needed in densely built-up areas of the city. The program still faces the significant challenge of including larger areas owned by the federal government and private institutions in the network of temporary use in order to further improve the supply of open space.

FURTHER INFORMATION

www.wien.gv.at/stadtentwicklung/06/22/01.htm

Michl Mellauner, *Temporäre Freiräume. Zwischennutzung und Mehrfach-nutzung: Potentiale für die dichte Stadt,* PhD diss., Vienna 1998.

Jutta Kleedorfer, "'einfach-mehrfach' - Ein Projekt der Stadt Wien," *anthos* 1/2006: 29–35.

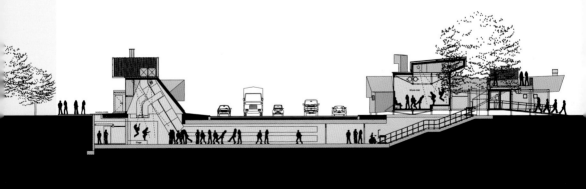

Cross-section of the pedestrian underpass at the Praterstern and temporary additions by architect Klaus Stattman. Thanks to mediation by the "einfach-mehrfach" program, an alternative site was found in an unused pedestrian underpass near the train station. Fluc 2 could be opened. (www.fluc.at)

OBJECTIVE: To revitalize empty urban areas and rescue endangered building stock

PROTAGONIST: Nonprofit association HausHalten e.V. as placement agency

USE: Cultural; associations, galleries, clubs, theaters, and other organizations

STATUS: Individual five-year leases

PLACE: Leipzig-West

TRAJECTORY: Association created 2004, first house acquired 2005, currently thirteen houses, ten of which are in the west of Leipzig, two in the east, and one in the north

Many Eastern German cities have lost residents on a massive scale since the end of the GDR in 1989. Suburbanization, low birthrates, and departure due to high unemployment caused in part by the change of political and economic system have led to a dramatic inner-city vacancy rate for residential and office buildings. Leipzig is no exception: more than a hundred thousand residents—roughly a fifth of all Leipzig residents—have left their city. Roughly fifty thousand apartments, or 16 percent of the existing stock, and 75,000 square meters of office space, much of it in the *Gründerzeit* neighborhoods that define the city's character, now stand empty. In the neighborhoods of Leipzig-West and Leipzig-Ost the vacancy rates are particularly high. Here about two thousand buildings are empty and in danger of decaying. Even a broad array of city planning measures, promises of support for potential investors, and the improvement of transportation infrastructure and open space have thus far proved unable to stem the decline. Since no renters or purchasers could be found by traditional avenues, most owners opted to wait for better times and barricaded their empty buildings to protect them from vandalism.

THE GUARDHOUSE MODEL

Inspired by the public discussion that took place in the framework of Leipzig's neighborhood management effort, the association HausHalten e.V. was founded in October 2004 with the goal of rescuing buildings at risk of decay by means of temporary use. The basic idea of the resulting *Wächterhäuser,* or guardhouses, is to preserve the houses by using them to the mutual advantage of owners and users. The owners are spared expense and also relieved of the acute anxiety about their buildings. The use of the buildings prevents vandalism and limits weather damage, since such damage can be quickly discovered and repaired by the users as on-site experts. Moreover, by making their buildings available to temporary users at no cost to themselves, the owners also receive a midterm prospect of standard market rents. Actors and initiatives that, despite the large space surplus, have thus far been unable to find appropriate spaces for realizing their ideas become *Hauswächter,* or "house guards," as temporary users. They get a lot of space for little money. Their job is to renovate their spaces, perform inspections, and make minor repairs. Particularly users who are likely to have a cultural or social impact on the neighborhood are considered as possible "guards."

The Wächterhaus in Demmeringstrasse with the temporary user
Kunstverein D 21 e.V., opening in summer 2006

THE ROLE OF THE ASSOCIATION

The association's members work on a volunteer basis. The city supports the cause by doing public relations work, setting up contacts with property owners, and providing financial help. Thus, the city's Employment Services Department made possible the creation of two government job-creation program positions that help with property management and public relations. In the meantime, the association has three permanent employees for the supervision of the users and owners, public relations, as well as project work. Additional government support came from various programs, including the EU program URBAN II. The association acts as a mediator between property owners, users, and the city. It contacts owners of empty buildings and if they are interested arranges for new users as house guards. Together with the owner, the association determines what safety measures are necessary; it helps the house guards with their independent renovation and repair work and the creation of usable spaces for public-interest purposes; and it organizes public support for investments. A shop unit in one of the guardhouses serves as a clubroom.

HausHalten e.V. has had its own small clubhouse in Lützner Strasse 30 since 2008. This pre-*Gründerzeit* building, like so many others in Leipzig, was vacant and approved for demolition. The clubhouse, with an office and a venue for events, could be renovated with the aid of funding from the national urban development policy program. Counseling sessions take place here for owners and user groups. There is a permanent exhibition on the guardhouse project. There is also a "guardhouse station" in the clubhouse where users receive tools and technical advice. A user exchange designed as a website contains information on activities, houses, and potential users.

LICENSE AGREEMENTS

The legal framework of the guardhouses is a *Gestattungsvereinbarung Haus*, or "License Agreement: House" between the owner and the association. In this document the usage rights are transferred to the association for five years. The association in turn passes these rights on, by contract, to the interested end users, that is, the house guards. The property rights and duties remain unaffected. In some cases the owner is required to invest in the building's basic safety and to ensure that it is provided with electricity, gas, water, etc. The usage rights are transferred from the association to the house guards by the *Gestattungsvereinbarung Raum*, or "License Agreement: Space." The temporary users bear the additional costs—property tax, costs for water, sewage, and garbage collection, as well as connection fees—and are free to use the hitherto empty rooms for social and cultural projects, as well as dwellings. In exchange they agree to maintain the space in good condition. Depending on the particular use concept, the renovation work is more or less extensive. It ranges from simply making it usable—for example, by installing wiring or painting the walls—to extensive renovation work, such as plastering or stripping the floors.

CONCLUSIONS

The association's long-term goal is to revitalize entire portions of the city by using them. In the meantime the work of HausHalten e.V. is already yielding tangible results. Eighteen houses in the western part of Leipzig are currently being cared for. Exhibition and performance spaces such as the Kuhturm ("cow tower") have been created, as well as shops, galleries, clubrooms, and the L.O.F.F.T. alternative theater. The structural and technical safeguarding of these houses that were previously in danger of decaying ensures that they continue to be worth preserving and worthy of preservation. The first guardhouse was already "released" in early 2007 and its use converted into a standard rental relationship between the owner and the existing house guard—three more have followed in the meantime. The released guardhouses are managed according to different conditions. One could be converted into a normal rental relationship, a second one was sold and is currently being renovated. A three-year follow-on contract was drawn up between users and the owner for another house according to similar conditions. An intermediate user intends to purchase this house.

Because the development of the west of Leipzig is now proceeding in a positive way due to the guardhouses there and what in the meantime have become numerous independent initiatives and house projects, HausHalten e.V. is now increasingly concentrating on those neighborhoods with an urgent need for development—these include those in the east and north of Leipzig. Two guardhouses have already been established in the east of Leipzig, and since 2009 a further one in the north. The association is currently carrying on discussions with additional owners in these neighborhoods.

The transferability of the model has been demonstrated. An idea was initially successfully transferred to the neighboring city of Halle/Saale, which also suffers from a dramatically high residential vacancy rate. The nonprofit association HausHalten Halle e.V. created here is working in collaboration with HausHalten Leipzig. Moreover, in recent years guardhouse initiatives were founded in Chemnitz, Görlitz, Dresden, Magdeburg, and an association in Rochlitz for Muldetal. HausHalten e.V. Muldetal is a fine example of the association's efforts to establish the guardhouse model in small towns and communities as well. Until 2009, this was funded within the scope of the national urban development policy program.

Reports in various media and an award have helped make the Leipzig initiative better known. Thus far, however, it has proved impossible to extend the project to city-owned buildings and *Wohnungsbaugesellschaften,* or municipal corporations for housing construction. The benefit of doing so can hardly be overstated, since they administer the great majority of empty residential buildings. Despite good cooperation between the association and the city government, negotiations between them stagnated for quite a long time. The city-owned corporation for housing construction pursued the strategic objective of reducing the city's total residential housing stock. Thus the recovery of the buildings in question, most of which were slated for demolition, was not regarded as desirable. The authorities also sought to justify this attitude by arguing, among other things, that there was sufficient space available in already renovated buildings and that they would prefer not to create competition in their own backyard. However, the city has departed from this strategy in the meantime: there has been a guardhouse since 2008 owned by the Leipziger Wohnungs- und Baugesellschaft mbH (LBW). A further cooperation with the LBW has been created within the scope of the *Wächterläden* (guard stores). A *Wächterladen* could temporarily be revitalized in the building owned by the LBW in Eisenbahnstrasse 91. Other buildings owned by the LBW have been passed on to groups who were looking for suitable properties without the guardhouse model.

The association has in the meantime been commissioned by the city of Leipzig to find new uses for salesrooms in Leipzig's Magistralen. First contracts have already been signed. The principle is the same as the one for the "guardhouses": vacant stores—and thus also the streets in which they are located—are to be revitalized by providing entrepreneurs, creative people, and the self-employed with the opportunity to bring their ideas to fruition on favorable terms. The financial risk is low and, if desired, the rental contract commitment is short.

FURTHER INFORMATION

www.haushalten.org

INITIATE

Large idle areas in the inner city—for example, old industrial facilities and abandoned buildings of the urban infrastructure for electricity, gas, and water—offer enormous potential for temporary use. This is especially the case if it takes years or even decades to develop such areas into commercial building sites. However, the problems that must be solved when activating an idle area generally exceed the capacity of individual users. In many cases, therefore, agents step in, often with the city's support, to facilitate alternative forms of urban development. To the extent that the establishment of temporary users does not already form part of the strategy for marketing the location (see "Exploit", p. 348), when owners initiate temporary uses at inner-city sites with poor development prospects they tend to have more practical objectives in mind: they hope that a temporary use will enable them to reduce their operating costs, contain vandalism, and ideally also improve the public perception of their property.

Common to all initiators is the goal of generating a critical mass of activity that will almost automatically give rise to further dynamism. Favorable framework conditions, above all low entry bars for space acquisition, are intended to meet the needs of a large number of users. The spectrum of techniques employed by initiators ranges from simple construction measures and the improvement of site access to leases and permits all the way to ideas competitions and the founding of associations. With measures like these they create a framework for action that opens up use possibilities for many actors.

As a rule, the profile of the use is at first undefined; however, it bears the stamp of the actors' ambitions and networks as well as that of the specific potential and surroundings of the area in question. From these, an individual cluster of uses then develops.

How the use is going to develop over the long term is something that is uncertain for the initiators at the beginning. Initiation has an experimental character. The decision regarding the future of the temporary use is left for later. If a project develops a dynamic of its own, the initial phase ends and so too does the task of the initiators. Depending on the context and the constellation of actors, various strategies may determine the further trajectory of a project. Some require sustained supervision (see "Coach", p. 304), others a consolidation of the use (see "Formalize", p. 322). With projects at sites under strong pressure to commercialize, the use ends or becomes embedded in the planning of the property owner or project developer, or else it is maintained through aggressive measures on the part of the users (see "Claim", p. 272).

AGENTS, ACTORS, MOTIVATIONS

Although agents, cities, and property owners share the common goal of activating unused urban spaces, they do so in the service of different interests. For the initial kick-off, favorable constellations of actors and places are the crucial factor. As "spiders in the web," agents have a special role in this process, since they are closely connected to the local structures. They negotiate a plan with the owner and licensing authorities that create opportunities for the activities of various users. They design use profiles for parts of the site and organize requests for proposals and ideas competitions to find sensible uses. They act as guides in the obtaining of permits, coordinate consensus formation among the participants, arbitrate conflicts, and oversee the communications strategy for the location.

When agents are not directly commissioned by the property owner or city to establish temporary uses, their motivation is often based on the ideal of an alternative form of urban development. They are concerned—like the initiators of the nt*/areal in Basel (see case study) or the RAW Tempel e.V. in Berlin—to understand urban development as more than merely a series of construction projects. On the contrary, they work to enable direct, action-oriented uses of space that also include noncommercial cultural and social projects. For the agents, the initiation of a temporary use is successful when it has a lasting influence on the way the place is used and when long-term possibilities are created for neighborhood projects and local initiatives.

Often the agents have experience from earlier temporary use projects. That gives them the courage and ability to instigate new projects. This is the case for Bibiena Houwer, initiator of the cultural temporary use on the grounds of the former Reichsbahnausbesserungswerk Franz Stenzer (Franz Stenzer Imperial Railroad Repair Works) in Berlin-Friedrichshain. As a resident, Houwer had looked at the disused factory for years before she had the idea of a temporary use of the former warehouse and administration buildings. After her decision, personal contact with the City Planning Councilor of the borough of Friedrichshain turned out to be the key to opening up the area. In order to facilitate a temporary use, the borough rented three of the buildings from the owner and sublet them to the association of temporary users. As an agent Bibiena Houwer then organized the formation of an association that became the umbrella for over thirty sociocultural projects. She has long since left the project, but the structure she created has been taken over and further developed by the users.

Noncommercial spaces in a context dominated by private-sector uses were also the goal of the architect Cedric Price in his project *Magnets,* developed in 1996. Price is one of the best-known champions of an interventionist approach that seeks to spark public appropriation of space by means of minimal architectonic interventions, independent of the interests of private investors. The building projects conceived by Price on his own initiative are meant to spark new uses in the city's public spaces, uses, however, that are deliberately *un*defined and left for others to develop.

Magnets was a plan for positioning mobile, variable, and recyclable elements in the public spaces of London. The term "magnets" stood for the effect of the objects on circulation flows and other activities, similar to that of a magnet on an electric field. Price placed his "magnets" primarily in highly commercialized locations. These physical interventions involved reusing elements of activities of construction. These were elements that defied monofunctional petrification. Cranes, electronic hydraulic systems, and pontoons were not only meant to make it possible to vary and modify these elements; they also implied the short life and temporary use of the objects themselves. His approach, which conceives of architecture as a process that does not simply confront the changing conditions of life with finished elements but incorporates those elements into the flux, is clearly recognizable in his sketches. The architectonic structures of the *Magnets* could be preserved, rebuilt, adapted, moved, or removed as needed. Price worked with the basic elements of architectonic connecting forms; his series of ten magnets consisted of elements such as "stairway," "walkway," "platform," "pier," "arch," and "arcade."

Conceptual diagrams for "Magnets" by Cedric Price and their locations in London and the surrounding area

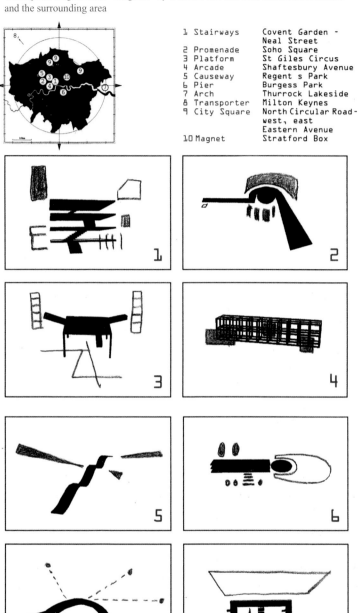

1	Stairways	Covent Garden – Neal Street
2	Promenade	Soho Square
3	Platform	St Giles Circus
4	Arcade	Shaftesbury Avenue
5	Causeway	Regent s Park
6	Pier	Burgess Park
7	Arch	Thurrock Lakeside
8	Transporter	Milton Keynes
9	City Square	North Circular Road-west, east Eastern Avenue
10	Magnet	Stratford Box

Implanted as public platforms at intersections and squares, on arterial roads, and over highways, the *Magnets* demanded the calling into question and inversion of the, often hierarchically dictated, use and development of space. However, the alternative use and design of the space—which was usually placed high up—was not only meant to raise the question of access to and ownership of space; it also sought to bring about a change in spatial perception, a redetermination and reinterpretation of the surrounding public space. As generators of unpredictable public phenomena with no fixed or permanent program, the Magnets served to promote the exploration of public space beyond all familiar functional determinations. In doing so, they sought to open up new forms of practice and reflection and places that had not previously been thought of. Price's *Magnets* showed how architectural interventions can enable and initiate temporary and even changing and evolving uses and how architects can become initiators themselves. Although his proposals went unrealized, they remain important conceptual contributions to new forms of urban development.

OWNERS AS INITIATORS

The motivation of property owners is completely different. As a rule they have a concrete development objective in view, but one that cannot be achieved in the short to medium term because of poor traditional prospects for commercializing their property or extremely large development time spans due to the area's size. In this context, the crucial factor in the decision to initiate temporary use is the owners' desire not to let the period between the abandoned and newly planned uses go by unproductively. Unlike the strategy of exploitation, initiation is less concerned with directly exploiting temporary uses as a tool for achieving more profitable ultimate uses. For this there is much too much uncertainty as to whether the ultimate development objective can actually be achieved. Rather, the owner is simply concerned that there be some kind of use at idle sites, in order to at least reduce operating costs and keep possible vandalism in check. A certain autonomous dynamic of the temporary activity and the formation of use clusters are welcome, provided their profile and programmatic orientation do not jeopardize the ultimate development objective. But for most owners—especially those of sites with poor development prospects—the initiation of temporary use is a stopgap solution that they put up with as a way of bridging the gap until hard times are over.

A good example is the history of the former Kaapeli cable factory in Helsinki. In the 1980s the Nokia corporation decided to close the inner-city factory with its more than 50,000 square meters of floor space. They stopped investing in the maintenance of the building, but rented the spaces—after vacating them in 1990—temporarily and very cheaply to cultural producers and young entrepreneurs. By doing so, the owners unintentionally initiated the development of a use cluster. The city planned to take the building over, then later tear it down and build a school, hotels, museums, and a multistory parking garage in its place. At an estimated cost of roughly € 80 million, the renovation of the existing building was not regarded as economically viable. However, before the plans could be finalized, four years went by. The users formed the association Pro Kaapeli and developed an alternative plan. Thanks in no small measure to a powerful response in the

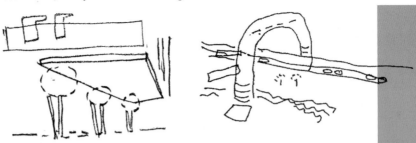

public media, the association was able to achieve the preservation of both the building and the existing use cluster. Now more than 200,000 people attend the performances at the former cable factory every year.

The initiation of a use dynamic by the owner is not always this unintentional and unsupervised. In the case of Spitalfields Market in London, for example, the owner commissioned an agency that already had experience in this area to establish temporary uses. During the real estate market collapsed in the early 1990s, serious doubt was cast on the plans to build an office complex on the grounds of the former produce market in London's East End. In just a short time, the agency succeeded in opening the area to a broad public by establishing athletic attractions and an arts and crafts market. With the return of the real estate boom in the late 1990s, the temporary uses, which were now successfully established, were replaced by office buildings. Some of them, however, were able to put down new roots in the immediate area. The example of Spitalfields Market shows how the initiation of temporary uses is vitally dependent on the conception and controlled realization of the project idea, but how it can also give rise to a development with a powerful dynamic of its own that can only be partially controlled.

CITIES AS INITIATORS

Cities become involved in initiating temporary use for a number of different reasons. Temporary uses offset local deficiencies that usually require a high degree of municipal engagement. They stabilize socially weak neighborhoods, create new uses for idle spaces, integrate marginalized social groups, help to maintain abandoned sites, and create attractors for new public life without the need for capital-intensive government investments. Sometimes temporary uses are deliberately initiated by agents of the city, as in neighborhood management efforts and liaison offices. But the stronger the autonomous dynamism of the use and the higher the actors' level of self-organization, the smaller the degree of municipal involvement. Sometimes cities also support the initiation of temporary uses passively, for example by providing lease guarantees and by entering into agreements with investors in city-planning contracts that ensure the creation of spaces for temporary use.

In the case of the grounds of the Kabel- und Drahtwerke (KDAG, or Cable and Wire Factory) in Vienna, which closed in 1997, the city initiated a cooperative planning process. After the loss of seven hundred jobs, they wanted to send a signal for new development prospects by involving residents and culturally appropriating the existing factory buildings. In coordination with eight construction holding companies—the new owners of the site—and cultural actors who were invited to participate, the decision was

made to initiate a temporary use of the factory halls, and in 1999 the governing association IG Kabelwerk was formed to coordinate and operate the uses. Equipped by the
city of Vienna with a (not insignificant) starting budget of € 260,000, the association
was extremely successful. The spectrum of temporary uses ranged from neighborhood
graffiti, theater, music, and youth projects to film festivals and exhibitions all the way
to commercial performances such as television shows and concerts. After six years of
intensive temporary use, a large portion of the factory halls was demolished in 2005.
Building on the 680,000 square meter site has now been completed. The temporary
cultural use of the factory halls was strategically positioned on the outskirts of the new
neighborhood. They had established themselves both spatially and programmatically at
the interface between the already existing neighborhoods and the new development and
thus contributed substantially to winning public acceptance for the latter. The mixture
of neighborhood culture and professional theater has now become a permanent cultural
institution. The city has made about € 5 million available for the construction of the
"Palais Kabelwerk." By initiating temporary use on the cable factory grounds, the city
of Vienna created space for local cultural life and promoted the commercialization of
the site. The determining factors for this kind of temporary use are less the degree of
institutionalization and commercialization than the ability to design long-term uses
processually, to integrate actors with insufficient capital, and to keep the site open to a
changing array of temporary activities.

   After years of disinterest, the Berlin city government has also begun to note the potential of temporary uses. During the 1990s, with expectations of a massive population
increase and an immense economic upswing, vast development areas were identified,
primarily on the outskirts of the city, and treated with master plans. Now, however, the
Berlin Senate is bringing its urban development policy into line with reality. The highly

optimistic predictions have not been fulfilled. City-planning projects are therefore being limited to strategic sites with a powerful development dynamic, for example traffic hubs like Schönefeld Airport and the area surrounding the new railroad station. By contrast, for development areas without sufficient demand—including the grounds of the inner-city Tempelhof Airport, which is virtually unused—models for activating temporary use are being formulated.

When flight operations were suspended in fall 2008, the airport's 380 hectares of open area and 28 hectares of building floor space immediately became the largest inner-city idle area in Berlin. Already in the late 1990s, the Senate Department for Urban Development had a master plan drawn up for reusing the airfield; it envisioned residential and commercial uses on 180 hectares. However, recent feasibility studies show that, due to the existence of other, more attractively located sites, there will be no demand in the coming years for the planned reuse of Tempelhof. What is more, the city does not have the money to design the area, alternatively, as a park. Because of the inner-city location, the administration is sticking to its long-term goal of a built development, but in late 2006 it decided to call for outside expert opinion on the possibility of initiating temporary uses as the opening phase of a sustained urban development project.

In contrast to traditional city-planning approaches, the idea workshop Tempelhof (Arge Michael Braum & Partner, raumlabor berlin, Studio Urban Catalyst) commissioned by the Senate placed the emphasis on the beginning rather than the end of the development process, that is, on the initiation of temporary use clusters. Strategies for the opening up and cultural exploration of the area, the activation of designated sites via pioneer usages, as well as initial measures for the development of a park will be integrated into a dynamic masterplan with long-term urban developments. In the process, the initiation of temporary uses at Tempelhof Airport that are being called for closely integrates "soft tools" (such as

the recruitment of users, the development of a visual identity, and process management) with "hard tools" (such as the mobilization of existing structures, measures for strengthening the infrastructure, and construction measures), which together make it possible to appropriate the area more effectively. Even when the selection of uses and spaces is meant to be initiated and directed by the city, a nonlinear, open-ended process will be recommended. The plan is geared toward the interaction of bottom-up and top-down strategies, the combination of firmly defined development parameters, and scope for self-reinforcing developments.

The airfield has been publicly accessible since 2010 and is currently being used primarily by people engaged in sport activities (flying kites, skating, bike riding, and jogging) and as a recreational and barbecue area. The newly founded urban development association has started a campaign for pioneer usages. To what extent pioneer usages will actually play a role in the development of the airfield remains to be seen.

CONCLUSIONS

The initiation of temporary uses in large building complexes has a special potential in the development of use clusters. For unlike scattered individual uses, use clusters give rise to intensive interchange and synergies among the various participants. Self-organized innovation clusters and production networks emerge. At the same time, they create important public places with strong identification value for a neighborhood or even an entire city.

The initiation of temporary uses involves relatively little risk of conflict between the owner, the agent, and the city, provided the use is desired by all three actors. Differences over the future of the building or site primarily arise when the temporary activities that then emerge lay claim to a particular use of space and touch off dynamics that can only be partially controlled. When the owner's interest in commercializing the property grows at the same time, the temporary uses come under increasing pressure. In such cases, the initiation of the use can easily be followed by its termination. Even when ideas for temporary use take all the planning and economic framework conditions into account, the realization of those ideas still remains an experiment. The effect of initiations on the mid- to long-range development of the city can no more be predicted than it can be planned. This argues for an open approach to planning that initially only sets approximate goals. Through possible use programs, through the relationship of undeveloped spaces to developed ones, and through webs of spatial relationships and densities, these goals must then be developed and gradually given concrete form.

FURTHER INFORMATION

www.kaapelitehdas.fi

www.raw-tempel.de

www.revaler5eck.de

www.wien.gv.at/bezirke/meidling/geschichte-kultur/palais-kabelwerk.html

Herbert Buchner, ed., *Kabelwerk. A Development Process as a Model. The State of the Art*, Stadtentwicklung Wien MA 21B, Vienna, 2004

OBJECTIVE: Development
of the site through intermediate use by means of socio
cultural projects; owner plans
to develop 700 apartments,
2,000 jobs, and a park

PROTAGONISTS: Philippe
Cabane (urbanist), Matthias
Bürgin (geographer)

USE: Over twenty projects
from the areas of socioculture
and art

STATUS: Two intermediate use
associations, k.e.i.m. and V.i.P.,
with rental contracts until 2011

PLACE: Disused freight
yard in northern Basel,
180,000 square meters; owned
by Vivico Real Estate and
others

TRAJECTORY: Initial study
and founding of association
1999, gradual appropriation
of area since 2000

COST: Lease: 850 square
meters at €29.00/square meter/
year on V.i.P. spaces. Owner
receives 50 percent of profit
from spaces leased by V.i.P.

Since June 2000 the Basel associations k.e.i.m and V.i.P. have been organizing various cultural temporary uses on the grounds of the northern Basel freight yard that has been idle since the early 1990s. The Vivico Real Estate Corporation, which owns the 18 hectares, plans to construct a new neigh-borhood there on the basis of two city-planning competitions held in 1996 and 2001, with seven hundred rental apartments and condominiums, 2,000 jobs, a shopping center, a school, and a preschool. A central park is meant to offset the striking lack of green spaces in the densely built-up area of Kleinbasel. The owner initially tolerated the temporary uses, and later explicitly welcomed them, above all due to the revitalization and enhanced image, but also in the context of the length of time it is expected to take to realize the development—fifteen to twenty years. A large proportion of the spaces will remain undeveloped for years to come.

STUDY AS INITIAL SPARK

The initial spark for the alternative use came from the study *Akupunktur für Basel* (Acupuncture for Basel) by the soci-ologist and urbanist Philippe Cabane and the geographer Matthias Bürgin, which the authors undertook on their own initiative. In it they examined models for realizing temporary sociocultural uses at the site. The study received intellectual and financial support from b.e.i.r.a.t.—Verein für Raum-wirklichkeiten (b.e.i.r.a.t.—Association for Spatial Realities ["*Beirat*" is a German word meaning "advisory committee"]), which had already initiated and implemented a variety of temporary uses in Basel in the past. Vivico found the study's idea of deliberately integrating temporary uses into the devel-opment of the location persuasive primarily because of a possible address formation and the prospect of regenerating the disused site.

In 1999, together with other interested parties, the authors of the study founded the association k.e.i.m. [the German word "*Keim*" means "seed" or "shoot"] for the development of urban sites and spaces with the goal of initiating informal, easily realizable uses of space at the disused railroad site in cooperation with actors from the adjoining neighborhoods. In 2003 they revived the Vereinigung interessierter Personen (V.i.P., Association of Interested Persons), a preexisting asso-ciation. While k.e.i.m. more broadly seeks urbanization and the initiation of public activities through temporary use, V.i.P.

concentrates on making unused open spaces in the western part of the area accessible to nearby residents and using them as venues..

With mounting success, the two organizations coordinated their efforts to rent two portions of the area from Vivico, the owner. Since then, the two associations have served as umbrella and magnet for an ever increasing number of temporary uses on the grounds of the former freight yard. Flea markets, art and landscaping projects, children's workshops, open-air bars and restaurants, a neighbourhood workshop space (Quartierslabor), and cult sport athletic fields (which young people helped to design) illustrate the diversity of the space appropriation and usages at the site. They have met with a high degree of public acceptance. Together with the initial study and the work of the two governing associations, the skilled intertwining of additional strategies actually continues to play an important role in the intensification of temporary uses at nt*/areal.

CATALYSTS

The parallel strategy of using commercially sustainable projects with positive connotations to gain legitimacy for action in terms of civil society has repeatedly proved successful at nt*/areal. The initiators achieved their first major success in 2000 with the opening of the Erlkönig restaurant in the former company cafeteria. The restaurant soon turned out to be

A broad range of temporary use projects
developed independently in situ, 2007

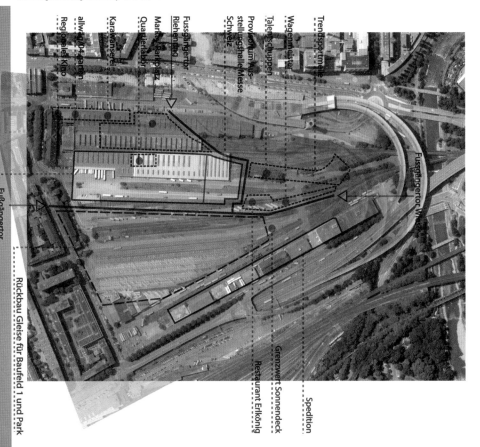

a catalyst for the informal development of the area. In just a short time its dining hall and lounge not only became a popular meeting place for a broad transregional public but also served as a platform for the culture, design, and architecture scene. The unconventional venue for meetings and social events has even become a favorite spot for decision-makers from administrative, economic, and political circles and Vivico. At the same time, it has also become an arena for a broad range of activities. The strong positioning of all temporary use activities via a publicly established facility like the Erlkönig allowed the initiators to launch additional informal and experimental projects. As a platform for association meetings but also for negotiations with prospective project developers and the owner, ideas took shape in the Erlkönig that became reality nearby just a short time later.

In late 2003, the Messe Schweiz AG invested CHF 12 million in the conversion of the huge former transfer halls into a temporary trade show hall. However, it was only used for several days a year for the most important watch and jewelry trade fair in the world, BaselWorld. Both partners profited from the nine-year cooperation between the trade fair—even intermediate users on the site—and the two associations.

With the securing under private law of rights of way in 2004 by the canton, "nt*/Boulevard" was created, which is fundamental for the overall planning. Marked out using very simple means, from the surrounding residential areas the road enables direct

Youths build a dirt jump track on their own, 2006

access to the nearby recreational area behind it. Moreover, the boulevard connects the individual intermediate use projects to one another and with the city and makes them accessible to a new public. Once the terrain became more accessible, the former perception of the site as a kind of no-man's-land has substantially improved.

CROSS-FINANCING

The strong commitment of the association's members has led to a very dynamic informal development beyond the formal planning process. New ideas are constantly emerging from the close-knit project landscape. For ten years now, the multifaceted activity has been attracting a growing public, which in turn has time and again provided incentives for new projects.

The V.i.P. and k.e.i.m. associations manage the uses in a way that allows them financial independence and provides development opportunities for as many public-interest uses as possible. Voluntary projects are indirectly cross-subsidized by commercially oriented temporary uses. For example, income is generated by using a large asphalt surface as a parking lot, the exhibitor's fees from a flea market, and leasing spaces to individual projects like the restaurant, the Quartierslabor, and studios. In this way the associations are able to finance special services provided by their members, including coordinating

activities, leading negotiations, and running a professional office. In order to support uses
with insufficient capital, the two associations provide space at no charge or at reduced
rents and invest in common infrastructure, and their members advise and coordinate projects. The bulk of the associations' surpluses are used to support the development of new
projects. Thus V.i.P. and k.e.i.m. do not just focus on maintaining the status quo but also
on expanding their activities and their support of similarly oriented initiatives elsewhere
in the city.

CONCLUSION

Work on the construction of the first 240 apartment units and the new municipal park
began in 2006. Both the owner as well as the canton operated with a strategy of domestication. Vivico terminated the intermediate use contract with k.e.i.m. in March 2009. This
development was to be expected in the case of the Erlkönig for, as agreed, the contract
ended with Vivico's transfer of the property to the canton. The Erlkönig subsequently
obtained an intermediate rental contract effective until 2011 directly from the canton.
In the long term, the canton plans to refurbish the building and then establish it as the
"Parkrestaurant." In the case of the automobile yard adjacent to the restaurant, Vivico

served notice. Because the property had not previously been transferred to the canton, in the association's view it was a breach of contract. They refrained from taking legal action. Vivico redesigned the small building and leased it temporarily on favorable terms to a new eatery, which does not operate within the context of the previous intermediate usages and runs a small mainstream club there.

The activities on the site administered by V.i.P. will also be subject to change. In summer 2010, the former transfer halls, in which V.i.P. rents about 650 square meters of floor space for offices, sociocultural activities, and food outlets, were sold as future building plots. The new owner has not yet made public his development proposals, however he is prepared to temporarily extend the intermediate usages. This is important, as the association's extensive free areas without interior spaces, which are not affected by this, could only otherwise be operated with difficulty.

SUMMARY

The city played a very small role in initiating temporary uses at nt*/areal. It supported uses in need of permits by granting temporary authorizations, but it has primarily focused on managing the formal planning process. Soon, however, the city will become the owner of the future public open spaces that form part of the area, and when it does it will have a special role in dealing with the temporary uses that have grown up there. As the owner it has the option of continuing to allow the activities, to transform the noncommercial qualities achieved into the newly developing district, or simply letting it run out. The communication attempts to date by the actors in the city's administration have met with a lack of understanding.

The owner, Vivico, has long taken a positive view of the temporary uses, not least because the real estate company uses the slogan "Urbanity is our most important product" to promote its locations and the various temporary uses have done much to create a vibrant public space. However, the closer the groundbreaking comes for the first construction site, the more the owner and investors commercially orient the quality of the urbanity and public spaces. Some of the current temporary uses are incompatible with the official target public of the new neighborhood. Before the search for a mutual solution could begin, the owner and the administration operated with barely veiled threats. After several unsuccessful offers for cooperation and with a formal commission, the former initiators of the intermediate usage no longer see it as their task to campaign for a transformation of the uses, which are beneficial to the quarter, beyond the former rental situation. Thus, as the initiators retreat, a vacuum is gradually developing. While local residents make intensive use of the range of offers, in the end, only a few are willing to make a long-term commitment and themselves assume responsibility for the area and the developments. Today, it is anything but certain whether the vital public milieus that have emerged on the grounds of the freight yard in recent years will be able to function as fertile soil for the long-term development of the neighborhood.

The associations are not demanding alternative areas. The operators place great value on developing usages from the specific examination of the location—in some measure they activate and join local and social capital. From this perspective, a simple relocation of the usages does not make sense.

If the future of the current intermediate use on the nt*/areal is itself also uncertain, then the associations' activities have had a strong influence on Basel's municipal policy. The newly instituted cantonal office for urban development policy recently begian working with the protagonists of the nt*/areal and has in the meantime commissioned them to point out possibilities for an urban development policy that is welcoming to intermediate usages. In addition, Basel City is already implementing the *Leitfaden Zwischennutzung* (Intermediate Use Manual), published in 2010 by the federal administration, on a local level. In doing so, Basel City is assuming a pioneering role among the Swiss cantons. This is not lastly the product of a reliable and high-quality tradition of intermediate uses in Basel and on the nt*/areal.

FURTHER INFORMATION

www.areal.org

www.neubasel.ch

www.zwischennutzung.ch

www.zwischennutzung.net

Matthias Bürgin and Philippe Cabane, *Akupunktur für Basel. Zwischennutzung als Standortentwicklung auf dem Areal des DB-Güterbahnhofs in Basel,* Basel, 1999.

Reto Westermann, Roman Züst, Tibor Joanelly (eds.): *Waiting Lands: Strategien für Industriebrachen* (Zurich: Niggli, 2008).

View from the outdoor bar of the first completed construction stage, 2010

SPITALFIELDS MARKET, LONDON

OBJECTIVE: To revitalize the property and increase its value through varied cultural uses

PROTAGONISTS: Private real estate development agency (Urban Space Management/USM); owner

USE: Retail trade, flea market, culture, sports, performances

STATUS: Legal, conflict with the users at the end

PLACE: Unused market halls in the center of London, 13,000 square meters

TRAJECTORY: 1992–1999 various temporary uses; 1999–2003 reduction in the number of uses and relocation to other buildings; 2003 construction begins on new office district

COST: € 400,000 for investments and lease

FINANCING: Private investment by owner

264

Cordelia Polinna

Rarely does the world of stocks and bonds come as close to a run-down neighborhood as in the case of London's Spitalfields on the eastern edge of London's financial district. Here the booming service location directly collides with neighborhoods marked by fading working-class culture and immigrants from the former colonies who have long filled the bottom places in poverty reports and social statistics. The temporary use of an empty market hall that was waiting to be converted into an office complex in the early 1990s functioned as a catalyst for the transformation of the entire Spitalfields area from a neighborhood where "no one went" into one of London's gentrified showcase districts. During the financial and service sector boom that followed the deregulation of the financial sectors in 1986, these spaces freed up by deindustrialization entered the sights of the City of London's town planners. While the conversion of neighboring Broad Street Station into the Broadgate office district went relatively smoothly, the conversion of Spitalfields Market turned out to be far more difficult. The large social and economic disparities between Spitalfields and the City raised doubts as to whether the area would be accepted as an office location.

In 1987 the Spitalfields Development Group (SDG) acquired the long-term lease on the lot containing Spitalfields Market with a term of 150 years. The building site included the Victorian-style market hall (Horner Buildings), an annex from 1928, and a parking lot on Bishopsgate Street. The market halls themselves are "hidden" behind a three-story shell development that contains shop units, small offices, and apartments. In 1991 the big fruit and vegetable market was shut down in preparation for the new development. Numerous attempts were made to redesign the choice parcel. A number of investors showed interest in the site, but all of them were ultimately caught up in the whirlpool of the collapsing 1990s' real estate market. When it became clear that it would not be possible to develop the site anytime soon, the SDG decided to open up the market halls for temporary use. The goal was to prevent vandalism and squatting, reduce maintenance costs, and increase acceptance of the planned office project on the part of residents and local actors. A request for proposals was published, and the firm Urban Space Management (USM) got the contract. Their managing director, Eric Reynolds, had already made a name for himself with the successful reuse of idle structures like Camden Lock and Gabriel's Wharf.

Interior view of Spitalfields Market
with temporary sports areas, early 1990s

OPENING DURING THE INVESTMENT CRISIS

For Spitalfields Market, USM and the SDG created the firm Spitalfields Space Management (SSM), in which each partner had an equal share and which invested £300,000 in the reuse of the halls. Tiny constructional alterations were undertaken to show the public that something was going on inside the halls and that a regeneration of the area lay ahead. Thus, forbidding metal blinds at the entrances were replaced by artistically designed iron gates, the exterior walls were painted, and colorful banners were hung to pique the curiosity of passers-by. In order to set the temporary use in motion, the members of the middle class who worked in the City had to be persuaded to enter the "no-man's-land" of Spitalfields. The plan was that covered soccer and cricket fields would first attract young men to the area for athletic activities and a beer after work. They in turn would bring along women and friends, and this would create the economic basis for the further conversion of the Horner Buildings. Smaller units in the shell development were rented to restaurants and bars, usually for five-year periods. The market was perfectly suited to this approach: the sports facilities could use spaces with high ceilings in the center of the halls, while the shell development offered flexibility and an architecturally attractive setting for a variety of uses. The tasks of overhauling the shop facades and developing the site were taken over by SSM.

The site's popularity and range of attractions grew steadily. Within five years the temporary use had solidly established itself on 13,000 square meters of floor space. Netball courts, photography studios, and restaurants and bars turned Spitalfields Market into a multifunctional center of attraction. Reynolds selected the tenants carefully. Uses like studios, which were not economically viable but desirable because of the atmosphere they created, were temporarily subsidized. Reynolds did not have long to wait before his marketing strategy bore fruit. After all, in London too there were increasing complaints about monotonous shopping streets and shopping malls. An organic and arts and crafts market in the halls attracted as many as 20,000 visitors to the area on Sundays. Spectacular projects were realized: in 1994 a building pit that had been dug for an office building and abandoned was turned into an eight-lane swimming pool.

THE END CAME WITH THE CONSTRUCTION BOOM

The building in the market halls of a temporary opera house with 540 seats, which was inaugurated by Prince Charles in 1993, was both the high point and the turning point for the temporary use. At this time the temporary use was so successful that Eric Reynolds offered to purchase the area from the SDG. Legally, however, the SDG, as owner of the lease, was in a stronger position. When the real estate boom took off in the late 1990s, it began to look like it might actually be possible to develop the planned office building, and in 1999 the SDG bought Eric Reynolds out of the company. Despite massive protests by citizens' initiatives, the sports facilities at Spitalfields Market were closed. The organic

and arts and crafts market stayed open for the time being. A number of temporary uses, including the indoor soccer fields and performance spaces, were temporarily housed at Bishopsgate Goods Yard, a disused freight yard that lay further north, until it was demolished in 2003 and they too had to be abandoned. The temporary users and other local community organizations formed the powerful citizens' initiative Spitalfields Market Under Threat (SMUT), which sought to prevent the office project and prolong the temporary use. SMUT organized demonstrations and signature drives against the conversion of the market, kept the public informed about the plans, and pointed out inconsistencies and irregularities in building applications and permits. However, once the battle against the radical redesigning of the market seemed lost, the group's actions began to peter out.

In 2003 construction began on the new Bishops Square office district in the western half of the market after plans by Foster+Partners. All the market's annexes were torn down except for a single building facade, which was integrated into the new development. In 2005 conversion work began on the Horner Buildings, with the goal of replacing the makeshift and somewhat dingy character of the market with a clean and orderly shopping center. At this point, many of the craftspeople moved to shop units in the surrounding area. Just a few meters away, in Truman's Brewery, a cluster of little cultural and media sector companies emerged, and portions of the market relocated to the distinctly less architecturally attractive halls and open areas of the former brewery.

The temporary use of Spitalfields Market is one aspect of the radical processes of urban redevelopment that have been underway in Spitalfields since the mid-1980s.

Because various desires and demands had built up there over time, a balanced course of development was virtually impossible. The Corporation of London and the project developer SDG (Spitalfields Development Group) were absolutely determined to build offices there. The administration of the Tower Hamlets district had an interest in seeing these plans realized, since for them it meant increased tax revenue and planning gain— the financial benefits and benefits in kind that the developer has to provide for the local community in order to receive a construction permit. While preservationists pleaded for the restoration of the historical building structure, after a preliminary and planning phase lasting fourteen years the SDG was able to use a generous package of financial and other measures to persuade the Tower Hamlets Council to authorize the office project, which was large but mediocre in its design. The political leaders of the district had to fight for an offer that would also convince the local population of the positive effects of the project. Ultimately, the planning gain financed 2 community centers, 118 units of public housing, an employment agency, and educational initiatives, and the Spitalfields Community Trust was sponsored to the tune of £ 5 million. The reason the SDG financed the temporary use and permitted it to go forward was to increase acceptance for itself and its future office project, not in the local community but among the City's companies and workers, who it was hoped would later lease the offices.

The Spitalfields Market develops to become a thriving shopping
center with international fashion stores and restaurants in new building
structures within the hall, 2009

CONCLUSIONS

The temporary use has undeniably brought about a change in the area's image. It has developed into an attractive service location with, in the surrounding area, a large complement of the kinds of businesses that grow up alongside offices. In the meantime, it is almost exclusively the flagship stores of the international lifestyle industry that can afford the commercial rents, which has meant that the former galleries and alternative concert and event venues have had to close or move elsewhere. While all of Spitalfields's social and constructional problems have not been solved, the area has clearly been saved from the prospect of total decay and isolation. Thanks to the short-term use, artists temporarily received not only affordable studios but an excellent opportunity to present their products to a broad audience. The local immigrant community only benefited indirectly from the area's transformation, for example through increased profits in nearby restaurants. But the larger conflict over the development of Spitalfields—of which the battle for Spitalfields Market was just one episode—led to some members of the immigrant population, which had thus far lived in isolation, being integrated into political processes for the first time; some were ultimately even elected to municipal office.

The losers in this process include Eric Reynolds, the initiator of the temporary use, who became a victim of his own success. The temporary users were only welcome as pioneers in the process of enhancing and increasing the value of the neighborhood; they were never envisioned as part of the long-term user structure. On the contrary, their job was to provide "proper" neighbors for the offices: restaurants where business meals can

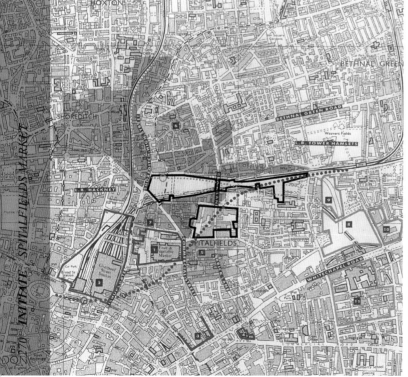

Development measures in the Spitalfields district of London

outlined in blue: existing and planned office locations

highlighted in blue: planned neighborhood development

outlined in black: development areas

outlined in green: individual areas worth preserving

highlighted in green: environmentally protected areas

Renovated eastern market halls and new office complex
on the grounds of the demolished western halls, 2005

be held in a civilized atmosphere and a stylish marketplace where staged entertainment
is offered at lunchtime and nothing is left to chance. However, the site will no longer be a
source of new impulses for London's art and culture scene.

I owe a special debt of gratitude to my conversation partners Eric Reynolds
(Urban Space Management) and Hugo Hinsley (Architectural Association).

FURTHER INFORMATION:

William Taylor, *This Bright Field—A Travel Book in One Place* (London:
Methuen Publishing, 2000).

Cordelia Polinna, *Towards a London Renaissance. Projekte und Planwerke
des städtebaulichen Paradigmenwechsels im Londoner Zentrum* (Detmold:
Rohm, 2009).

Jane M. Jacobs, *Edge of Empire: Postcolonialism and the City* (London:
Routledge, 1996).

Chris Hamnett, *Unequal City—London in the Global Arena* (London and
New York: Routledge, 2003).

CLAIM

Temporary users are usually pragmatists—they have a project they are interested in realizing; they need space at low cost in order to do so; and they are looking for the path of least resistance. When permits and agreements with the authorities are lacking, it isn't programmatic resistance but a tacit attempt to avoid running into difficulties. As a rule, however, temporary users do seek agreements with owners and authorities so as to be able to pursue their projects without running unforeseeable risks. Their goal is simply to find a constellation that comes close to matching their possibilities and wishes.

Some projects, however—and these are precisely the examples that tend to be better known—deviate from this paradigm. In these cases users and political activists fight for contested spaces and spaces for contested activities. The goals formulated for the development of important locations by property owners, town planners, and politicians are called into question, and alternative forms of urban development and use of space are demanded. What is at issue in cases like these is no longer primarily a pragmatic search for untapped potentials, but a conflict of interest between different actors and their different social ideas. The conflict is carried out in the public sphere, so that the shaping of public opinion via the media plays an important role.

TEMPORARY USE AS AN INSTRUMENT

Temporary uses play an important role on the way to this objective—first as the idea of a dynamic use from below that incorporates a wide variety of actors without defining the development in advance (see the example of Park Fiction, p. 282); second as a critique of the wasteful inefficiency of existing power structures and planning cultures, which often leave spaces unused for years and even decades in order to safeguard their own position (see the example of ZwischenPalastNutzung, p. 288); and third as a kind of "Trojan horse" within a strategy that uses small easy steps to pave the way for a long-term objective that conflicts with official planning. A prime example of this is the conflict surrounding Washington Square in Greenwich Village, New York This originated in 1952 when Robert Moses, who had sole responsibility for urban planning in

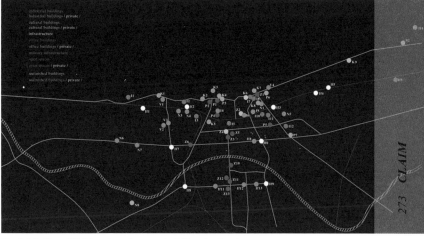

"Invisible Zagreb": Mapping of vacant buildings in the city center

New York City, planned the Manhattan Lower Expressway, which would have destroyed the park and the surrounding neighborhood as well. A citizens' initiative quickly formed in response, and together with the urbanist Jane Jacobs they not only demanded that the plans be abandoned but also that the street itself be removed. After seven years of struggle they achieved the temporary closing of the road through the park. This measure was such a positive experience for the residents that the street was permanently closed to traffic the following year.

A fourth aspect of temporary use in claim strategies is its strategic role in the social conflict. Primarily as a symbolic act, public space is occupied in the service of a certain objective, and that stimulates a public debate on the subject (see also "Subversion," p. 49). A prime example of this is the conflict surrounding affordable housing and homelessness in France in 2006–2007. The organization Children of Don Quixote set up 250 tents as emergency shelters for homeless people in an affluent Paris neighborhood not far from the Bastille in order to draw attention to the housing crisis and the problem of homelessness. This was followed by similar actions in Marseille, Nice, Orléans, Aix-en-Provence, and Toulouse. In addition, an empty bank building across from the Paris stock exchange was occupied and turned into a "Ministry for the Housing Crisis." The first fruits of these campaigns were a tenfold increase in aid to the homeless and the injection of the issue into the national political debate. However, time alone will tell to what extent such efforts are capable of producing a lasting change in housing policy.

All four aspects of temporary use in claim strategies have one thing in common: the temporary use is less an end in itself than a part and instrument of an overarching strategy. The activists' campaign is not simply based on a step-by-step approach—it stands in the service of an overarching long-term perspective from the very beginning.

The "Fette-Mieten-Parties" (High Rent Parties) are a current example of German housing policy. In protest at the excessive rents for small and medium-sized apartments in Hamburg, activists regularly disrupt the group viewing sessions of high-priced apartments.

Light installation in a former schnapps factory, Zagreb

Light installation in a former schnapps factory, Zagreb

Organized as a flash mob, the participants pass out sparkling wine and flyers and throw confetti. The actions are embedded in a fundamental critique of municipal housing and real-estate policy within the scope of the action alliance "Recht auf Stadt" (Right to the City). Since 2009, through a variety of artistic interventions, protest rallies, and media stagings, the network has been attracting a lot of attention and putting pressure on the urban development authority to draw up an alternative way of dealing with Hamburg's urban space policy. The action alliance has proved popular with Hamburg's residents and makes an enormous contribution to a broad debate over local housing and urban develop-ment policy. At the same time, in summer 2009 creative forces squatted the Gängeviertel, the last inner-city ensemble of working-class housing in Hamburg, in order to prevent its demolition and the construction of new housing. After intense debate, the city ultimately bought the property back from its Dutch investor, to whom they had sold it only shortly before. In the meantime, the initiative has presented its own development concept to the city and is engaged in negotiations. At the same time, the city is considering developing the area with the municipal building society Steg. It is currently unclear whether the squatters will be able at least in part to realize their vision for the space.

WISH PRODUCTION

For claim strategies, influencing public opinion is the key. The goal is to deprive existing town planning of its legitimation and gain an ideal majority for an alternative use and development scenario. The means for achieving this are not first and foremost protest, criticism, and negation, but the positive, constructive pursuit of one's own alternative idea and its gradual realization.

This realization takes place on two levels, which usually go hand in hand—first in the sense of wish production, that is, the awakening of the idea of a different, more desirable development in the minds of the public, and second in the practical implementation of that idea from the very beginning. However small, symbolic, and temporary these single steps

may be, they are nonetheless still capable of sparking a social dynamic in which more and more actors participate, so that the project keeps evolving.

There are many different ways to accomplish this: from symbolic appropriation by artistic means, walking tours, temporary occupations, and events to the communication of alternative scenarios through exhibitions and press and public relations campaigns to the use of symbolic gestures to anticipate future activities. A prime example of this is the work of the architects and media artists collective Platforma 9,81 in Zagreb. With their project *Invisible Zagreb* in 2003–2005 they explored the potential of inner-city wastelands for public use by the non-institutionalized cultural scene. The first step in laying claim to these spaces was to chart them on the "Invisible Zagreb Map." As a second step there followed the temporary appropriation of the sites by means of various cultural activities: a musical happening in a former slaughterhouse, a symposium in an empty movie theater, performances in a former underwear factory, an electronic music concert under a road bridge, an artistic light installation in an old schnapps factory. In other activities, for example *Operation: City,* all of Zagreb's important initiatives and independent cultural organizations were included. The result was to spur a public debate that ultimately reached the politicians as well, who agreed to make spaces available for independent cultural activity. These promises, however, have yet to be fulfilled. In view of new commercial real-estate and urban planning projects, a new initiative has formed under the name of "Right to the City" (Pravo na grad) with the same activists, who are now increasingly leveling criticism at official planning, the privatization of public space, and gentrification, and are organizing protests, such as, for example, sit-ins.

The initiators of claim campaigns like this are the potential users themselves as well as political activists and sympathetic agents—not, however, the property owners and politicians, with whom the initiators have a conflict of interest. Nevertheless, there are always key actors in city politics who endorse and support the project and play an important role in its realization. The fact that the legitimacy of existing planning is being called

into question in the media allows them to deviate from the existing official line, which has usually lost majority public support. As a rule, these political dissenters tend to be cultural politicians—for example, the Berlin culture senator Thomas Flierl in the case of ZwischenPalastNutzung (TemporaryPalaceUse) and the Hamburg Ministry of Culture in that of the Park Fiction project.

The initiators themselves are not primarily interested in realizing uses of their own. What is central for them is the desire to conquer a highly visible space of freedom for a large number of potential activists. As a rule the projects are not simply open to additional actors; more than this, there is an active effort to attract a wide variety of users. For the broader the coalition, the greater its public legitimacy. By establishing connections with prominent international actors, the projects gain additional weight and persuasiveness locally. In the case of the Park Fiction project this function was fulfilled by the invitation to participate in *documenta 11*, in that of the ZwischenPalastNutzung project by the repeated involvement of prominent cultural figures from Germany and abroad.

CONFLICTS OF INTEREST

Underlying the conflict between the users and the often public property owner is either a desire to exploit the property commercially (this is the case with Park Fiction and the Gängeviertel in Hamburg or MediaSpree in Berlin) or the planned demolition of an empty building (the case with the Palast der Republik, or Palace of the Republic, in Berlin-Mitte and the ZfzK in Halle-Neustadt). The latter case involved a railroad station that, since 2003, has stood empty in the center of Halle-Neustadt, a tower apartment block development from the GDR era that once had 100,000 residents but now has only 50,000 remaining. This dormitory town has always had services nearby, including a large shopping center, but it has no centrally located cultural institutions. Despite or precisely because of the dramatic shrinking of Halle-Neustadt, a broad array of cultural figures and town planners has stepped forward to work for the creation of a Center for Contem-

277 CLAIM

porary Culture (Zentrum für zeitgenössische Kultur, or ZfzK) in the disused railroad building. Their goal was to take the former transportation junction and bring it to life again as an urban center that would function as a strong source of identity for the area.

The center's initiation began with a series of temporary cultural projects, first in 2003 with *Rap Battles* in the context of the Theaterfestival Hotel Neustadt (Hotel Neustadt Theater Festival) by the Thalia Theater, and then in 2005 with a summer academy of the Internationale Bau-Ausstellung (IBA) Stadtumbau / Stiftung Bauhaus Dessau (International Building Exhibition on Urban Redevelopment / Bauhaus Dessau Foundation) and the Thalia Theater, for which a room of the building was converted into a bar to complement the indoor skateboarding facilities. In winter 2005–2006 there followed the exhibition *Shrinking Cities,* which drew five thousand visitors. For this occasion, with the approval of the city of Halle, the building was named "ZfzK" (Zentrum für zeitgenössische Kultur) and a neon sign to that effect was attached to it. An international curators workshop was held on the conception, and an association was founded. Since then, the association and the Halle city administration fought with the building's owner, the Deutsche Bahn (the German national railway), to prevent its planned demolition. After the building was closed in 2006 and the use agreement with the Deutsche Bahn was not extended, in 2007 the association installed a mobile ZfzK–"ZfzK Light 0.7"—which, among other venues, guested at the Festival della Creativität in Florence. This "cultural container" served as a vehicle for contemporary cultural activities at various locations throughout Halle. However, the association could not prevent the demolition of the train station—it took place in 2010.

It is also quite possible to have a situation in which the conflict of interest that underlies the claim strategies only arises in the course of a temporary use. This is the case, for example, where the temporary use was only briefly tolerated by the property owner and is now due to end to make way for a commercial exploitation of the property, but where the temporary use has thrived at the interim location and there is interest in it continuing

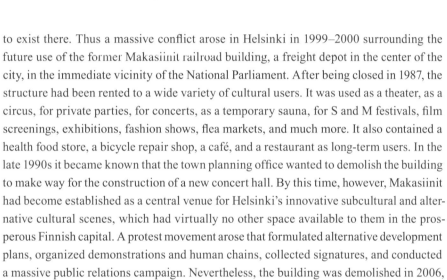

Concert below an inner-city street bridge, Zagreb

to exist there. Thus a massive conflict arose in Helsinki in 1999–2000 surrounding the future use of the former Makasiinit railroad building, a freight depot in the center of the city, in the immediate vicinity of the National Parliament. After being closed in 1987, the structure had been rented to a wide variety of cultural users. It was used as a theater, as a circus, for private parties, for concerts, as a temporary sauna, for S and M festivals, film screenings, exhibitions, fashion shows, flea markets, and much more. It also contained a health food store, a bicycle repair shop, a café, and a restaurant as long-term users. In the late 1990s it became known that the town planning office wanted to demolish the building to make way for the construction of a new concert hall. By this time, however, Makasiinit had become established as a central venue for Helsinki's innovative subcultural and alternative cultural scenes, which had virtually no other space available to them in the prosperous Finnish capital. A protest movement arose that formulated alternative development plans, organized demonstrations and human chains, collected signatures, and conducted a massive public relations campaign. Nevertheless, the building was demolished in 2006, accompanied shortly before by civil unrest.

TRADITIONS

Claim-based action strategies have a long tradition in the history of municipal conflict. In different ways, sit-ins, the campaigns of the Reclaim the Street movement, and the traditions of occupying unused houses and land are all versions of claim-based strategies. Like the sit-ins of the 1960s and 1970s, the happenings of the Reclaim the Street movement were short-term occupations of places that captured widespread public attention in an effort to press for their transformation and call into question the existing power structures with which they were associated. Sit-ins took place primarily at public institutions such as universities, government offices, and cultural and social institutions. The issue for the Reclaim the Street movement is the street as the space of automobile traffic, which they wish to reclaim for pedestrians and cyclists.

Occupations of houses and land generally aim at long-term use, but because they are illegal they initially have a purely provisional, temporary status. Depending on the political constellation, however, they are sometimes able to avoid eviction and establish themselves more permanently. Whereas the occupations of land that take place in South and Central America and elsewhere seek to gain the bare necessities of life for the poorest sections of society, the use of claim strategies in industrialized countries tends to revolve around cultural hegemony, local constellations of power, and social models that must be fought out between middle-class subculture on the one hand and the political and economic establishment on the other.

FURTHER IINFORMATION

www.contrast.org/KG/index.htm

www.rts.gn.apc.org

www.kangastus.org/makasiinit

www.gaengeviertel.info

www.pravonagrad.org

www.rechtaufstadt.net

www.magito.fi/makasiinit.net/historia.htm

autonome a.f.r.i.k.a. gruppe, Luter Blissett, and Sonja Brünzels, *Handbuch der Kommunikationsguerilla* (Berlin: Assoziation a., 2001)

Sonja Brünzels, "Reclaim the Streets: Karneval und Konfrontation," in *derive 2* (November 2000)

Gordon Mackay (ed.), *DIY Culture: Party and Protest in Nineties Britain*, (London: Verso, 1968)

Kimmo Oksanen, *Makasiinit 1899–2006* (Helsinki: Helsingin Sanomat, 2006)

Christoph Schäfer, *The City is Our Factory* (Leipzig: Spector Books, 2010)

Symposium in a vacant movie theater, Zagreb

PARK FICTION, HAMBURG

OBJECTIVE: to create a public neighborhood park instead of a private investment project

PROTAGONIST: citizens' initiative

USE: public park

STATUS: at first unlicensed activities, now legal and open-ended, managed and maintained by the district of Altona

SITE: 3,500 square meters of open space in Hamburg-St. Pauli, property of the Free and Hanseatic City of Hamburg

TRAJECTORY: citizens' initiative since 1994, main planning phase 1996–1998, realization 2002–2006

COST: Planning approximately €80,000 and a great deal of unpaid work, park approximately €2,400,000, gymnasium €3,900,000

FINANCING: Ministry of Culture, Ministry of Urban Development, Ministry of the Environment, and Ministry of Education of the Free and Hanseatic City of Hamburg; district of Altona; district of Mitte

Wanda Wieczorek

The demand for a park can be politically explosive in a neighborhood like St. Pauli. Here the needs of residents, tradespeople, investors, tourists, and nightclub patrons compete for satisfaction. St. Pauli is still one of Hamburg's poorest neighborhoods. It suffers from high unemployment and criminality and is forced to contend with more than its share of noise, traffic, prostitution, and drugs. It has a population density five times Hamburg's average, while living space per resident is 70 percent below the mean. Green spaces are small, few in number, and in high demand. But St. Pauli is also rich. A culture of critique has arisen here that stands for an independent approach to forms of living and dwelling. The squatting of the houses on Hafenstrasse in 1981 and the conflict over their preservation, which lasted a good ten years, are doubtless the best known examples. The dynamic of the housing struggles seized the entire neighborhood. Along with the spectrum of *linksautonom* groups, the struggles were marked by politicized artistic and subcultural scenes. Residents, the pastor of the nearby church, and neighborhood social institutions expressed their solidarity with the squatters. This network of supporters remained in existence even after the preservation of Hafenstrasse had been achieved. It extended its gaze beyond Hafenstrasse to everyday life in the neighborhood as a whole.

The shortage of open spaces and the increasing pressure from investors pointed the way for the coming struggle. Not far from Hafenstrasse was one of the last remaining undeveloped areas on the St. Pauli waterfront: the Geesthang by the Pinnasberg with a view of the Elbe and the harbor. In 1994 the Hamburg State Parliament approved a development plan for the area that envisioned the construction of a six-story residential building. But the neighborhood network presented a counterproposal. Instead of a closed waterfront development they called for the creation of a park. In 1995 two local artists signed up to the proposal. At the invitation of the Ministry of Culture they entered plans for Park Fiction in a competition for art in the public space (called *weitergehen : "going on" or "going further"*) and received the nod to continue planning. Thus, the neighborhood network had succeeded in bringing two different city departments into conflict, since the Ministry of Urban Development continued to insist on developing the land while the Ministry of Culture endorsed the planned park.

WISH PRODUCTION: "WISHES WILL LEAVE THE HOUSE AND GO OUT TO THE STREET"

Although the city administration continued to insist on developing the land, Park Fiction took its next steps in a parallel planning process—the initiators continued to plan the park without a commission from the city, without waiting for the authorities and other planning entities to come along. Numerous events, including exhibitions, parties, concerts, and lectures, were devoted to the public space of the city and examined its tension-filled relationship to private (living) space. The motif of wishes emerged as the central argument. The goal of the park planners was to learn to observe and name one's own needs, to encourage the residents to articulate their subjective thoughts and feelings, and hence to promote a different approach to the city and its planning. This position is at odds with the prevailing approach to planning—according to this alternative vision, the planning process should be guided not by the bureaucratic ordinances of planning authorities, brilliant architects, or managers of an "enterprise: city," but by everyday practices and the wishes of the city's residents. Many of the activities anticipated the desired use of the area, as an alternative to neoliberal planning fantasies, as a place of encounter, play, debate, and recreation.

CONSUMERS OF THE CITY BECOME PRODUCERS OF THE CITY

In 1997 the movement to create a park benefited from the aggravation of the political situation in St. Pauli. The announced closure of the Hafenkrankenhaus (Harbor Hospital) triggered a vehement wave of protest. In order to increase pressure on the Senate, the park activists occupied the Geesthang, cleaned it up, built benches, planted flowers, and proclaimed its use as a neighborhood park. The gamble worked—because it was in the middle of an election year, the city government was eager to deflate the situation, so it showed itself willing to negotiate and agreed to the construction of the park. The moneys appropriated by the Ministry of Culture were released; the planning process for the park— the collective wish production—could begin.

With the project money from the Ministry of Culture, AG Park Fiction developed various tools to ensure a process "in the public interest." A planning container was set up on site in which conversations and interviews were conducted, plans were sketched, and wishes for the park were molded in modeling clay. The wishes collected in this way grew into a wish archive. An infotainment series with lectures, discussions, and slide shows on various aspects of garden and public green space design along with visits to Hamburg parks stimulated the residents' imagination, and broadened the spectrum of what it seemed possible to wish for. The "action kit," a mobile planning suitcase, was used on house visits in the area around the park in an effort to gather the opinions of as many residents as possible. By the end of the planning process in summer 1998, more than

1,500 people had participated in the collective process of wish production with spoken and written words, drawings, and models.

FIGHTING BUREAUCRACY

By contrast, the implementation of the park planning was marked by bureaucratic delays: arguments between government offices, health and safety caveats, electoral calculations, and construction mishaps. There were neighborhood conferences at which all the wishes were presented, their transformation into reality was discussed, and the plans were adopted. Before the park was actually built, however, a tug-of-war ensued between the authorities and the residents that lasted for years, exacerbated by the fact that the boundary between two different districts runs right through the park, which greatly increased the number of responsible agencies and committees involved. The inconclusive discussions at the "round table" wore the park activists down and were largely responsible for the breakup of the core planning group. Many of the initially daring plans were ground down by the machinery of implementation. The fact that the park was realized at all is due to

the dedication of a small handful of people and not least to strong interest in the project on the part of the arts community. For in contrast to the official obstructionism there was growing public interest in Park Fiction, especially in the art world. The participation of artists had opened up a field of the conflict on which the city authorities were ill-equipped to fight–the struggle for legitimacy and symbolic capital. By 2002 at the very latest, when it participated in *documenta 11*, Park Fiction was in a position to set international renown against the delaying tactics of the local authorities.

CONTINUING CONFLICTS

The park exists—the residents have won. But its full potential has not been tapped. The challenge to established planning models that was represented by the *planning* of the park in St. Pauli sometimes seems to have its fiercest competitor in the *realization* of the park. For over the years the authorities' mills have administered the élan of the collective process of wish production to death and whittled down many of their demands. The participatory planning approach proved impossible to sustain during the construction of the park. The length of time alone that it took to complete it dampened the original dynamism. Children who in 1997 were still planning their own tree house have since grown up and are no longer interested in tree houses.

Now that it has arrived in the here and now, the park also has to defend itself against the commercial interests of the neighboring businesspeople. For the noncommercial use of the space is one of the most clearly followed principles of Park Fiction. What is more,

CLAIM PARK FICTION

St. Pauli is exposed to a massive process of gentrification. The demands of investors and the restaurant trade are growing, not least in connection with the overall conversion of the waterfront district into the "string of pearls" of the Hanseatic City of Hamburg. Thus, with the Empire Riverside Hotel, a large-scale project, part of the neighborhood's restructuring and displacement process, was erected in the immediate vicinity. Yet the residents gained substantial experience during the conflicts surrounding Hafenstrasse in the 1980s and the park in the 1990s. With the citizen's initiative NoBNQ, they are defending themselves against the subtle mechanisms of disinvestment, high vacancy rates, decay, redevelopment new buildings and rent increases and demand not only participation, but freedom for self-determined design and action in urban planning. Associated with the city-wide protest and action network "Recht auf Stadt" (Right to the City), previous experience, success, and personal continuity not only constitute symbolic capital; rather, specific forms of knowledge and practices are brought into the city-wide debates and conflicts.

FURTHER IINFORMATION

www.esregnetkaviar.de

www.no-bnq.org

www.parkfiction.org

Margit Czenki, *Park Fiction – Die Wünsche werden die Wohnung verlassen und auf die Strasse gehen,* film, FRG 1999, 16 mm, 61 min., screenwriter / director / editor: Margit Czenki ; text: Christoph Schäfer; cinematographers: Martin Gressmann and Margit Czenki; music: Ted Gaier and Schorsch Kamerun.

Christoph Schäfer, "The City is Unwritten," in Brett Bloom and Ava Bromberg, eds., *Making Their Own Plans* (Chicago: WhiteWalls, 2005).

OBJECTIVE: cultural use and preservation of the Palast der Republik

PROTAGONIST: cultural producers and architects (Urban Catalyst; ZwischenPalast-Nutzung e.V.; Volkspalast)

USE: cultural; theater, dance, music, exhibition, discussion

STATUS: legal; short-term leases

SITE: centrally located Parliament building of the GDR, property of the Federal Republic of Germany; 60,000 square meters

TRAJECTORY: concepts 2001–2002, realizations 2004–2005, demolition 2006–2008

COST: includes €100,000 for conversion for two-month use by VOLKSPALAST 2004; €650,000 for cultural program of VOLKSPALAST 2004 and 2005; rent in 2004 €6,000 / month, 2005 €12,000 / month

On September 19, 1990 the Palast der Republik (Palace of the Republic) was closed just fourteen years after its opening because of danger from asbestos. During the six-year process of asbestos removal, the inside of the building was gutted down to its basic static elements—a gigantic steel skeleton with floor slabs made of precast concrete components came to light.

Just shortly after the end of the GDR, the fate of the building and the future of the area seemed to be sealed. The demolition of the building had already been decided in 1993, and it met with resistance from only a small group of directly affected former Palast employees and a handful of intellectuals. Before the end of the year, a temporary simulation of the Berliner Stadtschloss (Berlin City Palace, the Prussian royal residence that had previously stood on the spot) was inaugurated amid great euphoria. The lobby of reconstructors positioned itself unambiguously and aggressively against a timid opposition who were branded *Ostalgiker* (a combination of *Nostalgiker*, or "nostalgics," with *ost*, the German word for "east," implying that they were nostalgic for the GDR). The winning entry in the town planning competition, hastily held in 1994, also seemed to capture the mood of the time: it envisaged the removal of the Palast and the reconstruction of the cubic form of the Schloss. Other than that, however, the proponents of reconstruction had no ideas regarding the possible content of the new structure, whether in terms of its use or with regard to whom the building sponsor should be. The answers to these questions varied throughout the following twelve years—the only constant was the desire for the Schloss facade. But the hope that another Berlin mega project would now be built on the fast track never quite got off the ground. On the one hand the asbestos problem made it impossible to proceed with the immediate demolition of the Palast; on the other there were signs that a hangover was setting in after years of a euphoric construction boom. The combined cost of €670 million for the building and reconstruction of the Schloss facade was more and more difficult to justify in the context of an economic crisis and empty public coffers.

NETWORK

Before the asbestos abatement was finished, various cultural actors—composers, artists, choreographers, opera houses, clubs, and others—expressed interest in the ruined building

as a place to realize temporary projects. At first, however, the proposals, all of which were put forward as isolated ideas, went unheeded—the planning decisions seemed too clear and too final, the prospect of using the ruin too costly and complex, and the resistance on the part of the state bureaucracy too insurmountable. In this situation, the research group Urban Catalyst approached the actors in spring 2002 and offered to perform a feasibility study in order to solve the existing problems with a common concept for a large number of uses. The state of the building itself made it necessary to link the various ideas—because of its dilapidated condition, any temporary use would require technical and constructional measures that would have far exceeded the possibilities and pockets of an individual user.

However, negotiations with the Federation as the owner of the building proved far more difficult. The responsible Oberfinanzdirektion (Regional Finance Office) and Bundes-vermögensamt (Federal Property Office, now the Bundesanstalt für Immobilienauf-gaben, or Federal Institute for Real Property Tasks), claimed that a temporary use of the building would cost €15 million and was therefore impossible. The owner's representatives regarded any further conversations as superfluous. Politicians and policy makers at the national level kept out of all discussions of the delicate subject. In the resulting political vacuum, the purely administrative elements of the government acted as they saw fit, and they based their view on the assumption that what was being proposed was a commercial exploitation of the building, something they initially regarded as impossible.

After developing a plan for a three-year use by the network consisting of Urban Catalyst and interested parties from the Sophiensäle, the Staatsoper Unter den Linden (Berlin State

Opera), the Deutsches Technikmuseum (German Museum of Technology), Club WMF,
activists involved in sociocultural youth work, and the artist Fred Rubin, the initiators
decided to go public with the project in order to put pressure on the Federation as owner
and the responsible politicians. In the neighboring Staatsratsgebäude (the building that
previously housed the GDR Staatsrat, or Council of State), they organized a three-day
exhibition, events, and a press conference. They made an offer to the owner according
to which the initiative formed for this purpose would organize a three-year cultural
temporary use of the Palast, making all the necessary technical arrangements and securing
all the necessary financing.

The public response was beyond all expectations. The opening of the exhibition in the
Staatsratsgebäude was already attended by several thousand visitors. More than a hundred
journalists reported on the event, and the resulting articles were almost entirely positive—
some of them were euphoric. The public's interest had now been aroused. Whereas none
of the many alternative construction plans for the Schlossplatz (the former location of the
Berliner Stadtschloss and now the location of the Palast der Republik) of the past ten years
had succeeded in sparking any sustained enthusiasm—if only because of the lack of certainty regarding the planned use of the building, building sponsorship, and financing—the
idea of the temporary use opened up an entirely different perspective. It started right in by
addressing the use and the program of events; it brought contemporary cultural production

After two years of tenacious struggling with politics and administration, independent cultural producers succeed in carrying out the two-and-a-half-month "Volkspalast" festival in summer 2004. Fifty-five thousand people visited the opened foyer.

to the site for the first time; it allowed a broad spectrum of actors to participate actively; and it could be implemented quickly. Thus, in addition to those who were actually interested in participating in the temporary use of the building, it also succeeded in winning the support of all those who were critical of the proposed reconstruction of the Stadtschloss, and who found in the project a focal point that confronted the official reconstruction policy with aggressive actions.

The success of the events at the Staatsratsgebäude also led to a consolidation of the cooperative network. Together the initiators created the Verein ZwischenPalastNutzung, or ZPN (TemporaryPalaceUse Association), which established an authoritative form for negotiating with third parties, making public appearances, and raising the necessary funds. The owner was now forced to concede that it was possible to use the building for a tenth of the cost it had previously estimated. However, it wasn't long before it threw up new bureaucratic hurdles to thwart the project. The new line was that the building could only be rented as a whole and that the renter would be required to cover all the associated costs to the Federation, which amounted to €140,000 per year. Moreover, the building could only be rented for individual projects; under no circumstances could it be rented for a program series. Leases would only be possible on condition that they be subject to termination on four weeks notice. Considering the substantial investment costs involved, these conditions made it effectively impossible to rent or lease the building.

TROJAN HORSE

The stagnating situation led to a change of strategy. The initiators decided to hold individual interventions at the site in order to sustain and strengthen public interest in the project. At the same time, these interventions would demonstrate that temporary use of the building was actually feasible, and they would even gradually begin to facilitate such use. In fact, public interest in the building was now so strong that the initiators were able to win the semiofficial agency Partner für Berlin (Partners for Berlin) as a collaborator. Minimal sums were invested for emergency lighting, fences, and staircase railings in order to make the building accessible to the public for the first time since the asbestos abatement, in the context of the program *Schaustelle Berlin* in July 2003. Thus, five thousand interested visitors were led along a path marked out through the Palast on walking tours that sold out in just a few hours. After *Schaustelle,* the security modifications made by the Mediapool event agency were left in place—they constituted an initial subset of the planned infrastructure for the temporary use of the building.

In September of the same year—after tough new negotiations—the initiative was able to take another step forward. With the concert series "Wagnerkomplex" by Christian von Borries in cooperation with the Brandenburgische Philharmonie Potsdam (Brandenburg

Façade republic within the scope of the "Volkspalast" festival, 2004. The Raumlabor group of architects installed an island landscape on the flooded basement floor. The area of water was officially approved as a fire fighting pond.

Philharmonic Orchestra, Potsdam)—realized by the Sophiensäle—the first public performances were held in the Palast der Republik, thus realizing one of the initiative's projects. This was possible, incidentally, only because the concert series was declared to be a "musical tour" shortly before it opened; with this designation the way was clear for obtaining a building permit.

Immediately after this first artistic event at the Palast and before September 2003 was over, the German Bundestag decided to demolish the building quickly, by the end of 2004. Following up on the first steps, Siegfried Paul of Mediapool carried out a new feasibility study for ZwischenPalastNutzung on the use of the Palast as a venue for public performances and events. Building on his many years of experience with temporary cultural projects and thanks to his close contacts with the building authority, he was able to come up with innovative solutions that would reduce the cost of the technical overhaul many times over, to €100,000. The concept was limited to reconstructing the former foyer. In parallel with this, the ZwischenPalastNutzung initiative developed the concept for a three-year use of the building as a cultural venue. In discussions with the international curators Hans Ulrich Obrist (Paris), Boris Ondreicka (Bratislava), and Hannah Hurtzig (Berlin), the initiative developed the concept *1000 Tage* (1000 Days), which defined thematic areas

and guidelines. The Palast was to be an innovative "open source" project, inclusive and nonhierarchical. The public presentation of this more highly elaborated concept took place in November 2003 (two weeks after the announcement of the decision to demolish the building the following year) with the support of prominent German cultural figures such as the film director Volker Schlöndorff, the opera director Peter Mussbach, and the urban development politician Karl Ganser. Once again the media echo was tremendous. But the situation with the Federation as the owner of the building failed to improve. However, because of the enormous public response, commercial entities now began to contact the owner regarding possible use of the building. The owner gradually came to recognize the building's potential, but it stuck to its negative attitude vis-à-vis the apparently difficult cultural producers and set its hopes on a lucrative commercial lease instead.

It was not until the Berlin cultural senator Thomas Flierl stepped in that the stalled situation began to show signs of movement. He arranged a meeting with the Verein ZPN, Federation and state representatives with responsibility for the issue, Bauaufsicht Mitte (the Mitte Building Authority), experts, and cultural figures. The goal of the meeting was to establish the framework conditions for a substantial cultural program at the Palast der Republik for 2004 and to approve the Palast for cultural use, in keeping with the recommendation of the International Commission of Experts from 2001.

The meeting opened with a "bombshell." The Bundesvermögensamt, the agency responsible for administering the Palast, tersely informed the gathering that a few days earlier it had rented the Palast to an Erfurt company that wished to use it for an exhibition

of copies of Chinese terra-cotta soldiers from the grave sites of Xian. This was a commercial exhibition that had thus far been held in tents on fields, primarily on the outskirts of a few big cities—an exhibition that wished to use the Palast simply as an attractive central location, without any substantive connection to its special character or historical specificity. The agency's thinking was transparent: a commercial business enterprise with no cultural or political ambitions seemed to be a more promising partner than a group of cultural producers with artistic as well as political and cultural ambitions. Nevertheless, before the meeting was over a compromise was reached, albeit a painful one. The Bundesvermögensamt did not reconsider its decision to rent the Palast for the exhibition, but it did make a binding commitment to rent the Palast to the Verein ZPN from August to November 2004 for a cultural program. Thus the way was now open for a cultural temporary use of the Palast.

Immediately after the decision to allow the temporary use of the Palast, the Staatsoper Unter den Linden withdrew from the joint project. The financial risk of using the venue seemed too high, and the period of just a few months seemed too short for realizing its opera project with Marina Abramovic. However, by returning the funds it had received for the project from the Hauptstadtkulturfonds (Capital Culture Fund), the opera house cleared the way for other projects at the Palast der Republik that now received these funds instead, thanks to the dedication of the curator Adrienne Goehler.

Since the ZwischenPalastNutzung project had always been a network, it offered to find new partners. It was the Theater Hebbel am Ufer (HAU) under the direction of Matthias

Lilienthal that spontaneously agreed to join the project and team up with the Sophiensäle to coordinate organizational activities. There was no question of the Verein ZPN serving as the organizer, since it had no way of assuming the financial risk. Also, the Bundesvermögensamt required that its contractual partner be a corporation. On the basis of the *1000 Days* concept, a condensed concept for a three-month season was developed under the artistic direction of Amelie Deuflhard, Matthias Lilienthal and Philipp Oswalt: VOLKS-PALAST (PEOPLE'S PALACE).

INTERVENTION

The VOLKSPALAST concept consisted in temporarily experimenting with the kinds of uses that would be capable of generating ideas for the future and at the same time of relating to the history of the site. The essence of the program was to take up the idea of the multifunctional cultural center, examine its contemporary relevance, and develop it into a twenty-first century institution. This basic idea necessarily meant appealing to an audience that went far beyond normal festival- and theatergoers. What was needed was a democratization of the audience. The strategy for this was to expand the audience not by making it shallower, but by making it more diverse. The organizers worked with figures from high culture all the way to sub- and club culture. The events encompassed theater and dance projects, a choral project, the staging of a Potemkin water city, a sports program for young people, an international architectural conference, music and film programs, and club events. All of the participating artists had to prepare works specifically for VOLKSPALAST. They were asked to treat the empty foyer of the Palast freely as a projection screen, with everything that implied. Temporariness was a fundamental principle, as was an antithesis to institutionalization. Programmatic in this connection was the symposium *Fun Palace,* a project proposed by Hans Ulrich Obrist in relation to the visionary architect

Cedric Price. The cultural projects were financed by public subsidies and admission fees, and the necessary construction measures were taken through cooperation with McKinsey & Company, T-Mobile, and the record label Motor, which were allowed to use the building for a few days in exchange for financing.

Even before VOLKSPALAST 1 was over, the date for demolishing the building was set for December 2005. Moreover, in October 2004—also while VOLKSPALAST was still underway—the minister of culture Christina Weiss and the Berlin culture senator Thomas Flierl decided to turn over the task of organizing the 2005 cultural program at the Palast to a public institution of the Federal state of Berlin. It is only because no suitable institution could be found that this task reverted to the original actors for 2005.

Meanwhile, other actors—cultural as well as commercial—had begun to express an interest in using the building. Even before VOLKSPALAST 1, the Bund der Deutschen Industrie, or BDI (Federation of German Industries) had held its annual convention at the Palast der Republik in June 2004, with the participation of leading national politicians. After VOLKSPALAST 1 there followed two theater productions, including Frank Castorf's adaptation of the novel *Berlin Alexanderplatz* by Alfred Döblin, a world break dancing championship, and an installation by the Norwegian artist Lars Ramberg, a gigantic neon sign with the word "ZWEIFEL" ("DOUBT"), which was mounted on the roof of the building and could be seen from a great distance.

The second round of VOLKSPALAST began under changed conditions: a date had been set for the demolition—end of debate. The installation *Der Berg (The Mountain),* by raumlabor and Club Real, dealt with the planned imitation of the Stadtschloss in the context of an absurd game. The mountain in the Palast was as senseless and as disconnected from social and spatial contexts as the romantic idea of reconstructing the Schloss facades. The mountain is transplanted from another space, the Schloss from another time.

The mountain creates a social body, a place for settlement and community, a place for free artistic production. The artists adopted it; the visitors climbed and discovered it. And they thought about socialist palaces, Prussian royal palaces, and mountains. A weakness of the project *Der Berg* was that it represented a more formal, primarily aesthetic intervention, whereas in this situation of imminent demolition, a strong politicization and thematization of the future of the site would have been desirable. An alternative proposal in that spirit for an exhibition project called *The Big Public Building / Urbane Kommunikationsräume für das 21. Jahrhundert* (The Big Public Building / Urban Spaces of Communication for the Twenty-First Century) had been refused state funding by the politicians despite the endorsement of the panel of experts.

The last temporary uses of the gutted Palast der Republik were the art exhibitions *Fraktale IV (Fractals IV)* and *White Cube,* which were held there toward the end of 2005. Both of them were highly successful and attracted some seventy thousand visitors. More than six hundred thousand people attended the over nine hundred events and performances held at the Palast during the year and a half that it was a venue for temporary use. In the course of 2006, more and more people came forward who wanted to hold performances and events in the building beyond the planned demolition date. Building on the experience of the temporary use thus far, the Berlin architect Claus Anderthalten presented the widely acclaimed concept *WeltKulturPalast (WorldCulturePalace).* It envisioned taking the Humboldtforum, a use that was planned for the newly constructed Stadtschloss, and housing it instead in a transformed Palast der Republik for a fraction of the cost.

In late summer 2006 a protest movement finally sprang up that opposed the demolition of the Palast with a broad range of actions in the months that followed, with demonstrations, happenings, picnics, press conferences, poster and postcard campaigns, and signature drives. Unlike the protest movement of the early 1990s, this one was carried by a younger generation that mainly came from Western Germany. They knew the building primarily from its temporary use and saw it as an important built witness to recent and contemporary history, as a symbol for the new Berlin and reunited Germany in all their ambivalence. The domestic and foreign press followed the conflict with great interest, usually with strong sympathy for the opponents of demolition. Despite the strong public pressure, the German Bundestag reiterated its decision to demolish the Palast in early 2006, and just a few days later the process began.

The older generation of politicians who were still socialized during, and traumatized by, the Cold War saw the demolition of the Palast as an additional, welcome, and this time symbolic destruction of the GDR, and neither objective arguments nor public pressure was able to dissuade them. In another sense, however, the temporary use was remarkably successful. The very fact that this central, most discussed, and perhaps most bitterly contested site in Germany could be appropriated for a year and a half for an alternative cultural use in which almost a million people participated was anything but a matter of course. It was also remarkably effective. It not only gave rise to a protest movement against the demolition—it also made the idea and practice of temporary use widely known and appreciated in Germany and internationally. Even if it is still unclear whether the establishment of new actors by the temporary use—*White Cube,* for example—will

have medium term consequences for the development of the site, there are nonetheless signs that this widely followed Berlin event is already having a positive effect on the discussion and potential of other sites in other cities. Last but not least, the site itself has been transformed. For many, after the temporary use the Palast der Republik no longer represented the central government building of the GDR but a laboratory for contemporary cultural production. The Palast had become the site of a social conflict that—aesthetically, culturally, and politically—reflected the difficult and extremely ambivalent process of German unification.

EPILOGUE

The debate over the temporary use of the site continued to be relevant, even after demolition began. Common to all the proposals was an attempt to continue the success of the temporary use of the Palast in modified form. The project *20,000 qm x 5 Jahre (20,000 m² x 5 Years)* for the temporary cultural use of the basement levels of the Palast, which following demolition provisionally remained in place, was rejected by the owner until the reconstruction by Urban Catalyst.

However, after intensive reporting in the media, the initiators succeeded in winning the support of state and national leaders for the construction of a new temporary art gallery, provided the project did not require any public money. The project *Temporäre Kunsthalle Berlin* tied in directly to the final use of the Palast as a temporary exhibition space for contemporary art, which was very positively received. Adolf Krischanitz designed the temporary Kunsthalle according to the concept of the white cube, whose facade was to be used as a convertible display and as space for visual arts projects in urban space. Seventeen exhibitions were mounted within a period of two years that were meant to introduce Berlin's contemporary art scene to a wider audience. The program met with an ambivalent response from both the public and the local art scene; it was not until toward the end of the program, after the art director had been replaced several times, that it met with general approval. With only 200,000 visitors, attendance was much lower than for the temporary use of the Palast. Although, besides the promotion of contemporary art, the motivation of the project's main sponsor, the patron Dieter Rosenkranz, was the rejection of the planned reconstruction of the Schloss, the program was consciously kept apolitical, and one that refrained from making any kind of explicit contribution to the site's potential. It is hardly surprising that in this respect the project had no impact whatsoever; by contrast, plans for a Kunsthalle in Berlin took root. Mayor Klaus Wowereit gave top priority to erecting a permanent Kunsthalle. Following the failure of an initial attempt to realize a Kunsthalle through a bidding process by private investors for a piece of real estate near the main train station, a renewed temporary realization, a stocktaking exhibition in summer 2011, was implemented at Humboldthafen and financed by public funds, including its temporary architecture. Berlin sees this project as a step toward a permanent exhibition venue.

The temporary Kunsthalle building at Schlossplatz, however, was purchased in late 2010 by the art foundation Thyssen-Bornemisza Art Contemporary (TBA-21), which in summer 2011 wanted to open it in Vienna for a period of five years and operate it as an art venue. The Austrian architect Krischanitz had already realized a temporary Kunsthalle in Vienna in 1993 that, following its relocation to the museum district, became a permanent venue.

The Kunsthalle was not the only temporary use at the Schloss site following demolition of the Palast. In 2006, the Senate carried out a landscape plan competition for the areas that were not required for the new subway line or archeological excavations. The winning design by relais Landschaftsarchitekten, which was later modified before it was actually implemented, fell in perfectly with the political specifications: allow grass to grow over the site and hinder its use by means of boardwalks. The client's goals had been clearly identified in internal Senate documents: "The open space . . . is to be greened in the simplest way possible and not configured. . . . Turning the grounds into a green space enables thwarting any use claims." A further element was added: the so-called Humboldt Box. The name was deliberately chosen in order to avoid the words "temporary use" and "Schloss," although the box's only purpose as a temporary use is to promote the Schloss proposal. After some delay, the Humboldt Box opened in spring 2011.

Carsten Nioclai, *autoR*, public intervention on the exterior facade of the Temporäre Kunsthalle Berlin, April–August 2010

It is financed by extensive outdoor advertising and operated by Megaposter GmbH. Thus, the commercialization of the prominent site is being tolerated.

While on the part of policy-makers the conflict over the temporary use of the site was still ongoing, the Schloss building project was advanced. The actual decision with respect to the project, above all the actual financing, was delayed as long as possible in order to first reach a "point of no return" by creating a general level of expectation. While the reconstruction of the facades remained a project constant, the use and financing of the building were modified over the course of a decade, depending on the prevailing political expediency. Policy-makers and several lobbyists skillfully pressed ahead with the project in the sense of a controlled request production. Ironically, the Schloss building project began with a temporary use: in 1993, a mock-up of the facade and an exhibition were installed at Schlossplatz. Since then, the government has used an intense and at times manipulative public relations campaign that sometimes works with deliberate misinformation to ply the public with a constant stream of untenable wish images, both with respect to financing and the structure's use. The responsible politicians and policy-makers are all too aware of the legitimation deficit. The project is dividing the public, and for a long time it was incapable of winning a majority among the population. And so the imposition of the facade simulation is accompanied by fictitious financing options, fictitious uses, and fictitious political decisions. The minutes of the German Bundestag itself selectively tell a quite sobering story: "Alternatives: none. Cost: cost was not discussed" (November 12, 2003). For the counterposition a central premise has changed with the demolition of the Palast. With the loss of the building it is deprived of a concrete site that can serve as a focal point and action platform for alternative scenarios. This makes it painfully clear how the control of space has a massive influence on the possibilities of social development.

In 2008, the design by the previously little-known Italian architect Franco Stella, who consistently implemented the Bundestag's strict specifications, won the international competition. Many saw the competition as a farce, for the specifications were so rigid that the winning design could only be a simulation of the Prussian city palace based on photographic similarity: thus, numerous internationally renowned architects failed to participate. An alternative design by Kühl Malvezzi that put forth an innovative interpretation of the specifications and which was favored by the majority of the jury and a large share of the media received a lucrative special prize, but was not taken into consideration. The client immediately launched the implementation of the winning design despite a great deal of doubt as to the architect's qualifications, rising costs, and a crisis in public funding. In June 2010, although the federal government officially announced the postponement of construction as part of an austerity package to ease the budget, the project pressed ahead behind the scenes. In the meantime, construction is planned for 2013/14, and completion for 2018/19.

FURTHER INFORMATION:

www.schlossdebatte.de

www.palastretter.de

www.zwischenpalastnutzung.de

www.kunsthalle-berlin.com

Amelie Deuflhard, Sophie Krempl, Philipp Oswalt, Matthias Lilienthal, and Harald Müller, eds., *Volkspalast* (Berlin: Theater der Zeit, 2005).

Philipp Misselwitz, Hans Ulrich Obrist, and Philipp Oswalt (eds.), *Fun Palace 200X. Der Berliner Schlossplatz. Abriss, Neubau oder grüne Wiese?* (Berlin: Martin Schmitz, 2005).

ZwischenPalastNutzung and Bündnis für den Palast in cooperation with Urban Catalyst, eds., *Zwischennutzung des Palast der Republik. Bilanz einer Transformation 2003 ff.*, Berlin, 2005.

COACH

The objective of the strategy of coaching is to train and strengthen self-organized users and uses. It is less about establishing prerequisites and framework conditions, not about merely investigating and enabling, and definitely not about merely making space available. Instead, coaching concerns itself with the activities and qualifications of the actors themselves. Whatever happens, the goal is not to formalize or exploit it—rather, the sole objective is to support the actors in whatever their own particular intentions may be.

Self-organized activity is usually subcultural and experimental—it therefore tends to be innovative, but improvised and amateurish as well. The users often lack experience, know-how, and access to networks and information. Especially during the launch phase, temporary users are usually so taken up with themselves and their immediate next steps that they lose sight of longer-term strategies and goals. Coaching seeks to address precisely these deficits, an endeavor that can take various forms. Entrepreneurial coaching provides support around issues of company organization, financing, legal questions, etc. Cultural coaching arranges contacts with important cultural networks and actors. Image coaching seeks to improve the public image of socially marginalized and sometimes illegal groups and activities.

And who is the coach? In contrast to modern management, in which professional consultants are paid for their services, this is out of the question for temporary users. Not only do they not have the money—their conception of themselves and their activities is often largely in conflict with the methods and values of management today, which is exclusively oriented toward short-term monetary gains.

SELF-COACHING

In self-coaching, the activists organize themselves for the purpose of mutual or collective consultation. Models like this are familiar from the histories of the labor movement, cooperatives, and later citizens' initiatives—for example, the network Selbsthilfe Berlin (Self-Help Berlin) and Wohnbund Darmstadt (Darmstadt Housing Coalition). In the current context of temporary use, the Berliner Clubkommission (Berlin Club Commission) is an interesting example. It was formed in 2000 and has just under a hundred members, including club owners, organizers, bars, agencies, and DJs. Some of them—for example, the Yaam or the Kiki Bloofeld—are still temporary users; others began as squats or temporary uses but have since become permanent. The goal of the Clubkommission is to improve the sometimes negative image of clubs as shady night spots, point up their importance for urban life and cultural production, highlight their role as economic players, and engage in political lobbying. The hoped-for result will be to simplify licensing procedures and eliminate bureaucratic hurdles. The group has also succeeded in negotiating a 20 percent discount for its members with the Gesellschaft für Musikalische Aufführungsrechte (GEMA, Society for Musical Performing Rights). By coming together to form a network the clubs become able to share experience; engage in further training (thus workshops are organized on entrepreneurial topics such as financing, licensing, taxes, and contracts); conduct public relations via websites, event calendars, press work, and events; and do marketing. Since 2001, a "Berlin club night" has been organized every six months to a year, during which a single inexpensive ticket gains admission to all participating clubs.

In 2010, the first "Berlin Music Week" took place in collaboration with various institutions, including Berlin's Senate. The program included music events as well as discussions, for instance about the developments and trends in digital production and distribution. Thus, the event served as a discursive platform for the music industry.

COACHING BY AGENTS

Related to self-coaching is coaching by sympathetic agents, that is, by artists and architects who are initially outsiders with respect to the temporary use. They don't stand in a classic contractor–client relationship but come to the project in question out of their own sense of engagement. They make their knowledge, networks, labor time, and sometimes their resources available free of charge. Interesting examples include Park Fiction in Hamburg and the project Ararat / Campo Boario in Rome. Here, outsiders whose personal background was totally different from that of the original actors joined preexisting projects. For example, Italian architects joined a group of Kurdish immigrants and artists joined a neighborhood group to support their efforts and strengthen them by contributing

Mapping of brownfield sites in the small Hessian town of Dietzenbach

Citizens of Dietzenbach were invited to depict their ideas for the use on postcards.

their own impulses. The difference between the agents and the core group is precisely what makes those coming from outside able to play a role like this, even if they themselves would never describe their activity as coaching. Their function is to develop long-term strategies and overcome the limited and limiting character of an approach that moves forward only by small steps.

GOVERNMENTAL COACHING AS EMPOWERMENT

Since the concept of coaching has much in common with new social policies of empowerment, one naturally also encounters the figure of the coach on government assignment and in various constellations. The most widespread example is neighborhood management initiatives, which first emerged in the 1980s in Great Britain and the Netherlands and later became established in countries like Germany and Austria as well. Neighborhood management efforts bundle government social work, business development, and city planning approaches and apply them to socially and economically disadvantaged urban areas where investment is low and vacancy is usually high. Hence in addition to a wide range of other activities, such initiatives also tend to become involved in temporary use of empty buildings and idle sites. Thus, in Berlin in 2001 and 2002, the Boxion project, which was part of the Friedrichshain neighborhood management effort, helped a number of firms to start up by offering empty shop units very cheaply, at the low rent of €3.00 per square meter, a gesture made possible by one-year rent subsidies and the cooperation of the owners.

Potential users were selected on the basis of their ideas. But the services provided to them went far beyond the mere provision of assistance during the initial phase (the hallmark of the strategy of enabling). The users were coached continuously—for example, the coaches organized events, did public relations work, created a user network, and offered one-to-one advice sessions. In the context of a neighborhood management initiative in Leipzig-Neuschönefeld from 2001 to 2004, an idle area was transformed into temporary

semipublic gardens. Participants in subsidized job-creation schemes prepared the ground for planting. It was coaching that sparked an interest in the project to begin with, and coaching that later eliminated difficulties which the users would have been unable to overcome by themselves. While neighborhood management efforts are sometimes limited to the support of preexisting private projects—this was the case, for example, in Soho Ottakring in Vienna—the opposite sometimes occurs as well: the forced animation of vacant spaces in an effort to simulate urbanity, an approach that is especially popular where empty shopping streets are involved. Thus, in the little town of Luckenwalde in Brandenburg in 2003, a local sculptor supervised the creation of artworks, also by participants in job-creation measures, for empty shop units as a means of promoting a commercial space rental exchange that opened at the same time. In this extreme form, coaching leads to a simulation of use and city life. Instead of independent activity, one finds the short-lived animation of a site, artificially produced by the government. No substantive personal interest really exists on the part of the users. While negative examples like these drastically point up the problematic nature of the notion of the "activating state," the productive potential of neighborhood management for temporary users is far from exhausted.

It is typical for neighborhood management efforts to bring actors from the administration and the economy together with local initiatives and unorganized residents. For this reason, neighborhood management is not a task that is generally taken on by the administration itself—instead, the city commissions and pays a local private agency whose offices are right in the middle of the neighborhood. This approach has proved to be a very positive one. By contrast, attempts to have the coaching of temporary uses organized by the administration itself have tended to fail, because as a rule such bureaucracies are committed to traditional logics of administering, decreeing, prohibiting, and permitting, and are unaccustomed to engaging in dynamic collaborations with independent and, what is more, informal partners. Problems like these hampered the realization of projects such as *100 qm Dietzenbach* (100 sq m Dietzenbach) and *Neuland* (New Ground) in Berlin-Marzahn.

In the case of *100 qm Dietzenbach*, the residents themselves were called upon to occupy the empty buildings that had existed in that satellite town since the bad planning of the 1970s. The project initiators—a consortium of the municipality and private and academic planners—used a public relations campaign to moderate the development of ideas. Later they organized, oversaw, and directly shaped the appropriation of space. As the project continued, however, it was overwhelmed by bureaucracy, prohibitions, and inspections, and its authors came away from it convinced that in future, municipal mechanisms should be left out of projects like these as much as possible.

The logic of temporary users is often just as much at odds with classic entrepreneurial strategies as it is with the mechanisms of administrative bureaucracies. Coaching that wishes to have any chance of succeeding has to recognize that fact. Assuming it does, however, then in addition to self-coaching, coaching efforts initiated and financed by the government can play an important role. Such efforts address the underfunded but engaged, self-organized, and innovative—in a word, subcultural—actors without attempting to make a hard and fast distinction between those who are temporary users in the strict sense and those who have developed along different lines. The coaching may focus either on a particular urban area, as in the case of neighborhood management, or on a particular activity, as with the Clubkommission.

MEANS AND ENDS

In addition to the types of communications- and media-related support and entrepreneurial training that have predominated thus far, future coaching measures might include legal advising on the process of legalization, technical advising on the specific constructional problems facing temporary users, and practical help through the loaning of resources. At the most fundamental level, coaching seeks to help actors achieve their optimal level of self-expression and self-development and helps them to eliminate obstacles and make use of idle resources.

For the city as a whole, the goal of coaching temporary uses is to strengthen them and so draw maximum benefit from their positive effects, whether in order to stabilize and develop social environments in threatened neighborhoods, as a new form of economic development in the era of the knowledge society and culture industry, or as a means of promoting public life and urban culture. At the same time, coaching respects the desires and goals of the temporary users themselves; it does not attempt to subordinate those goals to other processes and by doing so rob them of their own inherent qualities.

FURTHER INFORMATION:

www.clubcommission.de

www.stalkerlab.org

Gaby Grimm, Wolfgang Hinte, and Wolfgang Litges, *Quartiermanagement* (Berlin: Edition Sigma, 2004).

OBJECTIVE: To expand and connect a multinational cluster of temporary users and open it to the world

PROTAGONIST: Stalker, a group of artists and architects, as voluntary agents

USE: Sociocultural, various political and ethnic groups

STATUS: Tolerated

TRAJECTORY: Various users since the 1970s, expanded since 1999 to incorporate Kurdish groups and coaching

PLACE: Inner-city grounds of a former slaughterhouse, approximately 90,000 square meters, owned by the city of Rome. About 40,000 square meters informally used outdoor ground and 150 square meters for the building used as a cultural centre. Since 2003, besides sociocultural initiatives the principal renters at the site have been the Roma Tre university and the city, among others, including the Macro (museum of contemporary art)

310

Campo Boario, the grounds of a slaughterhouse inside the old Roman city walls that was shut down in 1975, is clearly cut off from the rest of the city by railroad tracks, the Tiber, and an old Roman garbage dump. As a result, it long escaped public attention and remained untouched by city-planning interventions, so that over the course of thirty years a self-organized coexistence of various cultures and milieus has been able to develop largely undisturbed. For five hundred years the site has been used again and again as a campground by the Kalderash gypsies, who live in trailers and specialize in working raw metals. After the slaughterhouse was closed, the Cavallari coach drivers used the old stalls to house their three hundred horses, which they use for touristic horse-drawn carriage excursions. At the other end of the site is the self-administered Villaggio Globale center, the most important of its kind in Rome, where intercultural activities are held throughout the year. Other parts of the site have been occupied by immigrant groups, especially from Senegal and North Africa; homeless Italians; and a Palestinian restaurant.

A PLACE FOR KURDISH IMMIGRANTS

In 1999 the Stalker architects collective was invited to participate in the Biennal of Young Artists of Europe and the Mediterranean, which was held in the immediate vicinity of Campo Boario. Stalker took the opportunity to make contact with the Kurdish immigrants in Rome. Shortly before this, during their fight for political asylum, these immigrants had built a protest squatter village out of cardboard, called "cartonia," near the Coliseum. The authorities, however, quickly shut the village down and dispersed its inhabitants to various Roman neighborhoods. Stalker occupied a house on Campo Boario that had thus far been used exclusively by drug dealers and organized a workshop there with Kurdish refugees, Roman architecture students, and the organization Azad. Afterward they took the building over permanently, renovated it, and turned it into a Kurdish cultural center. Under the name "Ararat," it became a gathering and meeting place and workspace for the city's Kurdish community. Most of Campo Boario's existing users and residents reacted with irritation, some of them with hostility, so Stalker stepped in as a mediator and attempted to ease tensions and create an atmosphere of trust. Crucial to this effort was the attempt to establish communication among the various groups at Campo Boario, who had thus far tended

Emergency shelters for Kurdish refugee families at Campo Baorio, the grounds of a former slaughterhouse in the center of Rome

to act separately; create a network including all of them; and spark communal activities. At the same time, Stalker opened up the site to the outside world. In doing so they were aided by the fact that the Ararat building is located right at the entrance to the area and has a roof terrace with a good view of Campo Boario as well as the neighboring streets.

Between 1999 and 2002 more than fifty events were organized without any governmental support: breakfast parties, the planting of a garden, games and artistic projects, book launches, exhibitions, Kurdish New Year celebrations, disco parties, seminars, workshops, and much more. While the first events focused on establishing communication within the group, later on communication with the outside world became more important.

COMMUNICATIVE EVENTS

In one of the first events, a *"carta di non identità"* (nonidentity card), was issued to everyone at Campo Boario as a playful and artistic way of expressing the fact that all of them shared an existence on the far side of "normal" as a common point of departure. In November 1999 a big collective breakfast, called "Pranzo Boario," was organized at a huge round table in collaboration with the Japanese artist and architect Asako Iwama. There were Kurdish dishes, "gypsy goulash," and Japanese seaweed. Since March 2000 the Kurdish New Year has been celebrated every spring. When the city administration had archeological excavations carried out in the Campo Boario courtyard (which, however, did not turn anything up), the group used the opportunity to plant a garden, the "Ortoboario," where the asphalt that was removed had previously been.

In 2000, the Stalker group began to use its projects to broadcast the themes of Campo Boario to the outside world beyond the borders of Rome. Invited to participate in several exhibitions—at the Villa Medici in Rome, the Architecture Biennale in Venice, and Manifesta 3 in Lubljana—they developed the project *Transborderline,* a three-dimensional spiral that represented a porous and habitable border and thus formulated a critique of contemporary forms of compartmentalization and exclusion. After showing it temporarily at Campo Boario, they installed it illegally on the European Union's external border, which at that time ran between Italy and Slovenia. In June 2000, while the installation was

The holes in the asphalt that were left after an archeological excavation are planted with trees by Stalker and residents of Campo Baorio.

still set up at Campo Boario, Stalker organized the so-called *Global Game:* two thousand soccer balls were thrown into the courtyard, and every resident of Campo Boario was asked to write down his or her personal migration story on one of the balls. In late 2000, with its notoriety increasing, Stalker was invited to participate in an exhibition organized by the Italian Ministry of Foreign Affairs, which focused on the multicultural Mediter-ranean region. For its installation, Stalker created a replica of the wooden ceiling of the famous, formerly Islamic Palatine Chapel in Palermo out of copper and ropes. Much of the paid work of producing the *Flying Carpet,* as the installation was called, was performed by the Kurdish immigrants of Campo Boario themselves. Thus, this project not only carried the themes of Campo Boario to the world outside but also supported the immigrants economically.

In ensuing years, the situation became increasingly precarious for the intermediate users. Even though the Kurdish community still operates the Ararat Cultural Center on the site, it still has not been officially acknowledged and constantly fears eviction. With their "Città dell'Altra Economia," the Romani community was the last to yield to an alternative market, which is operated by a consortium of organic and fair-trade grocers and was arranged when the old mayor, Veltroni, was still in office. Along with the Romani community, the Stalker group demanded that a metal workshop run by Romani also be installed. However, this was never realized.

A "*Carta di non identità*" (nonidentity card) was issued to the illegal residents of Campo Boario as a playfull and artistic way of expressing their existence on the far side of normality.

In collaboration with the Japanese artist and architect Asako Iwama, Stalker organized a large collective breakfast called "Pranzo Boario"—one of the first staged meetings of Romanies and Kurdish refugees at the Campo.

At the "Global Game," two thousand soccer balls tell the stories of immigrants. The spatial spiral *Transborderline* can be seen in the background.

In the meantime, another art and event venue has been established on the site. Besides the Campo Boario, the Museo di Arte Contemporanea di Roma (MACRO) and the architectrure department of the Roma Tre university organize events in the former slaughterhouse building. In contrast, following evictions, the Campo Boario is half empty and is closed off with nets and fences in order to prevent possible squatting. It is planned to set up the university of visual arts and communication, DAMS, here.

The reason why a solution for the development of the entire area has not be found up to now is the disagreement among the government decision-makers, the dogged determination of the informal actors, and the dubious offers made by private investors. With the introduction of a new law, which simplifies the privatization of common land and public facilities, the risk that the area will be sold to private speculators has risen significantly. The right-wing mayor Alemanno, who has been in office since 2008, is not only aiming at the stronger economization and formalization of the alternative market, he wants the entire area to be cleared. The future of the remaining informal uses is thus extremely uncertain. In cooperation with the citizens' initiatives, the Stalker group is currently making an effort to keep the public aware of the site and demanding alternative solutions for development.

FURTHER INFORMATION

www.stalkerlab.org

Francesco Careri and Lorenzo Romito, "Stalker and the Big Game of Campo Boario," in P. Blundell Jones, D. Petrescu, and T. Till, eds., *Architecture and Participation* (London: Routledge, 2005).

Peter T. Lang, "Stalker on Location," in Karen A. Franck and Quentin Stevens, eds., *Loose Space* (New York and London: Routledge, 2007).

SALBKE DISTRICT LIBRARY, MAGDEBURG

GOAL: Cultural reactivation of the central district and strengthening of the social network

PROTAGONISTS: Salbke Bürgerverein (Citizens' Group), Salbke Primary School, Aktion Musik e.V., KARO* with Architektur+Netzwerk, Magdeburg City Council

USE: Civically operated public library and associated outdoor library

STATUS: Completion June 2009, since then run by voluntary citizen organization

SITE: Derelict site of the former Salbke Public Library in Magdeburg

CHRONOLOGY: Concept study 2004, temporary intervention October 2005, set-up of the citizens' library 2005–2006, planning and construction 2007–09

COSTS: Price of lot €20,000 (488 m²), construction costs €325,000

FINANCING: Public funding

Stefan Rettich

The citizens' library in the Magdeburg district of Salbke has a stock of more than thirty thousand books that since June 2009 is in part also accessible in the associated outdoor library. The shelves are not closed, books can be borrowed around the clock. It is a library of trust, without bureaucracy or a borrower's slip—a development that at the beginning of the project in 2004 was hardly conceivable and which without participation and multiple authorship would not have been possible.

SITUATION

The outdoor library's lot is located in the center of the former fishing village, which during the Wilhelminian period was substantially transformed by industry. Use of the extensive industrial zones abruptly ceased in the 1990s. The disappearance of jobs triggered a severe downward spiral of outmigration, vacancies, and extreme unemployment. Salbke has since become a symbol for shrinkage and decline: the district center, transected by through traffic, has a vacancy rate of 80 percent. Where before the turnaround a baker, a butcher, an electrical appliance store, a *HO-Markt* (a former East German supermarket chain), a shoe store, and even an ice cream parlor bordered the almost village-like square, today there is only one shop run by a Vietnamese merchant. Its decline was admittedly already preordained during the period of the GDR. The unrenovated and neglected buildings suffered further due to a structural fire in the late 1980s: the library burned down and was not rebuilt. Thus the district lost its cultural center even before it did its economic base. It therefore seemed particularly fitting to initiate a process of renewal here due to the strategic location of the derelict site and the positive memory of the library.

TOWN ON TRIAL

The idea for a temporary sign and the construction of an outdoor library on the derelict site was discussed and met with approval in the district as early as the beginning of 2005 as the result of a study on the development of derelict sites commissioned by the City Council. However, there was no funding available for its implementation. After the architects were invited by the Galerie Aedes to contribute to a group exhibition in Berlin, they again took up the concept and the project gained momentum. The contribution to the exhibition was designed as an experiment with an open outcome and

consisted of initiating a process of participation in public space by means of a temporary intervention and from this deriving the form and function of a potential outdoor library.

An empty salesroom located directly adjacent to the derelict site served as a base camp for a one-week workshop in which, based on an urban model, designs and possibilities were played through and rejected, children and residents from the neighborhood built models, and at the end of the week a model of the most sustainable solution was constructed on a scale of 1:1. One thousand beer crates provided by a local beverage retailer served as the material for the temporary function test of a long set of bookshelves. An appeal for book donations met with a positive response all over town, and the books filled the shelves of the temporary installation. Although the improvised library furniture only defined urban space for two days, it developed a lasting impact. Immediately after disassembling the installation, the Bürgerverein decided to use the seven hundred books that had been donated to establish an informal citizens' library in the salesroom adjacent to the site and run it itself, without financial support. While the owner of the building made the salesroom available free of charge, the building had been shut off from the public utilities, which meant that there was neither drinking water nor a sewage hook-up, and power had to obtained via a construction site feeder pillar.

Within twelve months, the number of books had grown to ten thousand. Due to this dynamic development, upon the initiative of the architects an application was submitted to the federal government for funding of an ExWoSt-Forschungsprojekt (Experimental

Housing and Urban Development research project)—with the aim of converting the temporary solution into a permanent structure and implementing the idea for an outdoor library. In late 2006 the project was included in the research program as a pilot project and funding was secured for an outdoor library as permanent urban furniture.

SOCIAL DESIGN

During the ensuing planning phase of the building project, participation initially took place in the form of collaborative work, discussions, and the occupancy of a further vacant salesroom in the center of town. The idea for a *green living room* that is protected from street noise and provides a rest area in the neighborhood was further refined in a four-week planning camp. Besides its core function as a library, differentiated meeting places and venues, such as a stage and a youth center, were defined. The number of players also considerably grew during this period: there are eight groups who are now networked with each other via the project and an Internet platform developed specifically for this purpose. Among others, the primary school, a youth club, the congregation of the local church, and the municipal housing association have grouped around the Bürgerverein, which has assumed the leading role. The housing association also provided the salesroom for the citizens' library free of charge. The set-up of interaction loops such as this and the central aim of reactivating urban space by means of establishing and ordering social relationships thus constantly took on a more distinctive character. But of course there is another side to the coin. There is a reason for the state of the neighborhood and the lack of cultural facilities. Since German reunification, scarcely any municipal resources have gone toward the upgrading or redevelopment of the neighborhood. It cannot be in the spirit of responsible urban planning for volunteers and personal initiative to have to bear this burden on their own shoulders. Commitment also has to be rewarded, if not in hard cash then in the right to a say and the right to co-determination in policy decisions that concern urban development.

RECYCLING POSTWAR MODERNISM

The object's most noticeable feature is undoubtedly the facade of deep-drawn aluminum molding, whose modernist ornamentation is reminiscent of a department store facade from the 1960s. In fact, the facade and its substructure stem from a former Horten department store that was removed from a building in the Westphalian town of Hamm in 2007. The city council there provided it on favorable terms in support of the social project in Magdeburg. The point of departure for all of the considerations with respect to the facade was in turn the process of participation, during which several active players had spoken out in favor of the use of recycled material. The architects contacted the Hamm City Council, which ultimately led to this unusual idea for a facade. Yet this also led to conflicts. While citizens were enthusiastic about the suggestion, there were more and more objections on the part of the Magdeburg City Council. It was finally decided that the facade would not be bought due to unresolved legal issues. Because the option to purchase it was only in effect for a short period of time due to the demolition of the building in Hamm, citizens took things into their own hands and bought the facade at their own expense. At € 5,500, its purchase price was below the value of the raw material and posed no financial risks. Any

misgivings with respect to traffic safety could eventually be dispelled by the architects. Because there was no structural certificate for the forty-year-old facade, as is required in Germany in the meantime for all building elements, material testing had to be performed and an application submitted for approval as an individual case. As soon as approval was granted, the way was clear and the City Council ultimately bought the facade from the citizens. Today, the value of the facade as a unique feature and a new village icon is generally acknowledged: it signals the neighborhood's emergence following years of substantial demographic shrinkage. Yet for the architects, a large share of the project became advocacy planning. Good governance—this standard can only be maintained as long as the existing decision-making hierarchies are not called into question.

SITUATIVE DESIGN

As was the case for the facade, there was quite a bit of participative interaction between the players and the architects, which means that the boundaries of authorship are in fact blurred. After the first graffiti appeared on the concrete base of the structure during the construction phase, a competition, for example, was announced inviting all the youths

in Magdeburg to submit their tag, i.e., their personal graffiti signature. The youths themselves then applied the best tags. The only requirement was that they use the colors white, black, and chrome. It may be thanks to this action that youths who showed little interest in participating in the development of the project now comprise the largest group of users. However, there were some conflicts, for "chilling," which is what the youths prefer, does not correspond with the idea of contemplative "reading." Yet the situation is now stable, even after the first attack of vandalism in late 2009. This example shows that the project is not only a catalyst for urban development, but also monitors existing sociospatial conflicts that need to continue to be addressed and resolved with situative approaches.

Today, the site is used on a daily basis by passers-by to pause or borrow books. Two staff members subsidized by the department of employment help the Bürgerverein administer the bookcases. There is also a "green living room" where the "village" community can meet: the primary school bids farewell to its fourth-graders here, it provides the annual neighborhood festival with a center, and concerts, performances, and readings take place on the stage for both young and old. The range of offers is still in its infancy, but the Bürgerverein speaks of a new toy whose possibilities have gradually to be discovered.

FURTHER INFORMATION

www.karo-architekten.de

www.lesezeichen-salbke.de

CCCB Barcelona (ed.), *In Favour of Public Space* (Barcelona: Actar, 2010).

U. Altrock, R. Kunze, E. Pahl-Weber, and U. von Petz (eds.), *Jahrbuch Stadterneuerung 2008* (Berlin: Institut für Stadt- und Regionalplanung, 2008).

FORMALIZE

Temporary uses reach the point of formalization at an advanced stage in their development, when they are in transition to becoming permanent. The crucial prerequisite is that space be permanently available, ensured by long-term leases or the purchase of property. The impetus for becoming permanent may vary. Chances are good for successful temporary uses with excellent development conditions and a high degree of public acceptance, steadily subsidized social welfare projects, and thriving start-up businesses, all of which are welcomed by owners as solvent renters.

However, difficult development conditions and intense pressure to change can do just as much to encourage the formalization of a temporary use, because a situation of acute danger often provokes a reorganization of the use.

Because their existence is insecure, users are forced to grapple intensively with their internal organizational structure, be clear about their goals, communicate those goals to the public, and achieve them vis-à-vis others. The often weak initial position of temporary users—they only have meager financial resources and very few options if their lease is terminated—can become a position of strength if they are able to win public political sympathy for and acceptance of their project.

ACTORS AND MOTIVATION

The process of formalization is primarily conducted by the users themselves. Generally speaking, formalization becomes desirable for most temporary uses after a while, because it replaces short-term, situational action with planning security and the possibility of long-term investments. Beyond a common interest in having spaces that are permanently available, the goals of formalization vary depending on the actors. An economic interest may prompt users to develop solid business models, as in the case of the Arena in Berlin; associations may step in and support civil society projects in their neighborhoods, as in the case of the Verein RAW-Tempel (RAW Temple Association) in Berlin; or users may work for their own institutionalization, often with the support of politicians, as with the Tempodrom, also in Berlin.

Cities and towns are interested in perpetuating temporary uses when doing so makes it possible to take troubled urban areas and permanently offset the shortage of social and cultural institutions, create new jobs, generate new magnets for public life, or maintain existing public open space for whose maintenance public funding is not otherwise available. The following examples show how, despite tight budgets, municipalities support the formalization of temporary uses.

Unlike municipalities, owners and investors tend to have economic interests in view when they tolerate temporary uses or even promote their consolidation. Especially in the transformation of idle sites into new neighborhoods, an extremely important factor in motivating owners and investors to embrace the perpetuation of temporary uses is the hope that, by doing so, they can encourage the emergence in the medium term of a mixed-use urban landscape that will enhance the quality and value of commercially available properties. From the point of view of the property owner, there is only a possibility of allowing a temporary use to become permanent in cases where the image function of that temporary use continues to serve as an attractor for established uses even after its initial

phase is over, or in cases where the temporary initiatives are already so consolidated that the users are able to pay market rents, a situation in which the owner, as it were, has "cultivated" his own users.

There is no doubt that this entails the long-term exclusion of financially weak actors. With regard to formalization, the real estate industry makes a clear distinction between temporary uses that are economically interesting and those that are unprofitable, which it tries in advance to prevent from becoming permanent.

LEVELS OF FORMALIZATION

The formalization of a temporary use is a step-by-step process with several levels. As a rule, temporary uses have decidedly informal beginnings. In this way they reduce start-up requirements and avoid a whole range of obstacles that would otherwise nip their development in the bud. However, if the temporary use develops in a positive direction, the advantage of informality can become a disadvantage in the medium term. There is always a difficult-to-estimate risk that can fundamentally threaten the project's existence at any time. In this case the costs of informality outweigh those of formalization, as the Peruvian economist Hernando de Soto has shown with respect to informal economies in developing and newly industrializing countries.

Depending on the situation, the first step in formalization may be legalizing the use, that is, changing from an illegal appropriation of the site to an orderly, secure, and contract-based relationship with the owner. Additional steps toward legalization include obtaining a construction permit for a use that, as a general rule, does not correspond to the use that was previously made of the site in question, which sometimes entails consid-erable investment costs. A good example is the development of the legendary Berlin club

The RAW as a niche for start-ups: The instrument maker Roman Dill developed
a patent for tuning drums using bicycle tire inner tubes.

WMF, which originally came out of a clandestine squat and has changed locations repeatedly since then. In its fourth year of existence, the club moved into its third location and formalized its status, forming a GmbH (a corporation) and concluding a rental contract with the building's owner for the temporary use. Since then the club has operated as a legal enterprise without giving up its nomadic existence or its cultural creativity.

A further example of formalization, prompted by a change of location, is Mellowpark in the southeast of Berlin. With the district acting as a go-between, in 1998 the association alleins e.V. founded a youth club at the site of the former cable manufacturing plant. Over the course of the following years, the youths developed an internationally renown center for skateboarding and BMX culture on the industrial wasteland. Initially tolerated by the authorities as a temporary arrangement, the project's platform has continuously expanded: in addition to the skateboard course, dirt jumps, street ball fields, and a family park, the association operates a hostel, produces two scene magazines, and has several employees in a company that builds ramps. Thus, volunteer youth work is cross-subsidized with economically sustainable uses. The boundaries between recreational activities, volunteer work, internships, training, and entrepreneurship are fluid.

In 2008, the private owner's notice to terminate the contract threatened to end the project. The youths' untiring commitment persuaded the district, and beginning in fall 2009 it made a former 7-hectare sports area within walking distance from the former site available to the association for ten years. A major share of the previous programs could be taken up at the new site; however, its status is currently illegal. Instead of further active toleration, the responsible planning office introduced an intricate authorization process in order to ensure the publicly controversial transfer of the site. Spontaneous uses that informally developed at the old site are no longer permitted or have to be approved by the building authorities.

Parts of the RAW have been used temporarily for cultural purposes since 1998.

At the same time, the change of location involves an internal formalization of Mellowpark. Besides the association, Mellowpark is currently founding a building society and a consortium for the development of the site in order to be able to conclude contracts, apply for funding, obtain approvals, solicit sponsors, or professionally take on commissions. In addition to the cohesion of the Mellowpark actors, strong political backing as well as professional support through a research project contributed to the success of the formalization.

As was also the case for this project, the legalization of relations with the outside world is usually accompanied by an internal reorganization. From a loose collection of actors the use becomes a legally recognized organization, for example a partnership at will (Gesellschaft bürgerlichen Rechts, GbR), a corporation (Gesellschaft mit beschränkter Haftung, GmbH), or a registered association (eingetragener Verein, e.V.). Also at this point, work for the organization is often professionalized. Unpaid and volunteer work is increasingly replaced with paid labor. This reorganization is often accompanied by heated internal conflicts, debates, and power struggles. As structures that often only pretend to be nonhierarchical or loose informal hierarchies are replaced with clearly defined roles and responsibilities, former and potential future participants are marginalized or excluded, while key positions are filled by a chosen few. In principle, participatory business models such as cooperatives are also conceivable. However, in practice they are an exception. At the same time, the internal reorganization leads to a renewal of the project, which in many cases begins the development of long-term prospects in the first place.

The professionalization of organizational structures resulting from a conflict can substantially change the role of temporary uses that were originally set up to be only temporary, as the development of the former Reichsbahnausbesserungswerk (state railway repair workshop, RAW) Franz Stenzer in Berlin's Friedrichshain district shows. After its use was abandoned, the 10-hectare site sat empty until it was rediscovered by a local resident in the late 1990s and, based on good political contacts, made accessible for numerous

Development of the temporary use 1998–2008: The plan by the temporary users to develop the site on their own failed when the RAW was sold to an investor group in 2007.

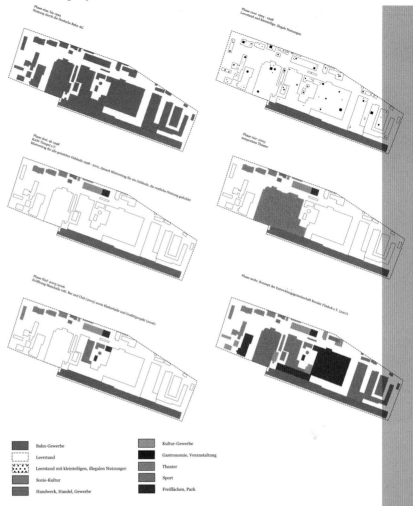

Bahn-Gewerbe		Kultur-Gewerbe
Leerstand		Gastronomie, Veranstaltung
Leerstand mit kleinteiligen, illegalen Nutzungen		Theater
Sozio-Kultur		Sport
Handwerk, Handel, Gewerbe		Freiflächen, Park

neighborhood sociocultural initiatives. The users initially organized themselves via the RAW-Tempel e.V. In order to enable the site's use, the district authority rented part of the site from its owner and transferred it to the association in return for payment of the operating costs.

After the restructuring of the state property owner into a commercial company, the development of commercial projects was kick-started on the RAW site. The rental contract with the district authority was terminated; the association was to vacate the site. In order to be able to continue the previous uses on the site in the long term as part of overall development, RAW-Tempel e.V. attempted to position itself in the development planning on several levels: by means of the further development of existing uses with conversions and installations; by exercising political influence on urban planning institutions and commissions; and, finally, by becoming actively involved in the cooperative communicative planning and participation process. An independent initiative formed that launched a public appeal for ideas for the development of the site, thus linking intense public relations

work to the state of development and possibilities of participation. In January 2007, the users finally achieved an important partial victory. After they succeeded in convincing the district parliament of their plan, the district scrapped their previous draft of a land-use plan, which had taken little account of the existing uses, and decided instead on internal development without a land-use plan. From then on, the district sought to preserve the uses that had developed informally—as an important basis for the further development of the site. Besides the association, other users had settled there, such as a skating hall, a club, and a climbing crag.

In order to be able to approach the authorities, the owner, as well as other businesses as a "serious" negotiating and cooperation partner and to emphasize their interest in long-term development, the users joined together to found the Revaler5eck e.V. development association. According to the development concept they submitted to the district, the existing halls were to be used for a mixture of community and entrepreneurial projects.

However, the owner, who had in the meantime changed twice, boycotted the discussion on the community development of the site with the aim of developing it to gain profit with a commercially oriented use concept. It was only at this late point that the structural weakness of the status of temporary use was revealed. As long as a formalization of the organizational structures does not involve the possibility of a long-term lease of the site or of acquiring it, the success of structural consolidation is questionable.

The new owner is currently pursuing a land-use plan in order to reserve the right for developing the site. The lasting cooperation between the district and the user group is now panning out in this process. The district is not only attaching separate conditions to the setting up of the land-use plan—among other things, the outstanding clarification of the rental contract with the association—it is also adhering to developing the site in collaboration with RAW-Tempel e.V. Its contributions to neighborhood culture and the alternative and self-determined forms of participation meet with a great deal of approval in the district—the social and local capital of the temporary users plays an enormous role even beyond formalization.

As the example of the former Reichsbahnausbesserungswerk (RAW) Franz Stenzer shows, the formalization of temporary uses also depends on their public presence and persuasiveness. Temporary uses rely on public perception, links to local milieus, and a distinctive visual identity. Being firmly implanted in public consciousness makes it easier to persuade political leaders, licensing authorities, and owners. Noncommercial users such as neighborhood projects and trailer parks also try to lend more formal public weight to their status by using websites, public relations campaigns, and events to communicate their goals and activities.

The users bequeath their own niche and a personalized, often homogeneous milieu for those who follow them.

LAST STOP FORMALIZATION?

Formalization alters the profile of a use. Uncertainty, a zest for experimentation, and informal structures give way to established procedures, predictable financing, and formal organizational frameworks. The planning security associated with a lasting use perspective and formalization is mostly reflected in investments in construction. Existing buildings are refurbished based on need or supplemented with new buildings. Leasing contracts lasting several years are a prerequisite for taking advantage of government funding programs.

Yet despite professionalization and planning security, it is still possible for projects to fail, as shown by the example of the Tempodrom in Berlin. In 1980 the Berlin nurse Irene Moessinger used her inheritance to buy a used circus tent together with her friends, in order to realize a long-standing dream of an alternative lifestyle. The Tempodrom was born as a platform for theater, concerts, and variety shows, and in the following years it developed into a well-known showpiece of the world of alternative culture, which enjoyed increasing support from government cultural subsidies.

The critical phase in the formalization of the Tempodrom began in 1995 when the federal government—for security reasons stemming from the future presence of the Bundeskanzleramt (Federal Chancellery) in the Spreebogen area—demanded that the Tempodrom relocate for the second time. In return it made € 3 million available as compensation, in order to guarantee that the popular venue would be able to continue operations in a new location. With intensive participation by politicians at the Berlin state level, it was also decided that this would be the occasion for the Tempodrom to change from a temporary institution housed in tents into a permanent one with a building of its own. Subsidies on a large scale came in from the European Union and the Stiftung Deutsche Klassenlotterie (German Lottery Foundation). The state of Berlin acted as guarantor for a loan of more than € 11 million.

When the structure designed by the Hamburg architectural firm Von Gerkan, Marg und Partner, whose towering form continues to play with the tent motif, opened in 2002, the original construction cost estimates had been exceeded by enormous margins. Wolfgang

Wieland, a construction expert and a then member of the Bündnis 90/Die Grünen (Alliance 90/The Greens) delegation in the Berlin House of Representatives, summed up the problem like this: "It's as if you and your family started out living in a tent for free. And then you get the offer to buy a condominium. The people also tell you, we'll put up our own funds—please use a bank loan to finance the rest. But the family income doesn't come anywhere close to generating enough to make the payments." Just two years after the festive inaugural gala, the Senate decided to place the completely overindebted project in bankruptcy in order to limit the damage. Meanwhile the Munich firm Treugast continues to operate the venue under the same name. Its commercially oriented program primarily consists of popular comedy, musicals, and show formats. Little has remained of cabaret or individual initiative. The initiator, Irene Moessinger, has long since ceased to have any involvement with the Tempodrom.

Ironically, with Tipi das Zelt (the TIPI Tent) there is now once again a performance space next to the current Bundeskanzleramt, which, however, is not pursuing an alternative cultural program. Apparently the former security concerns no longer exist.

MAINTAINING OPENNESS

The case of the Tempodrom dramatically illustrates that the formalization of a temporary use is an ambivalent process, which does not by any means automatically lead to improvement and success but in which the advantages and disadvantages of every step must be carefully weighed. Above all, it vividly demonstrates that formalization fails when it takes place along conventional lines, as in traditional cultural and investment projects. Precisely the process of formalization must recognize the differentness of temporary use as a potential and make the most of it. This may mean, for example, that a merely partial, incomplete formalization is beneficial. Thus it is not uncommon for users to reorganize their company while allowing the rental contract to remain informal. The converse is also conceivable. Private-sector actors have less of a problem with this than government agencies, whether it is a matter of issuing licenses, awarding grants, providing or arranging loans, or taking on payment guarantees. Here it would be important to find forms that accept a partially informal status of projects instead of insisting, as usual, on an extensive or even total formalization.

By contrast, a remarkable success story—in comparison with the Tempodrom—is the development of the ExRotaprint project in Berlin. The former industrial area, which was released in the late 1980s, was originally rented by different independent cultural, social, and commercial users for a fee just slightly higher than the operating costs. However, because the state of Berlin, its owner, neglected it more and more, at the initiative of two artists, in 2005 the users began organizing themselves. They founded an association and entered negotiations with the owner to take over the site. Yet at the same time, the state offered the property for sale on the open market and was negotiating with a real-estate fund in Iceland. The users fought for their development concept for two years in the form of protests, political networking, public relations, and refinement of their development concept. With the involvement of two non-profit foundations, they finally succeeded in purchasing the site and thus stabilizing a use mixture consisting of people engaged in the

End of a temporary use in tents: In 2004 the Tempodrom had to file for bankruptcy after it accrued debts for the construction of its own building by means of dubious public securities.

cultural sector, social projects, and commercial users. What had once been tenants acting individually became a project development alliance with shared activities. In the meantime, a café has opened and events take place.

FURTHER INFORMATION

www.exrotaprint.de

www.revaler5eck.de

www.tempodrom.de

Michael Rostalski, *Gelebte Orte – Geplante Stadt. Informelle Nutzung urbaner Räume und partizipative Stadtentwicklung – Das Raw-Gelände in Berlin*; PhD thesis at the Bauhaus-Universität Weimar, Würzburg, 2010.

Hernando de Soto, *Marktwirtschaft von unten* (Zurich and Cologne: Orell Füssli, 1992).

OBJECTIVE: To establish a diverse and financially self-supporting cultural center

PROTAGONIST: Actor and cultural entrepreneur Falk Walter

USE: Performances and activities in the areas of theater, art, music, events, sports, and dining

STATUS: Long-term lease with a period of 35 years

PLACE: Former bus depot in Treptow on the southern bank of the Spree, size of area 13,000 square meters, size of hall 6,000 square meters, property of Berlin boroughs of Neukölln and Treptow

TRAJECTORY: 1993 occupation by actors' collective, 1997 long-term lease and renovation, development of use clusters

FINANCING: Start-up financing of several million euros for renovation of the hall, since then self-supporting and profitable

Hardly any other place in Berlin has undergone as dramatic a transformation from an originally peripheral area into a cultural magnet since the end of the GDR as the grounds of the Arena near the strip of land left vacant by the fall of the Berlin Wall in the borough of Treptow. The site's charisma reaches far beyond its borders. The adjoining neighborhood on the Kreuzberg side, which is separated from Treptow by the Spree, has mutated into a creative industry hot spot in recent years. Fashion schools, record labels, clubs, design studios, and handicrafts workshops are part of a powerful development dynamic initiated in large part by the Arena.

In 1993, in the economically underdeveloped area of Treptow, which was still perceived as quite remote by the cultural scene of the Berlin of the early 1990s, the maintenance and storage facility of the Städtische Verkehrsbetriebe (Municipal Transport Services) was shut down. While the hall continued to be used as a bus depot, the neighboring administration building was taken over as living and work space by actors, artists, and students. In just a short time an intensive array of uses developed at the idle site. In 1995 the actor Falk Walter, together with a number of colleagues, founded Art Kombinat (Art Combine) as a nonprofit association with the goal of establishing long-term cultural activities on the grounds and in the hall itself. The first period of the use was limited to portions of the hall and also had to come to an arrangement with the other alternative users of the site. Only a few hundred square meters were rented as rehearsal and performance space. The first large-scale project taken on by the initiators of the Arena also fell in this period. Over 46 days, roughly 150 musical and theatrical performances took place. The project itself was a financial disaster for all involved, but it proved that the site was suitable for the visions of Art Kombinat.

FROM PIONEER TO ORGANIC PROJECT DEVELOPER
In the beginning, sustained development of the project was primarily threatened by the uncertain circumstances of the use. A lack of clarity surrounding the ownership of the area encouraged a rapid cultural appropriation of the site, but the "pioneers" had to be prepared that at any moment their activity could be ended at short notice. The Art Kombinat's initiatives were placed in question by other groups' claims on the halls.

Since 1994, the former bus depot has developed into one of Berlin's most popular cultural venues.

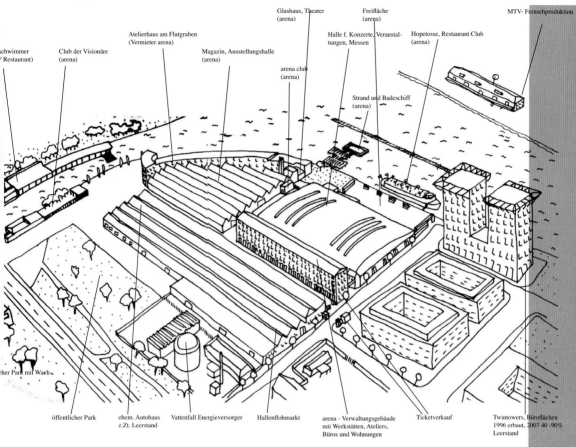

Glashaus, Theater (arena)

Freifläche (arena)

MTV- Fernsehproduktion

Atelierhaus am Flutgraben (Vermieter arena)

Halle f. Konzerte, Veranstaltungen, Messen

Hopetosse, Restaurant Club (arena)

schwimmer / Restaurant)

Club der Visionäre (arena)

Magazin, Ausstellungshalle (arena)

arena club (arena)

Strand und Badeschiff (arena)

her Park mit Waeh

öffentlicher Park

ehem. Autohaus z.Zt. Leerstand

Vattenfall Energieversorger

Hallenflohmarkt

arena - Verwaltungsgebäude mit Werkstätten, Ateliers, Büros und Wohnungen

Ticketverkauf

Twintowers, Büroflächen 1996 erbaut, 2007 40 -90% Leerstand

It was not until 1997, when the site was declared to be the property of the borough, that the users' status and prospects changed. Art Kombinat received a long-term lease with a period of thirty-five years. This lease was and remains contingent on the public-interest orientation of the association and hence on the primarily cultural use of the site. The manager of the Arena, however—that is, the performance hall—is Kulturarena Veranstaltungs GmbH (Kulturarena Event Corporation), which was created by the association and has much greater financial freedom. The organizational structure of the Arena was given its decisive stamp by Falk Walter, who together with two colleagues succeeded in asserting himself as the executive board of the association and chief executive officer of the corporation after internal disputes within the original actors' collective. At this point, Walter is one of the city's most important cultural entrepreneurs. His management strategy has brought about a situation in which today the Arena is no longer run as an alternative cultural center but as a commercial enterprise, an established institution that helps to shape the city's cultural landscape. The Arena supports itself as a cultural site independent of government subsidies, and Falk Walter regards his enterprise as a model in which culture and economy have a symbiotic relationship. The Arena welcomes roughly one million visitors a year.

The length of the lease was the deciding factor that catalyzed the use and development of the area as a whole. With these prospects in hand, in the coming years the users were

The "Badeschiff" (swimming ship) developed into a public attraction after it was opened in 2004. In the winter, the wooden platform and the barge are converted into a temporary sauna.

able to obtain subsidies from the European Union and to renovate and gradually upgrade and reconstruct the hall. The hall's renovation in 1999 was the precondition for professionally managing the Arena as a performance site. It made it possible to use the hall for large-scale concerts, trade fairs, shows, and events. In return the managers continue to make targeted use of these purely commercial performances to provide an opportunity to smaller projects. Many of these alternative projects have nothing to do with the hall. They take place all across the site, which the initiators have gradually appropriated and expanded in a kind of organic development process.

The second phase of consolidation was taken care of by the staging of Goethe's *Faust* by the internationally famous director Peter Stein in 2000/01, because it ensured that the hall was rented and used for months. While that production also influenced the future renting of the hall—it attracted an entirely different kind of audience to the site, which afterward greatly changed the profile of those who inquired about renting it—a restaurant on a converted Baltic Sea barge called the MS *Hoppetosse* indicates the focus for the development of the grounds themselves: the turn toward the water, the exploitation of the Spree. Thus, summer 2004 saw the opening of the swimming ship, another attraction in the area by the river. The swimming pool on the converted cargo barge was such a success with the public that the initiators have been able to forgo renting the MS *Hoppetosse* to big clients for private functions. The swimming ship is flanked by a bar. In 2005 the swimming ship was converted into a winter ship so that it could also be used in the cold-weather months.

The entire site constantly expanded and developed. In addition to the ANHALT restaurant, also opened in 2004, since 2005 the site has had a venue for electro parties the Arena-Club. In 2008, just in time for the European Football Championship, the Arena opened the "Fuhrpark," a public viewing location with a café in a former car dealership. However, the family-oriented range of offers did not meet with much acceptance; it is operating at a loss. The hall, the swimming ship and the Hoppetosse, together with a neighboring flea market, the Glashaus for smaller theatrical performances and concerts, and other clubs and restaurants—including the Club der Visionäre (Visionaries Club) and Freischwimmer Berlin (Free Swimmers Berlin)—form a conglomerate of cultural event spaces so highly concentrated that its effect is almost magnetic.

MULTIPROGRAMMING

The gradual establishment of specific uses is an alternative development strategy that has also substantially advanced the infrastructure of the borough. The Arena has helped to enhance the entire surrounding area, both in economic as well as in image terms, as more and more bars and shops have sprung up all around it over time. Unlike the new construction area nearby, where the office buildings are struggling with a vacancy rate of 60 to 100 percent, all of the spaces on the grounds of the Arena are in constant use.

This organic and gradual development process has made it possible to link together all of the projects at the site, a phenomenon that was not originally planned but is the

long-term source of the variety of the activities as well as the visitors and hence of the attractiveness of the Arena. Moreover, synergies are also created by visitors who come to the area privately and then later put on an activity of their own there. This mix of uses is what makes the area's financing concept work. It smoothes out fluctuations and enables the initiators to use the hall for this and that and thus to preserve the necessary flexibility as well as the ability to experiment. Otherwise the site would quickly become ossified. This variety and versatility are deliberate. The organizers have repeatedly provided a platform for specific groups, for example immigrants from Eastern Europe, the art and design scene, trade show visitors, fans of various music scenes, theater audiences, and businesspeople who use the Arena for company parties. At the site itself as well as in the surrounding area, the Arena has repeatedly been successful in creating new milieus and trends. Primarily thanks to the unusual diversity of its program, but also because it is constantly opening up new "spaces" in new ways. In addition to its special combination of place and program, the short duration of its projects has also contributed to the Arena's long-term success. In the meantime, numerous travel guides list the Arena with its wide range of offers as a place of interest; its informal quality is being marketed by the tourist mainstream.

Alternative culture as a location factor: Corporate presentation in the hall

THE LIMITS OF GROWTH

The Arena has developed from an alternative project into a cultural operation for the masses. As such it is now an economic factor that also provides added value to the borough and the city. However, in 2010, the site made headlines in the daily newspapers. Falk Walter had believed he would be able to transfer the Arena's success to a second cultural venue, the Admiralspalast in Friedrichstrasse, and backed the wrong horse, so to speak. After the theater's bankruptcy, the Arena is currently also in dire financial straits. The empire made up of individual businesses and associations is being threatened by the domino effect.

The lease, at any rate, is contingent on the use of the site in the public interest. In view of the financial difficulties, it remains open whether it can still be guaranteed in the future.

CONCLUSIONS

It is possible to see in the development of the Arena the consecutive stages of a gradual process of formalization. A long-term lease guaranteed the availability of space and planning security for construction investments and use programs, which were accompanied by a professionalization of the organizational structure and public relations work. The almost seamless interplay between these factors led to the rapid establishment of the Arena "brand" in Berlin's cultural landscape. Formalization initially leads to a consolidation,

which, however, is increasingly turning out to be a problem. The operator's constant push for growth is the cause of a struggle for economic survival. At the same time, homogenization and commercialization are being encouraged. With formalization, the attraction of unplanned appropriation and the continuous reinvention of the site are being forfeited.

FURTHER INFORMATION
www.arena-berlin.de
www.clubdervisionaere.com
www.freischwimmer-berlin.de

GOAL: To establish a long-term space for alternative cultural and lifestyle activities

PROTAGONIST: Voluntary event collective, now an independent association

USE: Cultural: parties, concerts, theater, alternative and youth culture

STATUS: Initially leased, now owned since 2003 property

PLACE: Former military airfield, 500,000 square meters, Mecklenburg-Vorpommern/ Germany; previously owned by municipality

CHRONOLOGY: Rented in 1996 ff. for a single weekend, since then gradual extension of the lease period to twelve months beginning in 1999, purchase of the site in 2003

COST: Ca. €1 million per year for running costs and improvement of the grounds

FINANCING: Fusion Festival; financial support in the area of youth and cultural work

Anyone who drives to the Müritz district, the northern part of *Nina* Eastern Germany, on the final weekend in June will sooner or *Brodowski* later ask themselves why this region is described as the most economically underdeveloped area of the Federal Republic. On this particular weekend the B198 highway is probably the busiest stretch of road in northern Germany. The reason is an event that has been taking place there annually since 1996 and that has been known to the fans of techno and electro house music as the Fusion Festival since 1997. With as many as 50,000 visitors, the Fusion, which at first glance looks like an oversize techno rave, gives rise almost overnight to the equivalent of a medium-sized city on the grounds of a former Soviet airport.

APPROPRIATING THE SITE

It all began entirely by chance. The U.Site System has been organizing noncommercial parties, events, and performances since 1994 and sees itself as a collective with a left-wing political coloring. It focuses on rejecting the capitalist logic of exploitation and creating, at least temporarily, spaces for (sub)cultural art forms and lifestyles and facilitating consciousness expansion in an atmosphere of mutual solidarity. At these parties and performances one feels as if one is at a combination of the peace movement, the Rainbow Family, and techno raves.

The parties and performances originated in a small circle of people who freely volunteered their labor and skills without receiving payment, as they still do today. Primarily organized via flyers and word of mouth, the parties and performances quickly became established among a circle of initiates. As time went on, the organizers increasingly looked for spaces outside the city for their all-night Goa-trance events. Thus aside from empty basements and halls (for example in the City-Süd areas of Hamburg), parties quickly established themselves in the more sparsely settled regions of Brandenburg and Mecklenburg-Vorpommern.

On its way to inspect a new party site in 1996, the U.Site Collective happened upon the former military airport in the vicinity of Lake Müritz. Lärz Airfield was abandoned by the Soviet army in 1993 after the end of the Cold War and with German reunification. There are twelve former airplane hangars on the site. Overgrown with grass, they once housed military vehicles that couldn't be easily recog-

Aerial photograph of the former Soviet military airfield near Lake Müritz during a Fusion Festival

nized by enemy aircrafts when the facility was operational, it used to accommodate a thousand soldiers.

In 1996, the collective had already organized a successful party at another nearby airfield and thus had a positive attitude toward sites of this kind. What really won them over in addition to the hangars, which make it possible to hold events in unusual spaces even in bad weather, was the location: the site lies more or less at the center of the triangle formed by the cities of Rostock, Berlin, and Hamburg, and it can be reached from each one of them in a reasonable amount of time.

The mayor of the time showed himself to be liberal and cooperative, especially since the neighboring town of Rettlin was accustomed to noise of an entirely different order from the time when the site was used militarily. Moreover, after reunification very few people were interested in the area, and inquiries regarding the site were rare. Thus, the collective was able to lease the site officially for a single weekend and, in the summer of 1996, the first Fusion Festival (which was not yet known by that name) took place as one of the very few *legal* U.Site parties, with some two thousand people. The organizers soon took advantage of the possibilities of this location, especially since the empty hangars made excellent freestanding halls and safe accommodation, and the district government was willing to extend the lease period to give extra time for preparing the event beforehand. From 1997, the U.Site Collective has regularly leased the site for four weeks every summer and used the time to set up and take down the stages and to build an entire infrastructure especially for the festival. In the two years that followed, the festival grew at a rapid pace. In addition to the open-air stages and music systems for round-the-clock sound, the need soon arose for sanitary facilities (portable toilets) and a freely available drinking water supply—especially since the techno and Goa festival meanwhile went on from Friday until Monday morning. The number of little stands or tents that offered food and drink also increased, initially with their own electricity generators but soon with electric power supplied by the festival organization.

FORMATION

In 1999 the organizers founded a nonprofit association, Kulturkosmos Müritz (Müritz Cultural Cosmos), and the lease was extended to the entire year, so that they could use the hangars for storage and reduce the cost of transporting material back and forth to the site. However, since the terms of the lease provided for termination with just one month's notice, the association began to work toward buying the 50 hectares, especially as it was now making massive investments in its own infrastructure (water conduits, etc.). Meanwhile, however, regional elections had led to a change of government. The new mayor, a former army commander, was not in favor of Kulturkosmos activities and sought to establish the southern part of the Müritz district as a refuge for older, affluent tourists. The region's conservatives saw the Fusion people as suspect and found their lifestyles, which were so different from their own, unacceptable. Thus, at the same time that the festival was becoming more and more established as an institution on the alternative scene, it was also engaged in a long and bitter struggle for the trust of the region's residents. Yet in the meantime, a cooperation developed within the region. The local taxi companies introduced a special fare and set up a group service to and from the nearest railroad station. The festival management ran a local shuttle bus to the corresponding railroad stations but also to the beaches at the nearby lake, where both the little hot-dog stand and the local supermarket probably do their briskest business of the year on these weekends in June.

Despite years of political conflict, in 2003 the festival organizers finally succeeded in purchasing the site. The purchaser was a corporation specially created for this purpose by the lessees, which has since then leased the site to the association. Thus the association bears no liability of its own, and even if the corporation were to go bankrupt, the association would be able to continue to operate. On the other hand, the initiators of the Fusion Festival also rely on this legal construct—the separation into corporation and association—to provide them with a kind of ultimate control over the use, despite the personal continuity that exists between the two entities: thus the lease is linked to the specific use of the property for the festival and particular framework conditions, so that despite the fluctuation of the volunteers and the association's members, the original idea of the festival can be preserved.

ФУЗИОН
LAGEPLAN

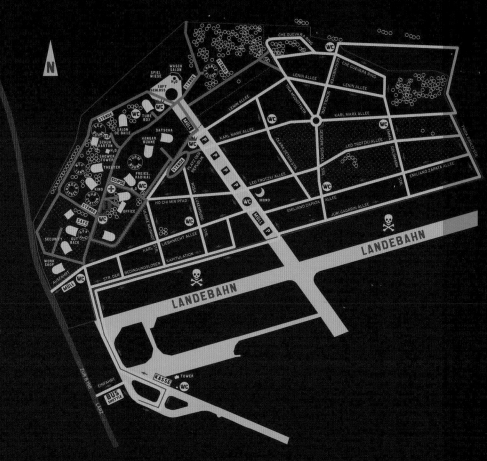

Unsere Parkplatzcrew ist bemüht, eure Wünsche nach Möglichkeit zu erfüllen. Aber dennoch gilt: Die Parkplatzeinweiser haben das letzte Wort und bestimmen, wo noch was geht. Heißt im Ernstfall, woanders campen als geplant...

Fast alle Wege sind Einbahnstraßen. Fahrtrichtung ist immer dem Pfeil nach.

Alle Wege sind auch Rettungswege und müssen deshalb unbedingt freigehalten werden, notfalls auch mit Hilfe des Radladers.
Platz für die Posse freihalten geht nur in gewissen Bereichen und dort nur in moderatem Rahmen.

A2 und A3 sind Family-Campingplätze und damit absolute Ruhezonen!

A4-6 und B1-3 am nächsten dran, dafür aber lauter.

D4-8 bleiben wegen Neueinsaat GESPERRT.

Für Gruppencamper gilt: Für Leute, die früh anreisen, die noch Nachzügler erwarten und die Ruhe und Abgeschiedenheit mögen, eignen sich C1-6. Hier gilt: Erst abparken, dann die Nachhut anrufen und verabreden, wo ihr zu finden seid.

D1-3 werden erst zum Schluss freigegeben.

E ist ein Ersatzparkplatz, wenn es ganz voll wird.

Hangar	
Autowege mit Fahrtrichtung	
andere Wege	
Grenze / Zaun	
Autogrenze	
Sperrgebiet / NO Camping	
A1	Camping
	Infopoint
+	DRK
SAFE	Safe-Area
ECLIPSE	Eclipse (psychedelische Ambulanz)
WC WC	WC und neu: WC deluxe!
MÜLL	Müllsammelstelle
☠	Landebahn - Lebensgefahr!
☷	Bäume/Wald

The overall choreography of the festival is centrally controlled, and over the years it has become extremely professionalized. Nevertheless, the festival is for the most part run by volunteers. At this point, more than 2,000 volunteer helpers and supporters work at and for the Fusion. Together they create, in just a few days, an infrastructure that supports 50,000 people. And the maxim is: all of the participants also work for their own fun. The sanitary facilities have been upgraded over the years: alongside portable toilets there are now also proper lavatories ("WC-Deluxe"), water stations and a converted "shower tower," garbage collection stations, and market areas for the stands. The campsites have names and are equipped with "access roads".

RAPID GROWTH

When the organizers purchased the site, they also began to relate to it in a new way. Since 2003 the Hamburg architecture firm Schwarz | Schmidt has been given the job of preparing an organic building plan which would transform the former airplane hangars into theatrical and musical stages. Most of the building work is being carried out by supporters of the Kulturkosmos. The site itself is occupied all year round by a handful of people, and it's open to anyone who wants to spend time there or lend a hand. Throughout the year the grounds are constantly being modified and improved and the halls prepared for the next festival. In 2005, with the construction of the Luftschloss, or Castle in the Air, the first new

In 2005, the event tent "Luftschloss" (castle in the air) was the first permanent structure on the Fusion site.

permanent structure came along to complement the preexisting hangars. Construction of the Kulturkosmos seminar and conference building commenced in 2009.

The festival has become an established large-scale cultural event in the Müritz region and become well known far beyond Mecklenburg. That's nothing unusual for festivals, especially in view of the fact that the festival and mega-event industry has been booming for years. But what sets Fusion apart is a certain edge in terms of psychological identification, an edge that goes hand in hand with a certain decrease in commercialism and consumption. Nevertheless, there's no doubt that the festival's growth and enormous success are also its biggest problem. In 2009, besides the 6,000 helpers and people with free tickets—as well as the usual "stowaways," as the organizers refer to them—just under 60,000 people attended the festival, some 15,000 more than the year before. The Fusion had already enjoyed a continuous increase—an average of 6,000—in the number of visitors each year, for whom campsites have to be leased from neighboring farmers. The festival is increasingly creating its own new ways of regulating organizational challenges, such as, for example, the "car toll," which was introduced in 2009 in order to deal with the large volume of traffic. Parking is free of charge on the landing runway in front of the campgrounds. It now costs €10 to park a car in front of the tents. The festival now also lasts longer than just a weekend, which was previously the case. The first "visitors" start to arrive mid-week.

The growth as well as the permanent nature of the festival are accompanied by a further problem. The extension of the infrastructure makes for costs that are not always covered by the festival's proceeds. In addition, the proceeds from ticket sales only just cover the running expenses. In order to satisfy visitor expectations as well as the requirements stipulated by the authorities, more and more money is being invested in upgrading the sanitary facilities (showers, washing stations, and toilets as well as the necessary fresh-water and waste-water/sewage connections). Added to this are the expenses for electronics, rents, and power for generators, cables, transformers, etc., as well as artists' fees (including travel expenses), GEMA fees, and the cost of new buildings, stages, and extensions. A greater number of visitors would generate higher proceeds in the short term, however it would mean further expenses on the infrastructure. Thus, for a long time the organizers sought to curb visitor numbers by means of less PR. In 2010, a limited number of tickets was made available for the first time. However, this also leads to stagnating proceeds or less takings due to the weather.

Over the years, awareness of the festival and the visitor structure have developed far beyond the original target group. The associated growth and transformation of the atmosphere elicit divided opinions. It's clear, however, what lies ahead financially. The fixed costs represent such a strain on the association that the festival management is constantly having to think of new methods of financing. Given the festival's left-wing political orientation, income from sponsors and advertising isn't an option. The festival's initiators are also determined to stick with the approach of having the bars run, not by the people who put on the festival, but by associations and political groups that agree to use their surpluses for their work or donate it to others. Instead, the tendency is to organize multiple parties and performances throughout the year—at a lower cost than before but on a larger scale. Moreover, a kind of permanent Kulturkosmos community is increasingly emerging, also for the alternative use of the site, for example for "family vacations" with like-minded people. The site can be used as a base for excursions on water and land, or as a refuge for alternative lifestyle activities.

BACKSTAGE

The festival sees itself as a locus of "FUSION." This is what the website has to say on the subject: "As diverse as the people who gather here is the range of what they are seeking and experiencing. [...] Fusion is and always has been a festival with a left-wing political orientation, and not a radical left-wing action camp with a cultural supporting program. The festival's program is contained in its name, and everyone who is willing to follow the clearly formulated guidelines is welcome and heartily invited, regardless of where they come from, how they dress, or how long they wear their hair." This leads to an interesting mix of people, since this region is known among other things for a strongly right-wing younger generation in the countryside. Thus on Saturday night techno ravers are side by side with barefoot dancing hippies and even young people in combat boots. Nevertheless, and despite the recurring potential for tension, conflicts of this kind have been decreasing in the past few years. One reason for this is that most of the visitors are not just passive consumers, but strongly identify with the festival. They follow movements and activities at the site throughout the year, and many of them also meet again at other U.Site.System events.

Over the years what began as a nighttime event has developed into a permanent institution on the alternative scene. Arguably, the site has even become attractive for other events, and the festival has had an impact on the structure of the region. In fall 2006 the theater and performance festival at.tension#1 took place for the first time at the festival site, supported in part by the Bundeskulturstiftung (Federal Cultural Foundation). The association has now become an established presence in the region, where it is primarily active in the area of alternative youth and theater work. Many young people's initiatives fund themselves and their projects with the proceeds from stands at the festival.

Moreover, the festival has come to be regarded as a positive economic factor by the underdeveloped region. Its local roots and cooperation with nearby cities and towns not only strengthen the festival organizers but also benefit the region (the association has seven employees from the region, and there are cooperations with the local employment office). The festival has attracted thousands of people to the Müritz district in recent years who otherwise might never have ended up coming here. Most of them now spend a few extra days in the region and/or plan their upcoming summer vacation in Mecklenburg in conjunction with their visit. In a rural area primarily known for unemployment and negative growth, a magnet that vitalizes the region has emerged over the years. In the process, the vision of those who pioneered the site has become a reality: what began as a single night has become a cosmos.

FURTHER INFORMATION
www.attension-festival.de
www.fusion-festival.de
www.kulturkosmos.de

EXPLOIT

Third parties may employ temporary uses as a means of pursuing their own economic interests. When this occurs, those uses become part of the entrepreneurial strategies of cities, companies, project developers, and property owners. By employing temporary uses, property owners usually seek to increase the value of their properties. For when temporary uses appear in a given location, that location becomes well known, and commercial users are attracted by the new image and milieu. Such uses are employed for similar purposes in city marketing. With properties that are difficult to rent, temporary uses can serve to "cultivate" renters over the medium term. Also, strategies developed in the temporary use milieu are copied in the marketing of lifestyle products.

CITY MARKETING

The range of possible applications for exploitative strategies is diverse. Such strategies can be of interest both city-wide, in district and neighborhood development efforts, as well as for individual properties. Provided they reach a certain critical mass, the cultural milieus generated by temporary uses are attractive for the image and location marketing of the city as a whole. Cities like Amsterdam and Berlin increasingly rely on their creative potential—more and more important in today's knowledge society—to increase their visibility and enhance their public profile. Thus, Amsterdam publishes an annually updated index of its cultural initiatives and creative small businesses, many of which come from the temporary use milieu. Berlin too is seeking to burnish an image tarnished by debt, unemployment, and stagnation. Mayor Klaus Wowereit's remark that "Berlin is poor but sexy" has become a slogan in a location marketing effort born of necessity. Temporary uses from the cultural arena in particular serve as image makers to attract commercial investors.

There are historical models for this approach, such as the development of Manchester and of SoHo in New York City. In the northern English industrial city of Manchester, it was recognized very early on that the music, gay, and immigrant scenes of the 1970s and 1980s, born in the empty buildings of the city center (see Kevin Ward's essay in this volume, p. 74), represent an enormous potential for changing the city's image—from an old, deindustrialized metropolis in crisis to a new, up-and-coming cultural capital. Early on, advertising and public relations campaigns were initiated that turned the existence of these diverse scenes to practical use for the development of the city. Finally, in 2004 the designer Peter Saville, who had designed album covers and posters for punk and new wave bands from Manchester in the 1980s, was appointed Creative Director for city marketing. As a rule, however, city marketing strategies only benefit one side. They are not symbioses. On the contrary, cities market temporary uses that are developing independently without in return supporting them or contributing to their development.

PROJECT DEVELOPMENT

A prime example of the beneficial incorporation of temporary uses into neighborhood development projects is the recent history of the area of the Nederlandse Dok en Scheepsbouw Maatschappij (NDSM) in Amsterdam. In Amsterdam the municipal government is the largest property owner in the city. For this reason it not only holds supreme planning authority but also acts as a project developer and investor. When use of the harbor in the northern part of Amsterdam ceased, the city planned the development of a new neighborhood. As an important catalyst for the future city planning measures, cultural initiatives were enlisted for the use of an enormous shipyard building and provided with start-up capital. The goal was to draw the populace to the neighborhood, which was thus far physically and psychologically untapped; to gain awareness for the project among potential investors and renters; and, over the medium term, to achieve a mixed use of the vast area.

Berlin's Media Spree regional management effort is another example of how temporary uses are sought after as location factors in neighborhood and regional management initiatives. In contrast to Amsterdam, however, here the authorities did not invest in temporary uses; instead, existing uses—whether Maria at the Ostbahnhof, Ostgut, Berghain, Bar 25, or Kiki Bloofeld—were merely exploited for marketing purposes. Soon after it began to become apparent that it would not be possible to realize the large-scale development plans in their entirety due to insufficient demand, the authorities sought to conceal the failure by emphasizing the already existing "creative milieu" and to communicate a positive image of the neighborhood. At the same time, within the scope of the Media Spree projects, attempts were made to press ahead with the commercial utilization of real estate together with the property owners, not least through the approval of large-scale reconstruction of the properties; however, this was a strategy that did not meet with much approval from residents of the affected districts of Kreuzberg and Friedrichshain. With the initiative "MediaSpree versenken" (Sink MediaSpree) a referendum was initiated that spoke out against the continuation of the master plan. The informal temporary uses on the Spree no doubt played a major role in this: they demonstrated alternatives to office buildings or auditoriums for mega events such as the O2.world-Die Arena from which other population groups also profit. In addition, the club operators supported the protest marches and

Nike as partner to the local club scene: During the FIFA World Cup in 2006, the "103" in Berlin-Kreuzberg became the "Casa 103."

interventions. Several of the temporary users have had to give in the meantime; however, the volume of authorized new buildings has been reduced, and the areas on the banks of the river to be made available to the public were enlarged. The conflict is still ongoing.

Changing images and building attractive addresses are also a determining factor for owners of individual properties. Empty buildings can be brought to the attention of potential renters and buyers by means of high-profile temporary uses. This becomes all the more relevant when, as in Berlin, economic stagnation leads to a surplus of buildings that cannot be rented or sold from a traditional perspective. In particular, temporary uses from the realms of art, culture, entertainment, and recreation generate a large amount of publicity, which can transform an unattractive location into a coveted object. Temporary uses create milieus that are essential for today's knowledge society and creative industries, so that commercial users increasingly seek them out.

Thus a Berlin property owner decided, on the advice of his project developer, to make unused spaces in the Edison Höfe available to the curator and gallery owner Rüdiger Lange rent-free for four years. Thanks to the enhancement of the property's image that resulted from the temporary gallery project *Loop*, the owner was ultimately able to attract conventional renters. For many owners, temporary uses can do more than merely enhance their property's image. They do not dismiss the temporary users after just a short time— on the contrary, they rely on the consolidation of activities at the site with the goal of "cultivating" their own renters. The owner of another empty building, a house on Berlin's centrally located Friedrichstrasse, made his spaces available to a few Berlin gallery owners, initially for free. The improvised scene soon produced a number of professional galleries, which then joined together under combined management and signed a ten-year lease for the building.

The cliché of street soccer is staged in ghetto style and with favela chic.

These two examples are not merely isolated incidents. The approach can also be pursued less haphazardly, that is, far more professionally, as the development of Berlin's Josetti Höfe shows. The empty former industrial complex in Berlin-Mitte had gone into receivership and was widely regarded as unrentable. By patiently and persistently making her case, Carmen Reiz—an agent with experience in neighborhood management projects—was able to convince the bank, which was reticent at first, to make the unrenovated building available for an experiment to the mutual advantage of the owner, the temporary users, and the agent. She presented a plan for dividing up the 12,000 square meter industrial complex into small sections and renting them out short-term to a large number of micro-users from the creative milieu. The limitations associated with the plan—a minimal standard of renovation and a notice period of just three months—are unattractive for traditional renters but meet the needs of many temporary micro-users, who also benefit from low rents. It was possible to secure more than 250 renters in this way and for a long time utilize the building to more than 90 percent of its capacity. The result was a deliberate and extremely diverse mix of tenants: short-term renters like film productions share the spaces of the industrial complex with individual renters and office communities from the creative fields. Acquaintance with the first renters led to additional contacts and the gradual building of a highly diversified contact network with a stable pool of potential renters. The bank benefited by having its day-to-day expenses taken over by the renters, as well as from the fact that once the project was underway it began to receive an—albeit modest—rental income. Moreover, the rental income also paid for the agent, who took over the labor-intensive task of micromanaging the many small and short-term renters and thus relieved the property owners of the burden of doing so themselves.

Carmen Reiz had the vision of the continued consolidation of circumstances at the Josetti Höfe by gradually improving the development standards and concluding long-term rental contracts. Yet the owner lacked insight into the requirements of such a strategy. While tea kitchens, lounges, and the foyer did not experience an improvement, she invested in conventional and expensive conversions that hardly improved the quality of use for users. In summer 2010, Carmen Reiz engaged a conventional property management that with respect to standardized and "professional" services fulfilled the bank's requirements, yet lacked a flair and the communication skills for dealing with the users' cultural and creative milieu. It is therefore doubtful whether it will succeed in carrying on the development strategy she began.

PRODUCT MARKETING

The employment of temporary users plays out differently from the exploitative strategies thus far described when the temporary use is part of a product marketing scheme. In these cases, what the organizers have in view is the hip lifestyle of informal activities in the recreational and cultural spheres. They seek to exploit the image of innovation and creativity associated with these milieus to market the products of sporting goods manufacturers (for example, Nike and Adidas), fashion companies (for example, Comme des

Street art and graffiti-style lettering. As is the case in all of their campaigns, the brand name Nike is not used, only the Nike "swoosh."

Garçons), and telecommunications firms (for example, Sony Ericsson). With this in mind, they primarily seek to enlist youthful target groups as trendsetters.

When efforts like this take the form of sponsorship, they are definitely something from which temporary users can benefit. In such cases, it is usually the users themselves who instigate the collaboration, knowing as they do that the association of particular projects of the temporary users with particular products of the sponsors can mean very effective and hence lucrative publicity for the investing companies. For example, money from sponsors made it possible to turn a former industrial hall on the grounds of the Reichsbahnausbesserungswerk (RAW, or Imperial Railroad Repair Works) in Berlin-Friedrichshain into an indoor skate hall. It was large-scale, high-profile events like the European Skateboard Championship that were decisive in persuading the sponsors.

In the late 1990s, however, many large corporations began to appropriate and imitate the methods of temporary users in their product marketing. The advertising strategies that go furthest in this respect are no doubt those of Nike, which used "urban marketing" to create a do-it-yourself image and thus lent the Nike label the "street credibility" that is so important in youth culture. Advertising is put in places where the consumer does not expect it; most important, it is not recognizable as advertising at first glance. These efforts seek the proximity of informal subcultural activities; the content presents itself as subversive and rebellious. Thus, in 1999 Nike put signs up at 250 Berlin playgrounds with slogans such as "Freedom lies behind bars," or "Please feed only with leather." This was followed beginning in 2000, also in Berlin, by a number of temporary uses in the empty subway stations beneath the Reichstag building, on the grounds of the former Stadion der Weltjugend (Stadium for the Young People of the World), in an empty department store,

In 1999, Nike placed advertising at 250 playgrounds in Berlin in the graphic design language of prohibition signs.

and in a series of bars. Analogous projects were carried out in London, for example in the empty Millennium Dome. There is no question that these campaigns also created new recreational offerings and helped to maintain public institutions and provide them with new athletic equipment. But these offerings go hand in hand with the commercialization and privatization of public space, which is now primarily supposed to be experienced as part of a branded environment. Finally, the companies that take this approach also have the advantage that their strategies for harnessing temporary uses only require a small amount of capital and are therefore highly cost-effective.

Companies like Nike, Comme des Garçons, and Sony Ericsson finance backdrops for activities that appear to be spontaneously organized, informal, even illegal. Using a camouflage strategy, they mobilize the visual language of the underground and harness anticapitalist codes to the realization of purely commercial interests. They use all the means of guerrilla warfare to infiltrate the subculture, recruiting actors, renting preexisting locations, seeking out the proximity of already existing activities that fit with their marketing, and infiltrating public spaces with logos.

INFLUENCING THE USE PROFILE

All of the various exploitative approaches described here have one thing in common: temporary uses and temporary users are employed to achieve an independent objective. Framework conditions for the activities involved are defined and formalized by those who are doing the exploiting. The types of use and users desired are selected, and the trajectory of the use is supervised. By influencing the profile of the use in accord with their goals, the external actors assume an important position of control. Temporary users are forced to adapt to predefined framework conditions and to accept the limits placed on their free development. Despite such exploitation, however, the temporary users are not necessarily reduced to passive agents of the property owners' designs. Depending on their behavior, they can even shape the use decisively and alter its trajectory and outcome.

In its effort to revitalize the hall of the Nederlandse Dok en Scheepsbouw Maatschappij (NDSM), the Amsterdam city government organized an ideas competition that temporary user groups from the subcultural milieu could enter with their ideas for the use. This way the city could select the programs and actors whose profiles were most advantageous for them. Carmen Reiz too was only able to realize her plan for the Josetti Höfe by proposing a specific temporary use profile. With her close contacts in the Berlin scene, she was able to attract temporary users from the creative milieu and in this way to shape the programmatic orientation of the industrial complex. Nike took an even more direct approach, hiring representatives of its customer target groups as "scouts." They became paid agents and opinion makers, who, for example, publicized the Nike Park on the grounds of the former Stadion der Weltjugend within their particular social networks.

BETWEEN PROFIT AND ANXIETY

The strategy of exploitation means harnessing temporary uses to the pursuit of entrepreneurial strategies. The examples show that informality and capitalization are not in conflict. The added value that owners and companies seek to achieve can lead to win-win situations: attractions and infrastructures are created without public funds and can be employed by temporary users as well as a broader public. In addition to win-win situations, however, there is also the case of the unilateral harnessing or cooptation of temporary uses. Commercialization with nothing in return does not create any added value, but leads to the exclusionary privatization of public spaces. Instead of the empowerment of marginalized groups and the participation of a broader range of actors, we see the staging of informality as a backdrop for new branded environments.

FURTHER INFORMATION

www.josettihoefe.de

www.ndsm.nl

Friedrich von Borries, *Who's Afraid of Niketown?* (Rotterdam: Episode, 2004).

OBJECTIVE: To exploit temporary uses for building and neighborhood development

PROTAGONISTS: City government of Amsterdam Noord, Kinetisch Nord

USE: More than 200 (socio)cultural users and users from the cultural sector

STATUS: Lease until 2027

SITE: 20,000 square meter shipyard hall in disused harbor area of Amsterdam Nord, owned by the city

TRAJECTORY: Plan and first uses 1999, 2000 feasibility study, 2000–2002 economic plan, since then gradual expansion of use

COST: Lease of € 1.00 / square meter per month in addition to operating costs; investments totaling € 25 million

FINANCING: Government subsidy of € 10 million. Loan being redeemed by rent payments from users; € 10 million invested by end users

The city of Amsterdam is divided by the river Ij. The vast majority of its residents live in the densely populated historic city center south of the Ij and the newer surrounding areas. Traditionally they have gone to work in the harbor and industrial areas north of the river. But since the 1980s these areas have fallen idle. As a result of the containeration of the shipping industry and the development of larger cargo ships, the riverbed became too small and the inland harbor ceased to be economically viable. At the same time, the postindustrial economic boom put pressure on the city center. The overheated real estate market began to displace the city's once so vital creative milieu. The city's residents began to ask, with an increasing sense of urgency, whether Amsterdam was at risk of being stifled by its own success.

Since the late 1990s the city government has sought to develop new alternative accommodations. Initially, new residential areas were gained for the growing metropolis on the southern bank of the Ij by means of land reclamation. In 1999, however, the city decided to brave the leap across the river. The former harbor area was integrated into a city-wide development plan and the respective master plan. The city as landowner planned a new neighborhood in the so-called NDSM area—the new neighborhood would be roughly 2 square kilometers in size with more than 3 million square meters of floor space, and it would be grouped around the empty shipyard hall of the Nederlandse Dok en Scheepsbouw Maatschappij (NDSM), which has 20,000 square meters of floor space. An unusual planning experiment was announced: the hall would become the engine and nucleus of the entire town planning development of the NDSM area. Temporary users would renovate the hall with government help and use it for cultural programs for a period of ten years. Thanks to the activity of a cultural center intent on popularity, this forgotten part of Amsterdam would once again become present in people's minds, and Amsterdam Nord would be rediscovered as part of the larger city. The aim was to attract potential investors and renters and to allow a vibrant mixture of uses to develop. In contrast to the monotonous residential and commercial satellites that were also typical of the 1990s, the area would see the gradual growth of the prototype of a highly diversified neighborhood with ample space for an urban culture to develop and thrive.

The original idea of a bottom-up development strategy, however, did not stem from the municipality alone. It was prompted in no small measure by an initiative comprised of squatters and people interested in using the industrial buildings along the Ij. This affiliation around Eva de Klerk and Hessel Dokum formed a working group that, along with municipal building societies, beginning in 1996 produced the strategy paper on the development of the harbor area, "*De Stad als Casco*," and presented it to the authorities.

The former NDSM shipyard and the surrounding industrial areas along the north bank of the river Ij are part of the largest inner-city development area in Amsterdam.

In 1999, the district of Amersterdam Noord solicited a temporary use
concept for the abandoned shipyard hall via a public call for projects.

Hier kunnen kunstenaars tot grote hoogte stijgen.

Wie houdt beide benen op de grond?

Welbekend van het 'Over het IJ'-festival en nu onderwerp van grotere plannen: de hal op het
NSM-terrein aan de IJ-oever in Amsterdam-Noord. De bedoeling is om de 30.000m² grote hal
plus omliggende terreinen te ontwikkelen tot een veelzijdige culturele verzamelplaats met ateliers,
werkplaatsen, oefenruimten, podia, studio's, etc. Voor gevestigde namen en jong talent. Voor groot
publiek en select gezelschap. Voor commercieel succes en experiment. Voor evenementen en
manifestaties én kleine exposities en theater.

Daarom zoeken we een **creatieve ondernemer** die culturele belang-
stelling weet te combineren met nuchter zakelijk inzicht. In eerste instantie zijn we geïnteres-
seerd in uw visie en een concreet beheer- en exploitatieplan. *Ziet u 't al voor zich?*
Zet uw ideeën voor 8 november op papier. Vraag een informatiepakket aan bij Gerard van Horn
(tel. 020.634 94 39) van het Stadsdeel Amsterdam-Noord, postbus 37608, 1030 BB Amsterdam.

stadsdeel amsterdam-noord

De Theatergroep Zonder Olga

MUNICIPALITY DEFINES FRAMEWORK CONDITIONS FOR TEMPORARY USE

The city of Amsterdam was able to use its considerable room for maneuver to realize
its plans. The municipality not only possesses supreme planning authority; it is also the
owner of most of the spaces within the city limits, and assigns these for long-term use with
hereditary leases. Moreover, after local industry had departed, the NDSM hall reverted to
the city. The municipality became involved in a series of individual investments—each of
which was not economically viable, but in which the measures turned out to be economically advantageous. Thus, temporary users established themselves and a ferry service was
set up between the NDSM hall and Amsterdam's main railroad station.

The temporary users' experience of the city's powerful position proved to be ambivalent. On the one hand, they owed their very existence as temporary users to that position.
At the same time, however, their existence formed part of the municipality's pursuit of a
larger strategic objective, and the city sought to influence the character of the temporary
use with a series of binding framework conditions. This was precisely not a magnanimous
gesture, but a neighborhood development project by other means, with clear economic
objectives.

THE BROEDPLAATSFONDS

Amsterdam was able to make use of a tried and tested tool to finance the initial measures
and the later stages of the process. Since 2000, the city has organized and financed the
Broedplaatsfond Amsterdam (BPA). The purpose of the Broedplaatsfonds, or "breeding

ground funds," is to promote and assist the city's creative industries. These funds were the result of fierce protests and conflicts between the city and Amsterdam's alternative and creative scene. The protesters demanded the preservation of building projects and creative, subcultural sites, the transfer of the respective real estate, and the support of self-determined initiatives for the development of independent objects and projects. The provision of subsidies and making inexpensive spaces available in unused buildings were to counter the crowding out of actors who were financially weak but important to city culture, and who in the wake of the real-estate boom in the 1990s were almost completely driven out of Amsterdam's city center. Between 2000 and 2006 the fund invested € 40 million in 37 city-center breeding ground projects. In all, roughly 2,000 studios and workshops and 1,000 cultural producers were supported in this manner. Breeding ground projects can come about in various ways—through the legalization of squats, through competition between creative groups, and through the initiative of owners or that of the Broedplaats-fonds itself. The formerly disused areas are given over to the cultural groups for a period of ten to fifty years. The fund's initial phase ran from 2000 to 2010. The NDSM shipyard has become one of the BPA's most prestigious assistance projects. A total of € 10 million of public funds has been invested in the redevelopment of the hall.

THE IDEAS COMPETITION

The realization of the NDSM project started in 1999. The city began by holding a public ideas competition with the aim of finding an organization to realize the temporary use

of the NDSM shipyard hall. The competition was won by an initiative created for the purpose called Kinetisch Noord, which came from the former Amsterdam squatter scene. Their idea envisioned a cluster of theater groups, handicraft enterprises, studios, start-ups, and performance spaces. The hall would be divided into thematic zones: "Kunst-stad" (10,000 square meters); a skate park (2,000 square meters); facilities for youths (3,000 square meters); "Nordstrook" for exhibitions, cafes, galleries, and apartments (6,000 square meters); "Oostvleugel" for theater studios (2,500 square meters); and the temporary outdoor spaces "Dazzleville" (during the reconstruction of the warehouse a performance area of 9,000 square meters). Other artists, craftspeople, youth projects, and creative firms would be able to apply to Kinetisch Noord for inexpensive spaces.

The advantages of this procedure for the city are obvious. First, the well-publicized competition aroused strong public interest, which not only enabled the administration to present itself as creative and responsive to the needs and desires of its citizens but also gained public awareness for the new neighborhood. Second, the competition allowed the city to select and shape the profile of the users in keeping with its goals. Third, the city laid down the framework conditions of the temporary use in the competition announcement, and potential users had to accept them in order to participate. In this way, for example, the city was able to insist on the formation of a management structure as a precondition of the temporary use and thus avoid being drawn into time-consuming and costly negotiations with individual temporary users. The use was limited to a period of ten years. As early as 2000, following protests by the initiators for more planning

security, the duration was extended to 25 years. For the total area of 26,000 square meters, a leasing rate of € 11 per square meter per year was established, to be paid annually beginning in 2003 after a free transitional period. The city also insisted that its contractual partner constitute itself as a corporate body in the form of a foundation. Immediately after the competition was decided and long before the conclusion of the contract in February 2002, a group of 40 artists and cultural entrepreneurs moved into the hall. Their need for space was so great that they put up with the improvised use in the leaky, unheated hall. A container village was set up with a construction-site electricity supply and temporary toilets. It was not until after 2002 that the conditions for use normalized, once the roof was repaired and heating was installed.

INFLUENCE AND CONFLICTS OF INTEREST

The city also controlled the trajectory of the use once the competition was over. It exerted considerable influence on the formation of the management structure, in turn ensuring that it would remain in possession of long-term opportunities for control: as head of the building management of Kinetisch Noord and coordinator of the by now more than 200 users, a director was appointed from within the city government. He was originally endorsed by the users—among other things because they hoped for the professionalization in dealings with formal requirements. However, this decision had enormous consequences. The director concentrated less on financing the loan and the targeted independence of the project and more on a short-term and prestigious public image, for example by purchasing expensive art objects. An expensive submanagement instrument was installed without having approached the foundation for their approval. In order to bolster marketing, the city insisted on large-scale, high-publicity events in the hall.

Despite a successful start, various conflicts soon arose between the users (represented by a foundation set up specifically for this purpose) and the city. The imposed framework conditions were increasingly experienced as difficult and restrictive. In addition, it was more complicated than expected to coordinate all of the participants. The spirit that was important to the initiators around Kinetisch Noord and strongly characterized by the tradition of Amsterdam's alternative scene got lost in the power struggles between the participants and the increasing anonymity due to uninvolved new renters. At the same time, after the shift to the right, the goals of municipal policy in the Netherlands changed. As a result, the city continued to reject the demand for the transfer of ownership. This would not only have allowed independence in the design of the project, but also point a way out of the current financing dilemma. The € 10 million of subsidies from the city and the € 10 million the temporary users had thus far raised themselves were just enough to renovate half the hall. Yet the temporary users were required to pay the lease for the entire hall. In order to be able to rent the other half of the hall, which had thus far gone unused, it would have to be renovated. As security for granting the necessary credits, the banks required ownership by the users. The users rejected the option of financing the investment by raising the rents, since they feared this would lead to the commercialization of the uses.

The lasting conflict between the city-controlled building manager and the foundation that represented the temporary users has been resolved for the time being. Criticism of mismanagement and undue influence on the program of events and performances ultimately led to the appointment of a new building manager in 2007.

The project's initiators regret the increasing disintegration of the overarching concept. As the pilot of the overall project, the municipality in the meantime concludes different leasing contracts in individual areas. The users are increasingly forming subgroups

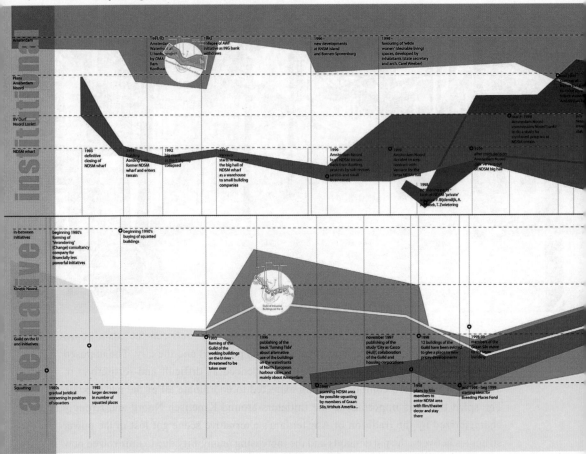

representing particular interests. In the meantime, the city has offered the hall to a private project development on terms that would also have been affordable for the current users.

CONCLUSIONS

Has the strategy been successful? From the city's perspective the answer is definitely yes. Even if the paradigms of city planning have changed after a political shift to the right, the advantages of NDSM remain obvious, even for an approach to urban development more strongly oriented toward commercial perspectives: many of the building projects in the area surrounding the hall have already begun, and thanks in part to the success of NDSM renters have been found, including users from the creative industries, such as MTV. Moreover, the users of the hall are responsible for the lease and operating expenses.

The temporary users initially experienced the development process primarily defined by the city as predominantly positive. Initial negotiations took place in a relaxed atmosphere and there were no particular objections to the city's gently smothering "embrace." It seemed that the framework conditions defined by the city were reconcilable with the objectives of the temporary users. The advantages outweighed the disadvantages: there were new spaces and new possibilities, opportunities for self-development and self-expression.

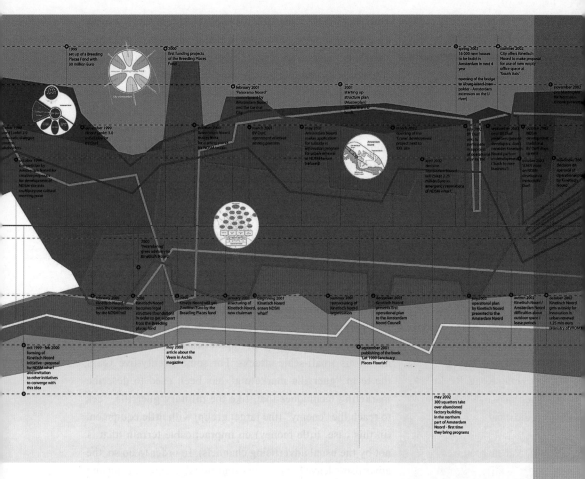

It proved possible to establish a broad and varied spectrum of users. Programs and activities were positively perceived not only in Amsterdam but elsewhere in Europe as well. Yet if one takes a look at the conflicts of interest, the founders evaluate their relationship with the city critically. Although they have been able to defend the cornerstones of the use profile and resist the mounting pressure to commercialize the area, the longing to be independent remains. Instead of municipal subsidies and a lease, ownership and financial autonomy are preferred.

FURTHER INFORMATION

www.evadeklerk.com

www.ndsm.nl

OBJECTIVE: Marketing of
fashion articles

PROTAGONIST: Young small
business owners as well as
fashion companies

USE: Store

STATUS: Rent for several
weeks up to 12 months

TRAJECTORY: 2004 first store
in Berlin, since then various
stores in Warsaw, Basel,
Athens, Hong Kong, Reykjavik,
etc. Time span of a store one
year at the most

PLACE: Vacant premises

FINANCING: Rent by person
running the store; merchandise
on commission

"Guerrilla stores" is the name given by the fashion label Comme des Garçons to a series of stores that never stay more than a short time in any one place. Temporary use as a subcultural strategy is turned into a marketing instrument. *Propaganda Camp / Popular Occupation / Alliance / Independent Base / Revolution / Radical Supplement / Disappear / Reoccupation Starts*—this is the text on the posters that refer to the guerrilla stores. But what do politically charged terms like guerrilla, revolution, and propaganda have to do with clothing stores?

Friedrich von Borries

GUERRILLA MARKETING

Guerrilla is a military term. In the eighteenth and nineteenth centuries, guerrilla, or the "little war," refers to tactical deceptive maneuvers intended to tie up enemy forces beyond the actual battlefield. With the Wars of Liberation against Napoleon, the term guerrilla comes to be used for irregular resistance fighters who attempt to weaken the enemy, who is superior in terms of numbers and equipment, with surprise maneuvers, usually on impracticable terrain, and with numerous small-scale attacks. For some twenty-five years, the term "guerrilla marketing" has been used to describe marketing techniques that, like the military guerrilla, seek to reach the "enemy" (the target group) with little equipment (in this case, little money) on impracticable terrain (that is, not by the usual advertising channels). In order to do so, the advertisers leave behind their traditional terrain of print and TV and enter the space of the city.

CAMOUFLAGE

An important technique used by guerrilla fighters is camouflage: it is imperative that they not be recognized as combatants. Guerrilla marketing also tries not to be recognized as marketing. Hence it frequently uses the expedient of slipping an accepted mantle over the actual marketing technique. In Hamburg, for example, the coffee producer Senseo financed a temporary art festival.[1] Nike opened clubs and bars in various German cities together with partners from the club scene[2]—as a brand it kept in the background the entire time. With these camouflage strategies, the brand is intended to penetrate the consciousness of the target group only subliminally.

View into a guerrilla store in Berlin-Mitte, 2006

TEMPORARINESS

Time is an important factor in all guerrilla techniques. The intervention ultimately draws its effectiveness not from its degree of force but rather from the element of surprise. So it has to be fast—"disappear" and "reoccupation" are the corresponding buzzwords of the Comme des Garçons guerrilla stores. All guerrilla marketing campaigns are short-lived—they draw their power from the reciprocal persistence of the "attention economy": it is more efficient to be known in the target group by word of mouth than to reach a broad audience. Fashion is a fast-moving business; two collections a year is the norm. Actually, however, this tempo only applies to the products, not to the sales venues. In the wake of guerrilla marketing strategies, however, the fashion industry has also discovered the temporariness of sales spaces. Whether Adidas, Levi's, or Nike, for certain "hip" products it is increasingly becoming standard practice to open temporary stores that only exist for two or three months and then vanish. The company that goes furthest in terms of "making itself scarce" is Clemens en August. Like a street peddler, the fashion label travels throughout Germany and makes guest appearances in the cities it has selected for its route, never staying for longer than three to five days. As partners for these guest performances, however, it seeks out institutions that have a positive image in the target group—an art gallery, for example. In this process the exclusiveness of the product is generated not by the factor of money (because it dispenses with the usual more expensive distribution structures, the label is actually relatively inexpensive) but by knowledge of place and time. Thus, compared to the more classical competitors, the guerrilla strategy gives its practitioners an economic edge (the product can be offered for sale more cheaply) and enhances their image as well. In a society where time is the most precious commodity for the rich, scarcity of time becomes a distinctive feature.

A NEOLIBERAL PRINCIPLE

The Comme des Garçons guerrilla stores are the most thorough and systematic current implementation of guerrilla marketing in shop concept and retail design. The first guerrilla store opened in Berlin in 2004. The setting was a little former bookstore at the northern end of Friedrichstrasse, away from the tourist hotspots but still easily accessible. The former bookstore was not elaborately renovated but merely retooled with the barest necessities. In this respect it follows a strategy of temporary use that is encountered especially frequently in the cultural scene of Berlin: with a small amount of money, an empty retail store is refurbished for use as a gallery or workspace. A mere € 3,000 were spent on setting up the store, which for a fashion boutique is actually a ridiculously small sum of money. In this case, however, it was a conscious principle and a strategy of differentiation. For sale in this store were clothes from the current Comme des Garçons collection, Second Season/ Vintage (remnants of earlier collections), and special editions not available in ordinary stores. As a special highlight, every two weeks the inventory was completely replaced. The Berlin guerrilla store was so successful that it gave rise to a shop model of its own, with guerrilla stores all over the world—in Athens, Barcelona, Basel, Glasgow, Helsinki, Hong Kong, Cologne, Copenhagen, Ljubljana, Reykjavik, Singapore, Stockholm, and Warsaw. All the stores are temporary, and after a year at most they change their location, their ambience, and their interior design. In a world in which everything is fast and ephemeral, the stores must be flexible too. Moreover, the locations selected and the furnishings are quite eccentric. The label that wants to spend little or no money has to travel different design paths from the usual smooth and aestheticized surfaces of established retail design. In Reykjavik the guerrilla store is located in the industrial harbor; deep-sea vessels are visible through the window, and the clothes are presented on standardized europallets instead of expensive racks. In Singapore the guerrilla store is located in an industrial warehouse, in Cologne in a former slaughterhouse—the expensive articles of clothing hang on old meat hooks. Design that is different from what one knows. The global brand acquires a local face. An exciting adventure for the global Comme des Garçons community: where can I find a guerrilla store, how is it designed, and what vintage products can I find there?

PROPAGANDA
CAMP
POPULAR
OCCUPATION
ALLIANCE
INDEPENDENT
BASE
REVOLUTION
RADICAL
SUPPLY
DISAPPEAR
REOCCUPATION STARTS
26 MAY 2006,
BRUNNENSTRASSE 152,
10115 BERLIN

COMME des GARÇON*
+49 30

But guerrilla stores do more than just mimic the aesthetic of cultural scenes, which are
forced to resort to temporary use by economic reality. The economic principles of temporary cultural use are transferred to the guerrilla stores: flexibility, locality, fast response
time. Until now Comme des Garçons clothing was found in exclusive fashion specialty
stores with a good reputation in their area. However, Comme des Garçons has no influence over how the stores are set up. The store owners select clothing from the collection
as they see fit and buy it from the company. What doesn't sell lands in the discount bin at
the end-of-season sale or else continues to hang on the rack. Comme des Garçons has no
influence on the store's corporate policy.

In order to have more say over how they appear to the consumer, in the past ten years
many fashion companies have therefore built so-called flagship stores. But flagship
stores are expensive—a large amount of floor space in a good location costs money.
The decentralized principle of the guerrilla stores is much more efficient. A shop is
opened, and right from the outset it is only designed to last for a short time. If it works,
it moves on to a new location, if not then not. And unlike with Nike, Adidas, and Levi's,
the phenomenon of temporary occupation and the simplicity of the design are an inten-
tional part of the concept. Now one might think that, with its guerrilla stores, Comme
des Garçons had copied the informal strategies of the cultural scene in a particularly
intelligent manner. But that is not the case—on the contrary. Here, actors from the

PROPAGANDA
CAMP
POPULAR
OCCUPATION
ALLIANCE
INDEPENDENT
BASE
REVOLT
RADICAL
SUPPLY
DISAP...

COMME DES GARÇON
+354

GUERRILLA
Store

OCCUPATION STARTS
24 SEPTEMBER 2005,
MÝRARGATA 2-8
101 REYKJAVIK

cultural scene approached Comme des Garçons and successfully presented them with their idea of a whole different kind of store, with the full intention of running the shops themselves.[3] With roots in the local scene, they have a better feel for the place and what is locally "hip." And even more importantly, as the operators of the store they shoulder the economic risk themselves. As small business owners they set up the shop themselves and negotiate the rent with the landlords—and since this is a genuine temporary use, and not just an aesthetic imitation of one as with Nike or Adidas but economically real, the rent is extremely low. The operators of the Basel guerrilla store apparently do not even have a lease, but set up their guerrilla store in a basement, as "squatters." Comme des Garçons is responsive to these small business owners: they are not required to buy the clothes, but sell them on commission. This reduces the risk and necessary start-up capital for the operators and gives Comme des Garçons control over the inventory. Thus they are able to completely change the inventory every two weeks, which not only means greater responsiveness to the wishes of local customers but also more efficient inventory management. Instead of high rents there are cheaper shipping costs. Everything is efficient and hip at the same time.

In addition to these economic advantages there are also psychological ones: the operators of the guerrilla stores do not perceive themselves as personnel, as employees of a multinational corporation (nor is that their legal status), but as freelance creative professionals who search out exciting locations in their city, design clever and also cost-effective interiors, and have a partner standing beside them with hip products and a good image to help with their realization.

GUERRILLA STORES AS AN EXPORT HIT

One might say that guerrilla stores are the ideal pairing of the current economic imperative of flexibility and the individual desire for independence and self-realization. A lifestyle reproduces itself as a marketing instrument. Accordingly, other businesses have capitalized on the principle of the pop-up store. In the summer of 2010, for example, the Suhrkamp[4] publishing house opened one in Berlin—flexible use of space, decentralized organization based on a high degree of personal engagement, integration of creative capital, and cost-effective advertising by word of mouth: a highly efficient economic principle. The top-down approach of classical planning (which also includes so-called strategic marketing) is replaced by the bottom-up strategy of the cultural self-marketers. The Comme des Garçons and Co. guerrilla stores stand for the transformation of the principle of temporary use: an alternative form of the use of space is turned into an instrument of its neoliberal marketing. In the meantime, however, the innovation potential of capitalism has reinverted the principle. Rem Koolhaas developed the "Transformer" for Prada, a temporary architectural construct that rotates around its own axis, thus sustaining the guerrilla pop-up principle as an upper-class mega-event.

And what has become of the guerrilla shop in Berlin? Its founder turned it into what she probably always dreamed of: a small fashion shop with clothes by Comme des Garçons and others. But it is not temporary: it is open Tuesdays through Saturdays, just like any other store.

NOTES

1. The Ding Dong! Senseo Art Festival was an arts event that lasted for a few weeks in a vacant department store complex in Hamburg-Altona. See also http://www.senseo-art-initiative.com.

2. There were Presto Lounges in a number of German cities, and during the 2006 World Cup there were so-called Nike Casas in a number of cities where World Cup games were played. For example in Berlin in cooperation with Club 103, and in Hamburg in cooperation with the clubhouse of the strongly left-wing St. Pauli soccer team—Nike meets the skull and crossbones.

3. A graduate of the architecture department of Technische Universität Berlin (Berlin Technical University) and a Berlin fashion designer approached Comme des Garçons. The young architect is now employed by Comme des Garçons and responsible for the worldwide coordination of the guerilla stores.

4. Designed by the author of this text

A decade after the beginning of our involvement with temporary and pioneer uses, they have now become a permanent part of current discourses on urban development and urban planning. The practice of maintaining scope for experimental uses as a necessary resource of urban development has not only asserted itself in regions affected by economic crises or outmigration, but also in cities experiencing heightened pressure to develop.

HafenCity Hamburg, for example, currently one of the largest urban planning projects in Europe, recently updated its master plan. The eastern section, which was previously scheduled for development, will for the time being be left open in order to gain space and time for an open-source process involving temporary uses. It is suspected that behind this decision there is an instrumentalization of temporary uses in order to better market property, yet at the same time it is associated with a noticeable paradigm change in the development of the flagship neighborhood that is due, to a great extent, to ramifications of the worldwide economic crisis.

The collapse of the financial markets at the European level, triggered by the real estate crisis in the United States, has been directly reflected in a building freeze, the pull-out of investors, and the abandonment of real estate projects, as well as in vacancies, above all in retail and commercial properties. To date, this has resulted in only very few new options for temporary uses, as many investors are attempting to "wait out" the vacancies in anticipation of a renewed upturn. The fact that temporary uses are in many cases used to bridge a gap in a crisis-ridden real estate economy is not new. However, it is interesting to note that for those places affected by the crisis, the overlap of two completely opposing systems—a delocalized financial market that has lost control and a network of locally rooted temporary uses—presents itself as nothing less than a challenge to realign previous policy.

With the collapse of real estate financing, the crisis of the financial market exposed the dysfunctionality of a purely monetarily controlled urban development system. It was the tentative climax of an entrepreneurial urban policy that had been propagated for more than twenty years and which was increasingly geared toward the interests of financial investors and their thinking in terms of benchmarks and returns on investment. With the uncoupling of owners and property, this system turned away from real urban uses. In fact, investors are largely unaware of the specific projects in which they have invested their money. A maximum abstraction from property occurs due to the diverse forms of pyramiding and repackaging of financial products. The system is no longer able to trace the real values that stand behind the property titles. This is not only a problem for risk assessment and the well-founded evaluation of property titles; it also reduces property to purely quantitative fiscal dimensions. Any other dimensions of property—be they, for example, social obligations, local commitments, or environmental awareness—are completely blocked out.

Traders take advantage of quick transactions to gain a maximum of capital out of short-term value fluctuations. The system works as long as buyers can be found to speculate on further increases in value. However, if demand collapses, as it has during the economic crisis, asset value is no longer accompanied by equivalent value, and the interim purchaser is left with his piece of property. Because few owners are willing to ease the development rights and enhance the asset value of the property, a large number of properties and pockets of land become derelict.

In many places there is talk about recovery after the crisis and a revival of the markets. Yet there continues to be a deep mistrust toward an abstract financial and real estate market, to whose rules urban neighborhoods are subject. With the growing awareness of the fact that one's own way of life is directly connected with the production of one's living environment, people are taking the initiative to again exercise immediate influence on the design and use of their environment. Temporary uses are not a cure-all, but they are evidence of this change in thinking and lead the way toward an organic urban development.

PRACTICE URBAN DEVELOPMENT WITHOUT CAPITAL
Temporary use allows groups of the population with insufficient capital to actively design the city. At the same time, other territories are introduced into the urban design. The increasing capitalization and commercialization of society are countered with the valorization of non-monetary resources.

USE AVAILABLE RESOURCES
The transformation of what already exists is the key to the urban development of tomorrow. It is about how what is given can be perceived, used, changed, or removed. Existing structures, structural atmospheres, and structural environments are valuable resources, and it is essential that they be integrated into development concepts.

APPRECIATE THE INCOMPLETE

Vibrant cities do not originate in test tubes but develop over time. The focus is not on urban design, but urban use. The incomplete, the dissimilar, the transitory, the temporary become part of the cityscape. They harbor the chance for fields of tension of a more hybrid and multifaceted city.

ENABLE GRADUAL DEVELOPMENT

Temporary uses can constitute an important impetus for a new form of processual urban development concerned with the recoding and reprogramming of existing space. The present book presents examples for intelligent growth in which urban development is not viewed as an urbanistically structured accumulation of building mass, but as a successive condensation of activities, programs, and networks that also structurally manifest themselves in phases.

PROMOTE COPRODUCTION, SHARE VALUES

Temporary users are spatial entrepreneurs. They develop their projects in a trial-and-error process irrespective of market and location analyses. What is done is what the location yields and whose use stands the test. Unlike spatial consumers, who use the objects executed by architects and planners, spatial producers build their city according to their own ideas. Coproduction means winning over temporary users as partners in development. This involves both participation in responsibility as well as in economic success.

COMBINE TOP-DOWN WITH BOTTOM-UP METHODS

Temporary use does not exclude long-term planning. Direct space appropriation and the built vision are still frequently perceived and treated as two mutually exclusive extremes. But a city that would like to constantly reinvent and rejuvenate itself needs both: on the one side, open spaces for unanticipated uses from "below," and, on the other side, spatial-programmatic specifications and designs from "above." Development concepts that dovetail with both have to be augmented by new instruments alongside classic planning tools.

The issue of temporary use transcends itself. It is the antithesis of the monetary urban developed outlined above. To put it hyperbolically: the urban production of financial markets is exclusively based on the organization of money flows that are completely uncoupled from issues concerning the use of urban space. Conversely, temporary use is urban development without financial means that is solely based on the use of urban space. It can be understood as a particularly striking example, the prototype of a new urban practice conceptualized in more universal terms.

Urban Catalyst is therefore an appeal to again make the use of the city as the gateway to urban development—in contrast to the paternalistic practices of the classic welfare state and the neoliberal concept of the entrepreneurial city.

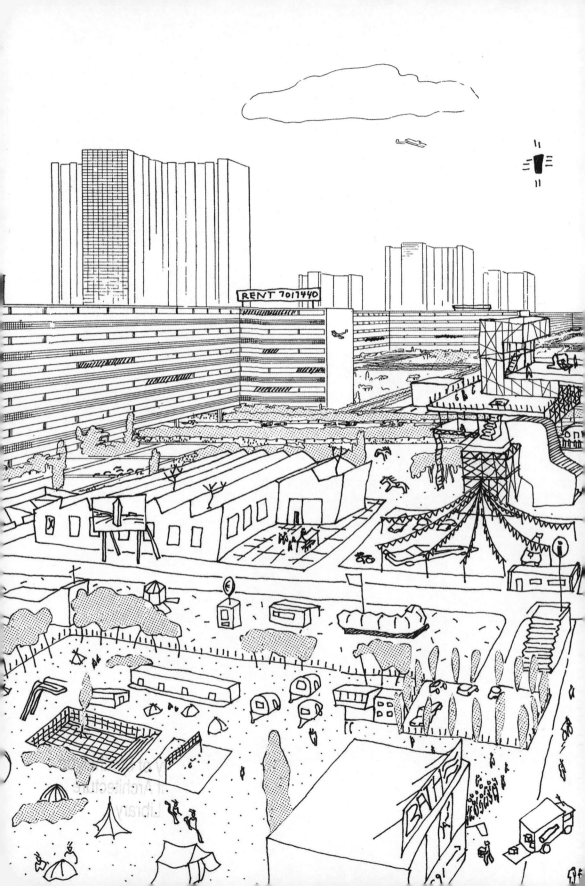

Contributors

Azra Akšamija (b. 1976, Sarajevo, Bosnia and Herzegovina) is an artist, architect, and historian living in Cambridge, Massachusetts (USA).

Peter Arlt (b. 1960, Linz, Austria) is an urban sociologist; he lives in Linz.

Tobias Armborst (b. 1972, Düsseldorf, Germany) is an architect, professor at Vassar College, New York State (USA) and cofounder of the firm Interboro; he lives in New York (USA).

Aram Bartholl (b. 1972 in Bremen, Germany) is an artist, currently artist in residence in Berlin (Germany).

Eyebeam New York City (USA) member of the group F.A.T.Lab; he lives and works in Berlin (Germany).

Friedrich von Borries (b. 1974, Berlin, Germany) is an architect and founder of the firm Raumtaktik; he is a professor at the Hochschule für bildende Künste Hamburg (HFBK) and lives in Berlin.

Nina Brodowski (b. 1979, Hamburg, Germany) is a cultural critic and lecturer at the HafenCity University Hamburg, Germany; she lives in Berlin and Hamburg.

Claudia Büttner (b. 1965, Buchholz in der Nordheide, Germany) is an art historian and curator; she lives in Munich (Germany).

Kees Christiaanse (b. 1953, Amsterdam, Netherlands) is an architect, professor at ETH Zurich, and owner of the firm KCAP; he lives in Zurich (Switzerland).

Margaret Crawford (b. 1951, Long Beach, California, USA) is a professor of history and theory of architecture, urbanism, and urban history at the College of Environmental Design, University of California Berkeley (USA).

Jesko Fezer (b. 1970, Stuttgart, Germany) is an architect, author and runs a bookshop; he is a professor at the Hochschule für bildende Künste Hamburg (HFBK) and lives in Berlin (Germany).

Christa Kamleithner (b. 1974, St. Pölten, Austria) is a cultural critic and research associate at Universität der Künste Berlin (Berlin University of the Arts); she lives in Berlin (Germany).

Rudolf Kohoutek (b. 1941, Vienna, Austria) is an urban researcher; he lives in Vienna.

Michl Mellauner (b. 1960 in Bolzano/Bozen, Italy) is a landscape architect and co-founder of PlanSinn GmbH; he lives in Vienna (Austria).

Philipp Misselwitz (b. 1974, Jena, East Germany) is an architect, coordinator of the research project Urban Catalyst, professor at the University of Stuttgart and since 2012 member of Urban Catalyst [Studio]; he lives in Berlin (Germany).

Jurij von Ortenberg (b. 1977, Würzburg, Germany) is an architect, tutor at the research project Urban Catalyst and visiting lecturer of architecture at Shenzhen University; he lives in Shenzhen (China).

Philipp Oswalt (b. 1964, Frankfurt am Main, Germany) is an architect and author, initiator and coordinator of the research project Urban Catalyst, Director of the Foundation Bauhaus-Dessau and professor at the University of Kassel; he lives in Berlin and Dessau-Roßlau (Germany).

Klaus Overmeyer (b. 1968, Rhede, Germany) is a landscape architect, initiator and coordinator of the research project Urban Catalyst, founder of Studio UC/ Klaus Overmeyer, since 2012 Urban Catalyst [Studio] and professor at the Bergische Universität Wuppertal (Germany); he lives in Berlin (Germany).

Cordelia Polinna (b. 1975, Berlin, Germany) is a city and regional planner, visiting professor at TU Berlin, co-founder of the initiative Think Berlin and of Polinna | Hauck Landscape | Urbanism; she lives in Berlin.

Arnold Reijndorp (b. 1948, Amsterdam, Netherlands) is an urban sociologist and professor at the University of Amsterdam; he lives in Rotterdam (Netherlands).

Stefan Rettich (b. 1968 in Ebingen, Germany) is an architect, partner of KARO* and co-founder of the architect's network L21; he is a professor at the University of Applied Science Bremen and lives in Hamburg (Germany).

Saskia Sassen (b. 1949, The Hague, Netherlands) is a sociologist and professor at Columbia University and the London School of Economics; she lives in Chicago (USA).

Rudolf Schäfer (b. 1942, Berlin, Germany) is a professor of building law and building administration; he lives in Berlin.

Kevin Ward (b. 1969, Barnet, United Kingdom) is a professor of human geography at the University of Manchester; he lives in Manchester (United Kingdom).

Wanda Wieczorek (b. 1978, Karlsruhe, Germany) is a cultural critic and cultural mediator living in Berlin (Germany).

Urban Catalyst was initiated as a research project (2001–2003) by Philipp Oswalt and Klaus Overmeyer. After finishing the research project Philipp Oswalt, Klaus Overmeyer and Philipp Misselwitz founded the interdisciplinary platform for research, design, public intervention, conferences, exhibitions and publications of the same name. Urban Catalyst aims to support the public discourse about contemporary urban issues and to develop new concepts and models of action for urban development.

This publication is based on the result of the research project as well as a series of further projects, publications and exhibitions by Urban Catalyst.

EU research project Urban Catalyst (2001–2003) —Strategies for Temporary Uses

Twelve partners in five urban metropolis coordinated by the Technical University Berlin studied temporary uses in local test areas and developed tools that enable their potential to be harnessed be used for urban developments.

Idea and concept

Philipp Oswalt und Klaus Overmeyer

Direction and coordination

Philipp Oswalt, Klaus Overmeyer and Philipp Misselwitz with Ali Saad, Thomas Hauck, Melanie Humann, Jurij von Ortenberg as well as Penny Herscovitch, Tashy Endres, Christian Mika

Project director

Kees Christiaanse, TU Berlin, since 2004 ETH Zürich

Coordination EU

European Commission DG XII-D.1.4./ Vincent Favrel

Partners

Helsinki University of Technology – Christer Bengs, Helka-Liisa Hentilä, Timo Kopomaa, Kaisa Schmidt-Thome, Helsinki

Gallotta + Tischer - Marcella Gallotta, Stefan Tischer, Naples

CPA Città Paesaggio Archeologia - Francesco Escalona, Claudio Finaldi-Russo, Fabrizia Ippolito, Pepe Maisto with Maria Ceretta, Franco Lancio, Neapel

Florian Haydn Architekt – Florian Haydn, Robert Temel, Mirko Pogoreutz, Vienna

Magistrat Wien, Magistratsabteilung 18 – Brigitte Jilka, Ina Homeier, Jutta Kleedorfer, Micheal Mellauner

Nyenrode Business Universiteit – Annemieke Roobeek, Erik Mandresloot, Damian van der Bijl, Amsterdam

Stadsdeel Amsterdam Noord – Ted Zwietering, Rob Vooren, Con Vleugel

Stealth Group – Milicia Topalovic, Marc Neelen, Ana Dzokic, Rotterdam

Deadline – Britta Juergens, Matthew Griffin, Berlin/ London

Nexus – Hans Luidger Dienel, Malte Schophaus, Berlin

Berlin District Administration Friedrichhain-Kreuzberg – Matthias Peckskamp, Frank Vettel

Scientific advisory board

Joost Schrijnen, Rotterdam

Robert Mull, London

Arnold Reijndorp, Rotterdam

Reports

Law –Rudolf Schäfer, Petra Lau, Technische Universität Berlin

Tactics of Users – Peter Arlt, Berlin/ Linz

Economy – Rudi Kohoutek, Christa Kammleithner, Vienna

Acknowledgements

We would like to thank Kees Christiaanse for providing an institutional framework for the project as well as giving advice and support, Ina Homeier-Mendes for support during the process of application and negotiating with the EU, Vincent Farvel for monitoring the project during its development, Rüdiger Lainer and Job von Nell for valuable advice, and all contributors to the book for their patience with the long process of development of the publication and all temporary users, from whom we learned so much.

For further information about Urban Catalyst see:

www.urbancatalyst.net

As a part or result of the research project, the following further publications have been produced:

Bündnis für den Palast/ ZwischenPalastNutzung e.V./ Urban Catalyst, eds., *Zwischennutzung des Palast der Republik, Bilanz einer Transformation* 2003 ff, Berlin, 2005

Florian Haydn, Robert Temel, eds., *Temporäre Räume/ Temporary Spaces* (Basel: Birkhäuser, 2006)

Panu Lehtovouri, Helka-Liisa Hentilä, Christer Bengs, eds., *Tilapäiset Käytöt. Kaupunkisuunittelun unohdettu voimavara/ Temporary Uses. The Forgotten Resource of Urban Planning* (Helsinki: Espoo, 2003)

Magistrat Wien, Magistratsabteilung 18, *Urban Catalyst, Werkstattbericht Nr. 60* (Vienna: Magistrat Wien, 2003)

Philipp Misselwitz, Hans Ulrich Obrist, Philipp Oswalt, eds., *Fun Palace 200X. Der Berliner Schlossplatz. Abriss, Neubau oder grüne Wiese?* (Berlin: Martin Schmitz Verlag, 2005)

Senatsverwaltung für Stadtentwicklung Berlin, ed., *Urban Pioneers* (Berlin: Jovis 2007)

As well as many articles in magazines and books.

Image Credits

ACG Wien: p. 254

Adams, Daniel: pp. 162 bottom, 163

Akšamija, Azra: pp. 46, 62–66 (processing by UC)

Baltzer, David/Zenit: pp. 291–296

Bartholl, Aram: pp. 192, 195

Brade, Nikolaus: p. 232

Buttenberg, Lisa: p. 287

Comme des Garçons: pp. 367, 369, 370

Crosby Homes, Manchester/London: p. 79 left

Czenki, Margit: p. 286

Dickson, Bob: p. 76 right

Falco, Michael/The New York Times: p. 161

Förster-Baldenius, Benjamin: p. 184

Gemeente Amsterdam Noord (aerial photograph) p. 357 (processing by UC)

Good, John: p. 31 top

Haushalten e.V.: p. 243

Helander, Marja: p. 40

Hinsley, Hugo: pp. 265–267

Holtmann, Sebastian: p. 36

Honnef, Klaus: p. 144

Howitz, Sam: p.18 top

Hueners, Michael: p. 191 top

Kanton Basel (aerial photograph): p. 258 (processing by UC)

Karo Architekten: p. 317

Kinetisch Noord: p. 358

Knuutila, Tomi p. 16 bottom

Kraak, Ronny: p. 341

Kulturkosmos e.V.: p. 343

Lembke, Marcel: p. 345

Maaß, Malte: p. 213 top

McLain, Ross: p. 31 bottom

Manchester City Council, Library and Information Service, Manchester Archives and Local Studies: p. 75 (processing by UC)

Media Wien: p. 252

Misselwitz, Philipp: pp. 79 left, 214, 215

Moore, Ari: p. 30 bottom

Moore, Peter: p. 141 bottom

Nagl, Michael: p. 241

Oswalt, Philipp: pp. 23 bottom, 27 bottom, 28 top, 44, 200, 204 top, 299

Oswalt, Walter: p. 48

Overmeyer, Klaus: pp. 16 top, 18 bottom, 19 top, 22 top, 23 top, 25, 26, 27 top, 28 bottom, 29 bottom, 203, 212, 213 bottom, 334–339, 359, 361

Pamer, Volkmer: p. 253

Park Fiction Archiv: p. 285

Petras, Christoph: pp. 34, 289

Pfister, Michael: p. 42

Platforma 9.81 Zagreb: pp. 273–281

Polinna, Cordelia: pp. 268–269, 271

Price, Cedric: pp. 249, 251

Pritzkuleit, Benjamin © Carsten Nicolai, VG Bild-Kunst, Bonn 2010, Courtesy Galerie EIGEN + ART, Leipzig/Berlin and PaceWildenstein: p. 301

Projektbüro Philipp Oswalt: pp. 20 top, 21

Projektteam Dietzenbach 2030: pp. 306–308

Schäfer, Christoph: p. 283

Schelle, Rupert: p. 331

Schläger, Philip: p. 24 top,

Schulz Jorgensen, Peter: pp. 362, 363

Schulze, Hinrich: p. 284

Schwartau, Eric: p. 20 bottom

Seidel, Torsten: pp. 69–70 (processing by UC), 72

Stalker: pp. 311–314

Stealth: pp. 364, 365

Stattmann, Klaus: p. 240

Studio UC/Klaus Overmeyer: pp. 17 top, 53, 57, 233–235, 237

Thalia Theater Halle: p. 147

Ullstein: p. 328

Urban Catalyst: pp. 22 bottom, 59, 60, 71, 201 bottom, 202, 204 bottom, 205–207, 209, 224–229, 290, 325, 327, 333, 378–379 (after a sketch by Le Corbusier)

Verein V.I.P. Basel: pp. 208, 210 top, 259, 260, 263

Vivico Real Estate: p. 257

Völkel, Thomas: pp. 319–320

von Borries, Friedrich: pp. 350, 351, 353, 354

Weber, Sven: pp. 210 bottom, 211 bottom

Willats, Stephen: p. 145

Wirth, Matthäus: p. 54

Wünsche, Michael: p. 191 bottom

The *Deutsche Nationalbibliothek* lists this publication in the *Deutsche Nationalbibliografie*; detailed bibliograpic data are available in the internet at http://dnb.d-nb.de.

ISBN 978-3-86922-261-5

© 2013 by DOM publishers, Berlin/Germany
www.dom-publishers.com

Editors and Concept

Philipp Oswalt, Klaus Overmeyer, Philipp Misselwitz

Urban Catalyst (Philipp Oswalt, Klaus Overmeyer, Philipp Misselwitz) is the collective author of all texts included in this book where an external author has not explicitly been named.

Editorial Team

Philipp Oswalt, Klaus Overmeyer, Philipp Misselwitz with Nina Brodowski, Lisa Buttenberg, Christiane Kania, Melanie Klofat

Copy Editing

Nina Brodowski, Nicole Minten, Rudolf Stegers, Ruth Ur

Translation / from German into English

James Gussen, Antje Pehnt, Rebecca van Dyck

Proofreading

Mariangela Palazzi-Williams

Graphic Design

Tom Unverzagt

Printed by

Tiger Printing (Hongkong) Co. Ltd., Shenzhen/China

Acknowledgements

We would like to thank Albert Ferre, Roswitha Koskinas and Anna Tetas and all other persons who made this publication possible.

This publication was supported by the EU's Fifth Framework Program in the context of the Urban Catalyst research project.